Policy problems are inherently complex and hence difficult to solve. Charles Phua's book is well embedded in complexity thinking assumptions and ventures to cross fertilise the best of corporate strategy into policy strategy. This interdisciplinary entrepreneurial book is essentially about practical problem-solving methodology and has immense potential for problem solving in other disciplines.

Professor Carmine Bianchi, *Professor of Business and Public Management, University of Palermo, Italy, and Scientific Coordinator for CED4 Systems Dynamics Group*

To make public policy and business strategy work together for the greater good requires more than just rhetoric. It requires tools. This is precisely the focus of The Policy-Strategy Innovation Primer and practitioners will benefit.

Professor Craig Calhoun, *University Professor of Social Sciences, Arizona State University, former president of London of School of Economics and Social Sciences Research Council (SSRC)*

When in need of a tool, a toolbox is extremely useful, if its contents are well organized and cover many contingencies. Charles Chao Rong Phua has assembled a conceptual toolbox composed of elements of strategic pragmatism for policy strategy-innovation that draws selectively on complexity, policy and strategy literatures to create an effective repository of conceptual devices to aid practitioners' practical wisdom.

Professor Stewart Clegg, *D.Phil, D.Litt, Ph.D, John Grill Institute for Project Leadership, School of Project Management and Faculty of Engineering, The University of Sydney*

In an era when governments the world over face seemingly insurmountable challenges, public administrators need more of the kind of "strategic pragmatism" that Charles Chao Rong Phua advocates in this book. Readers will find Policy Strategy and Innovation Primer brimming with optimism that governmental organizations can adapt and innovate to meet the many demands of our time.

Prof Cary Coglianese, *Edward B Shils Professor of Law and Professor of Political Science; Director, Penn Program on Regulation, University of Pennsylvania Carey Law School.*

A sweeping and intellectually challenging analysis of policy- strategy innovation, especially its complex inter-disciplinary nature and written with an eye for politicians and civil servants. A text for the times.

Professor Christopher Coker, *Director, LSE IDEAS*

I think the future of interesting research and writing sits as the intersection of arenas and disciplines rather than within any particular one. This is what Certified Management Consultant Academic Fellow Charles Phua has accomplished in his latest book. Here, in Policy Strategy and Innovation, the worlds of public policy and business strategy are inter-twined to produce a practically oriented text designed to appeal to the research community and practitioners alike.

As chair of the Academic Fellows with the International Council of Management Consulting Institutes and a fellow Certified Management Consultant Academic Fellow, I fully endorse the bridge building between the leading edge of practice and communicable insight that Charles has achieved.

Prof Simon Haslam, *CMC-AF, Visiting Professor, University of Durham Business School and Chair, International Council of Management Consulting Institutes (ICMCI) Academic Fellows*

In this lively new book, the author lays out an approach to public policy that escapes the usual US and Westminster boundaries to the broader fabric of public policy puzzles throughout the world. He lays out strategies for innovation that are rooted in the emerging new reality of policy complexity. That creates a rich new lens through which to view the big issues facing governments around the world.

Professor Donald F. Kettl, *Professor Emeritus and Former Dean, University of Maryland School of Public Policy*

Business and policy scholarly disciplines have professionalised through the decades. But the increasingly complex topics as technology and sustainability are necessitating cross-fertilisation and cross-learning across disciplines. Having done doctoral training in public policy and business strategy, Charles Phua's cross-fertilisation of business strategy tools into the policy process will advance the complexity discourse in public policy. A novel and commendable feat!

Professor Sarah Kreps, *John L. Wetherill Professor in the Department of Government, Director, Cornell Tech Policy Lab, Cornell University, and non-resident senior fellow, Brookings Institution.*

Policy Strategy and Innovation Primer: Process, Praxis, Tools is very relevant to policy scholars and practitioners because innovative policies are needed to solve complex problems of today. Under this context, Professor Phua clearly articulated and elucidated the strategies in innovation for the policy domain. I am confident that this book on policy strategy and innovation will greatly impact the building of theory and practical know-how in the field of public policy.

Professor Hae Young Lee, *Professor of Public Administration at Yeungnam University, S. Korea, former President of Korean Association of Public Administration (2014) and former Chairman of Korean Government Evaluation Commission (2014–2018)*

In the fast-changing world that we live in today, where innovation outstrips policy formulation and regulation, and where the longevity of a political party, let alone a politician, is increasingly elusive, the public-private debate takes on heightened emphasis. Charles does an excellent job of addressing this head-on, questioning if a dichotomy truly exists or should be allowed to prevail.

Lim Hwee Hua, *Former Minister in the Prime Minister's Office, Singapore, Rector, Tembusu College, National University of Singapore, and author of Government in Business - Friend or Foe? (2014) and Government in Business - Leading or Lagging? (2021)*

Good policy strategy requires a sound outstanding of context and strategic levers. Good policy innovation requires focus on objective and agility in design and implementation. Charles Phua's book offers a unique blend of how corporate strategy and innovation tools could support better strategies and innovation in public policy. Both government and business worlds should operate with the citizen-user in mind.

Professor Lim Siong Guan, *Professor in Practice, Lee Kuan Yew School of Public Policy, National University of Singapore, former Head of Singapore Civil Service, former Chairman of Economic Development Board and former Group President of GIC*

As the world advances towards a post-pandemic future amidst intensifying technologization and geopolitical upheaval, greater clarity than ever is needed for sound policy making. This book provides a strategic and practicable framework to answer those imperatives.

Professor Lim Sun Sun, *Professor and Head of Humanities, Arts and Social Sciences, Singapore University of Technology and Design, former Nominated Member of Parliament, Singapore.*

This book is based on the author's belief that corporate strategy and innovation tools and practices have much to offer in the practice of public policy – a conviction formed through Charles Phua's two-decade experience as a bureaucrat-nonprofit entrepreneur, researcher, and adjunct faculty at various universities. By breaking down the public policy process into steps, and through the use of diverse examples, Charles illustrates the potential application of corporate strategies, in a manner that permits it to be transferable across political systems. Those interested in public policy are likely to find much food for thought offered in this book.

Professor Ling San, *Deputy President and Provost, Nanyang Technological University, Singapore*

Classical military strategists such as Sun Tzu have inspired corporate strategists. Public policy strategy as a growing field could benefit from learning from corporate strategy. This nexus is well articulated in Charles Phua's book which strings relevant corporate strategy frameworks to their matching policy strategy process. A highly commendable interdisciplinary effort, useful to practitioners, academics, students and public-conscious citizens.

Professor Hwy-Chang Moon, *Professor Emeritus, Graduate School of International Studies, Seoul National University, and author of The Art of Strategy: Sun Tzu, Michael Porter and Beyond*

In the early years of its independence, Singapore attempted any method, regardless of orthodoxy or elegance, that delivered favourable outcomes to it citizens. Several public- sector leaders also led government-linked companies, thereby gaining valuable cross- sector experiences. Charles Phua's book is a timely reminder that despite professionalisation of disciplines, corporate strategy may have something useful to offer the public sector in pursuing solutions to time-honoured problems.

Joseph Y. Pillay, *Rector, College of Alice and Peter Tan, National University of Singapore, former Chairman (2005–2019), Council of Presidential Advisors (Singapore), and, former Chairman, Singapore International Airlines (1972–1996).*

What makes certain decisions effective and outcomes successful will very much depend on having an in-depth policy strategy and innovation. What are the necessary inputs for formulating good policies and why some worked and some do not, are highlighted, and explained carefully in this book. This book shows that much of that often requires in turn, a good knowledge and use of business strategies as well. The author comes from an interesting mix of background experiences from utilising a variety of tools and applied techniques to bear on a number of real-life scenarios. This book is strongly recommended to readers who have keen interest in how real problems may be solved.

Professor Euston Quah, *Albert Winsemius Chair Professor of Economics, Nanyang Technological University, Singapore; President, Economic Society of Singapore*

As a practicing city designer, where we think everything is political and everything is inter-disciplinary, it is a refreshing way of analysing and dissecting policy strategy innovation. It is a must read for policy makers as well as city practitioners such as us where we need consensus to design and plan future cities and future of our current cities.

Chintan Raveshia, *Cities Business Leader, Southeast Asia, Arup*

Dr Charles Chao Rong Phua has put his practitioner experiences and academic expertise in government and corporate to good use to integrate corporate and policy strategy in this Policy Strategy-Innovation Primer. He has provided imperative synthesis and meaningful contributions. Strategic approach and design are vital for successful entrepreneurs and this primer provides readers with a fundamental understanding of these topics.

Professor Amir Reza, *Dean, Babson Academy for the Advancement of Global Entrepreneurial Learning, Babson College*

Charles has laid out a comprehensive array of toolkits from the private sector that can be invaluable for public policy-making. These business practices may just be able to help develop solutions for addressing some of our most wicked problems in society today.

Seah Chin Siong, *President, Singapore Institute of Management, and Chairman, National Volunteer and Philanthropy Centre*

Policy strategy and innovation is growing field and often seen as a central force for increasing economic prosperity and improving economic inequality. The writer incorporates the business strategy framework into public policy process for formulation innovative public policy. The book is recommended for the policy practitioners and scholars even for the MBA students. It offers different views how to formulate innovative policy.

Professor Agus Soehadi, *Vice Rector, and former Dean of Business and Economics School, Presetiya Mulya University (Indonesia)*

Industry 4.0 and the many disruptions the world is facing, even before the Covid-19 pandemic and the Ukraine war, has accelerated the rate of change to a level where business models, policies and skills are becoming obsolete at such a rapid pace that society as a whole struggles to keep and catch up. Policy makers cannot rely on past models because what worked in the past will also quickly become outdated. In business, cross-disciplinary knowledge has shown to yield superior results. In the book, Charles has cleverly suggested that policy making needs to also take an inter-disciplinary approach of adopting innovation and business concepts, tools, and strategies from business disciplines to yield robust policies that the world badly needs to keep the peace and prosperity of the world. Current and future policy makers should use this as a reference and guide as they take over helms of politics and policy making.

Professor Inderjit Singh Dhaliwal, *Former Member of Parliament, Singapore, Entrepreneur and Adjunct Professor, College of Engineering, Nanyang Technological University and President, Global Start-up Committee, WBAF (World Business Angel Investment Forum)*

Public policy impacts everyone's life, it does not take place in a void and not just for policy practitioners or scholars. As the nation's challenges get more complex and the people more educated, it needs to open itself to more public participation in policy making. It is equally important that active citizens are able to understand and participate more meaningfully in discourses on public policy. Charles Phua's new book fills an important gap to facilitate this by providing a primer and applied guide on strategy-innovation in public sector. You can sense Charles's enthusiasm to share his deep knowledge as he has always been keen to drive more active citizenry in policymaking. Given his role as a trainer and management consultant, this book is both useful and practical.

Professor Tan Thiam Soon, *Institute Professor and former President, Singapore Institute of Technology*

It is a great project, very valuable for both academics and practitioners, especially those who want to learn and integrate latest business practices in strategic management into the governance and decision making in the public sector.

Professor Wang Xiaohu, *Professor and PhD programme coordinator, Department of Public Policy, City University of Hong Kong*

This book on Policy Strategy and Innovation by Charles Phua provides many interesting perspectives on the subject. In doing so, he enables readers to have a broader yet insightful understanding of what policy strategy is all about. It is also a well-researched piece of work.

Professor Wee Chow Hou, *PhD, BBM(L), PPA, FMIS(Hon), Adjunct Professor for Strategy and Marketing, Nanyang Technological University and Singapore University of Social Sciences, author of 5 books on* Sun Zi Bingfa

In this volume, Charles Chao Rong Phua continued his strategic pragmatism thesis and embedded it in the policy strategy process. His infusion of corporate strategy tools into the right policy process sequence is novel and requires a deep understanding of both public policy and business management disciplines to do so. This book opens the door for greater cross-fertilisation of knowledge between policy and business disciplines through policy strategy and innovation cases. Highly recommended for government and business practitioners and academics alike.

Professor Xufeng Zhu, *Executive Dean, School of Public Policy and Management, Tsinghua University*

POLICY STRATEGY AND INNOVATION PRIMER

Phua focuses on applying the best of corporate strategy and innovation tools and praxis into the policy process with the aim of devising a coherent policy strategy–innovation framework and process.

Government and business strategies differ in their operating assumptions and variables, but the strategy process is more similar than is often perceived. Phua debunks the government versus business dichotomy and demonstrates the potential for cross-learning between both domains. Readers will benefit the most by reading this book in tandem with Phua's other works on strategy also featured in this series.

This book is an essential primer for academics, practitioners and learners of public policy, strategy, innovation and applied problem-solving.

Charles Chao Rong Phua now runs Solaris Strategies Singapore (and chairs Solaris Consortium of Management Consultancies) dedicated to pragmatically solving complex problems supporting governments, corporates and underserved nonprofits at national, sector and enterprise levels. Charles also presides over Association for Public Affairs (Singapore) spearheading active citizenry in policymaking and served as chief judge for Singapore Model Cabinet and Parliament organised by government. He is an internationally certified management consultant – academic fellow amongst global top 100 professor-author grade management consultants (International Council of Management Consulting Institutes) with doctorate in public policy, postgraduate/degrees in international relations, security management, education, accounting, systems thinking, organisational psychology, strategy and innovation, HRM, Ops, marketing, digital business/leadership, supply chain management and law, Charles completed executive education in strategy, innovation, entrepreneurship, marketing and sustainability from leading business schools: Harvard, MIT, Stanford, Wharton, Kellogg, Berkeley, Babson, INSEAD, Cambridge, Oxford, London Business School. He currently serves as series editor for Routledge series for strategy, wisdom and skills with a commitment to codify academic + practitioner wisdom in applied and interdisciplinary fields. He has taught applied problem-solving at four universities in Singapore Civil Service College (Singapore), University of St Gallen (Switzerland) and is currently program leader/success coach for Chief Strategy, Chief Technology, Chief Data and AI Officer programs for NUS Business and Computing schools with Emeritus. He was a Fulbright fellow and completed resident fellowships at Brookings, Columbia and Johns Hopkins.

Part of this book was adapted from his course materials. He seeks to bring the best of corporate strategy into public policy academia and practice, in the right sequence and for the right purpose.

Routledge-Solaris Focus on Strategy, Wisdom and Skills

The Series is advised and edited by Charles Chao Rong Phua, the Chairman of the Solaris Consortium of Management Consultancies.

Strategic Pragmatism in Foreign Policy
Comparing the US, China, and Singapore
Charles Chao Rong Phua

A Humanist Approach to Sustainable Investment
The Green Dot Score
Janek Ratnatunga

Principles of Political Thought
Lee Hae Young

Cultural Pragmatism for US-China Relations
Breaking the Gridlock and Co-Creating Our Future
Charles Chao Rong Phua

Designing the Future of Education
C J Meadows

Policy Strategy and Innovation Primer
Process, Praxis and Tools
Charles Chao Rong Phua

Managerial Accounting Analytics
A Primer
Janek Ratnatunga

POLICY STRATEGY AND INNOVATION PRIMER

Process, Praxis and Tools

Charles Chao Rong Phua

Routledge
Taylor & Francis Group
LONDON AND NEW YORK

Designed cover image: BrianAJackson / Getty Images

First published 2023
by Routledge
4 Park Square, Milton Park, Abingdon, Oxon OX14 4RN

and by Routledge
605 Third Avenue, New York, NY 10158

Routledge is an imprint of the Taylor & Francis Group, an informa business

British Library Cataloguing-in-Publication Data
A catalogue record for this book is available from the British Library

ISBN: 978-1-032-30908-8 (hbk)
ISBN: 978-1-032-30909-5 (pbk)
ISBN: 978-1-003-30722-8 (ebk)

DOI: 10.4324/9781003307228

In loving memory of Tan Sway Moi @ Monica

my mother who bravely bore me under difficult circumstances
our entrepreneurial Ma who successfully managed a
million-dollar enterprise
our dedicated Ma who lovingly managed a tasty home kitchen
our fighter Ma who sequentially fought multiple illnesses
our survivor Ma who jovially embraced pain with smile and zest
our role model for optimism, courage, grit and selfless love

Professor James G March (1928–2018)

a titan in organisational management covering political science,
sociology, economics, business and education disciplines.
an author with Herbert A. Simon (1993) Organizations, with
bounded rationality and many more concepts on decision science
at the individual, groups, organisations, firms and society.
a teacher to me who kindly hosted me twice at
Stanford University
and we spoke about many things under the sun.
His breadth of work and impact remain an aspiration to many.

CONTENTS

FIGURES

TABLES

PREFACE

First, does the world really need another policy textbook?

I am probably biased, but I think it does. The nature of any policy, politics, political philosophy or public administration is heavily influenced by the precise place in which the lines are drawn between these various categories. Most politics textbooks tend to bear the tacit influence of political philosophy and also touch upon public administration topics. Meanwhile, policy and public administration textbooks are often heavily – though not always consciously – influenced by the political a priori of the authors. Thus, US-based textbooks tend to assume a strong separation of powers system in which the judiciary has a significant influence. British textbooks tend to focus to a far greater degree on the tensions between civil servants and political actors, and the differing deontologies of each group. Meanwhile, books in continental Europe are far more accepting of the idea of the "administrative state" in which the bureaucracy functions almost as a separate power. East Asian textbooks, on the other hand, tend to take a more business-like approach, reflecting the corporatist approach to public management that tends to prevail throughout China, Japan, Korea and neighbouring countries. Textbooks tend to focus in a very granular way on project management, differing only from MBA course materials insofar as that it is necessary to remove profit motives and financial indicators and replace them with other factors more appropriate to a public context.

There are advantages and disadvantages to this approach. On the one hand, it means that the content can be used by most – if not all – civil servants, regardless of the political and national contexts in which they are operating. On the other hand, however, a studied ignorance of politics can lead readers to underestimate the influence of political forces on the implementation of policy. Potentially more seriously, an unwillingness to question the sources of political instructions or the ideas that underlie bureaucratic actions can reduce bureaucrats' willingness to argue against unethical policy suggestions or to question their groupthink and received ideas that they encounter in their work.

Nevertheless, I would argue that the solution to this problem is not to create books that are a hodgepodge of politics and public policy, but rather to draw clear dividing lines between the various academic disciplines relating to political and policy action. While I am well aware that a bureaucrat or a student of bureaucracy requires a solid understanding of both the politics of their state and the political philosophy upon which it was founded, these two things can easily be obtained from other books.

This book would not have the temerity to presume that it will be the only volume that its readers will ever peruse. I assume that our audience has a reasonable level of education and an interest in the subject, and moreover that they are well aware that public policy does not take place in a void untainted by the world of politics. I have thus decided to avoid – as far as possible – adopting any particular philosophical assumptions or presume a particular political background on the part of the readers. This is not because such things are unimportant, but simply because readers can easily find these things elsewhere. What is much harder to find in other books is an extremely detailed step-by-step description of the methods that can be applied to achieve public policy goals. I make no assumptions regarding the rightness or wrongness of the policies that the readers will be aiming to implement or impede; my aim is merely to give them the tools to do this, operationalising policy strategy–innovation for complexity thinking in public administration.[1]

Second, what is Policy Strategy–Innovation?

(1) Policy Practitioner: "Policy strategy should only be designed by policy practitioners for policy practitioners" (assumption: policy scholars do not know policy contexts adequately well to be useful in practice);
(2) Policy Scholar: "Policy strategy should be designed by policy scholars for policy practitioners" (assumption: policy scholars have more time, clarity of thought and past knowledge created to better strategise policy; policy practitioners are too busy "fighting fire").

Both responses have some merits of truth but are sub-optimal by themselves. An inclusive approach is possible. This book starts "where *Towards Strategic Pragmatism in Foreign policy* (Routledge, 2021) and Cultural Pragmatism in US-China relations (2022)" left off. No matter the policy/philosophical paradigm, the sector or the problem involved, it is important to bear in mind that policymaking follows a reasonably standard and logical process. This begins with identifying the problem (problem-finding/agenda setting), policy formulation (user data collection, data analysis and idea generation), decision-making, implementation and evaluation.

In this book, I tried to embed strategic pragmatism framework in the policy strategy–innovation process, essentially, the idea that it is good to be inflexible when it comes to goals but flexible when it comes to the means that one uses to attain them.[2] While this idea was originally developed in a foreign policy context, its adaptability to a more general policy context has been demonstrated by Clemons and McBeth (2020).[3]

Its novelty is in the fusion of geopolitical and policy contexts, with strategy–innovation–entrepreneurship framework that I learnt from top business schools into a coherent policy strategy–innovation framework and process. I will focus primarily on problem-finding and formulation phases, breaking the process down into specific steps and borrowing from various different concepts that will be familiar to readers with a business school background, but not necessarily to policy specialists. Every Biz school has their pet strategy tool/s: Harvard strategy (Five Forces, Diamond) and disruptive innovation, MIT systems thinking, Stanford design, Wharton strategy and entrepreneurship, INSEAD advanced strategy, Babson entrepreneurship, Kellogg marketing, Berkeley open innovation, LBS and Cambridge sustainability, Oxford scenarios, etc. The uninformed policy scholar or learner may be at first confused by the plethora of corporate strategy tools which prima facie may seem irrelevant to policy problems. Each corporate strategy tool is designed for a specific purpose, and NO ONE tool can cover the entire policy process.

The utility of corporate strategy tools is high if they are re-rationalised in the right policy process sequence: (1) pre-agenda setting benefits from SWOT; (2) policy design/formulation requires data collection which Stanford Design is useful, data analysis which Oxford Scenarios and MIT Systems Thinking are useful, and further idea generation can benefit from INSEAD's blue ocean strategy, Harvard's job-to-be-done; (3) policy implementation and (4) evaluation can benefit from Stanford Design, Agile and Scrum. To show the versatility of the approaches provided, I gave real-world examples from around the world, showing how the methods described can be and have been implemented by public sector actors to achieve their objectives.

This book seeks to illustrate ONE possible approach in combining a specific set of tools to support a specific policy process stage. There are many other possible approaches and combinations. There can often be a resistance among policy specialists towards the adoption of methods from the business world, since many tend to cling to the idea of the public service ethos as being "above" financial motivations. However, an important part of pragmatism involves being flexible over the tools one uses to achieve pre-ordained goals. However, this does not necessarily mean that public sector actors should simply adopt practices from the private sector wholesale and without applying a critical eye (note: New Public Management paradigm was essentially adopting market principles wholesale into public sector to check state failure and fat bureaucracy; we now know the result of losing the "public" orientation as we face the consequences of privatisation, deregulation, management by KPIs, etc.). Each of the business tools that I describe later was designed for a specific purpose and will not necessarily translate to any given circumstance in the policy domain. Instead, they must be analysed carefully in order to identify possible parallels in the policy world, and the likely advantages and pitfalls of porting them over. Making this more complicated is the fact that the policy implications of a commercial strategy may not always be entirely obvious.

In the context of this book, I have striven to tease out the implications of each strategy to elucidate its potential applications in the policy world. In doing this, I drew on my experience as a trisector practitioner and doctoral training in public policy and corporate strategy to straddle between the two and optimise the interdisciplinary possibilities. The litmus test of utility should be the ability to holistically solve a wicked problem (phronesis market test prevails over any intellectual argument of epistemic correctness). If they work for you and improve your organisation's performance, then they are good strategies. If they can – as we hope – tackle wicked problems in a comprehensive manner, then they have achieved what we set out for them to achieve.[4] If not, find the next best possible tool to help your policy strategy and innovation journey.

The examples were deliberately chosen from a wide variety of cultures and political systems, the goal being to show that, however, political choices may be made, competent management remains competent management. The methods and techniques that produce competent management are largely transferable between political systems, and thus this book can be used as a guide by readers in almost any country. Indeed, it is hoped that it will provide useful background on potential approaches to adopt for policymakers, students and citizens aiming to take a more active role in public life. I hope that you will get as much enjoyment and utility from reading this as I did from writing it.

The **ASPIRATION** of this book is towards Strategic Pragmatism in Policy Strategy–Innovation where (1) **problem**: complex wicked problems necessitate pluralistic perspectives and tools to solve the problems (pragmatically); (2) **possible solution**: corporate strategy tools thrive in corporate problems and have evolved and refined through iterative feedback loops (with consumers) and hence worthy for consideration for policy usage; (3) **solution**: corporate strategy tools can be useful to policy problems provided they are used correctly and in right sequence; (4) **holistic paradigm**: strategic pragmatism framework with the apt fusion of corporate strategy tools in the right policy process presents itself as a possible (operational-level) framework to support complexity paradigm (at strategic level) in public policy. Its application in a complex yet impactful topic such as complexity in smart city governance merits further research.

Charles Chao Rong Phua (humbly, from Singapore)

Notes

1 Mitleton-Kelly, Eve, Alexandros Paraskevas, and Christopher Day, eds. *Handbook of research methods in complexity science: Theory and applications*. Oxon: Edward Elgar Publishing, 2018.

2 Phua, Charles Chao Rong. *Towards strategic pragmatism in foreign policy: Cases of United States of America, China and Singapore*. Oxon: Routledge, 2021.

3 Clemons, Randy S., and Mark K. McBeth. *Public policy praxis: A case approach for understanding policy and analysis*. Oxon: Routledge, 2020.

4 Perry, James L., and Robert K. Christensen. *Handbook of public administration*. New York: John Wiley & Sons, 2015.

1

PUBLIC POLICY AND PUBLIC ADMINISTRATION/MANAGEMENT

Paradigms, Practice and Paradoxes

Public policy is as old as human organisation, and the earliest policy memos go all the way back to the ancient near east, in the form of letters exchanged between bureaucrats and rulers recommending or warning against particular courses of action. The Amarna letters found in the early 20th century describe diplomatic relations between ancient Egypt and its neighbours in the second millennium BC. In them, diplomats and officials describe the problems they face and argue in favour or against particular courses of action.

1. The Origins of Public Policy

These are policy documents, but they are also entirely contingent responses to present circumstances: each recommendation is an ad hoc strategy based on the issues faced by a given official.[1] None of the authors attempts to suggest that a solution that they have found to a problem that they encountered could profitably be generalised throughout the nation. It is in ancient Chinese documents dating back to the Western Zhou Dynasty (1046–771 BC) that we find the earliest descriptions of policy as we would understand it: government regulations designed to be applied to all instances of a given phenomenon, absolving bureaucrats of the need to make subjective case-by-case decisions. Take, for example, this instruction to judges regarding criminal cases that do not seem to be covered by existing statutes, taken from the *Book of Documents*:

> In doubtful cases . . . you must class them with the next higher or next lower offences, not admitting assumptive and disorderly pleadings, and not using obsolete laws. Examine and act lawfully, judging carefully, and proving yourselves equal to every difficulty. Where the crime should incur one of the higher punishments, but there are mitigating circumstances, apply to

DOI: 10.4324/9781003307228-1

> it the next lower. Where it should incur one of the lower punishments, but there are aggravating circumstances, apply to it the next higher. The light and heavy fines are to be apportioned in the same way by the balance of circumstances.[2]

In ancient Rome, by contrast, regulations tended to focus on the structure of the bureaucracy rather than how it was intended to behave. Officials were appointed and not only given a charge but also given a relatively high degree of liberty in how they were to achieve their pre-set targets. Many Roman laws and regulations were customary rather than the result of government decisions, and the bureaucratisation of public administration did not really set in until after the fall of Rome in 476 and the development of written legal codes in the Byzantine Empire. As Justinian put it:

> While we are occupied with cares of the whole state, and matters of importance demand out attention, having to see that the Persians remained quiet, that the Vandals and the Moors remain in obedience, that the Carthaginians retain their former liberty, recently regained, and that the Tsanians, now first subjected to the Roman sway, be received as our subjects – something which God had never granted to the Romans till under our reign – many private affairs, too, are brought before us by our subjects, all of which we decide in the proper manner. But remedies frequently enjoyed by individuals, may, if embodied in a law, be of enormous benefit to all who are in need thereof; and we have, therefore, thought best to incorporate them in a law which itself with grant the remedy, making frequent imperial orders in future unnecessary.

In this chapter, we will focus on Public Administration/Management (PAM) paradigms and their evolution, starting with the birth of bureaucracy in China and ending with the most exciting new topics in the domain: complexity and wicked problems. This thus serves as an introduction to the following chapters, explaining why modern policymakers need to have a diverse toolkit for dealing with the problems that they face, and to be able to deploy this toolkit in an agile manner. Fortunately, this does not need to be built from scratch. The corporate world has already been working on similar challenges for many decades, and in most cases, there is no reason why their various frameworks and methodologies cannot be used by public sector agents.

However, there are also key differences, notably, the fact that the private sector tends to have much tighter feedback loops, thanks to the presence of financial metrics by which the success or failure of a policy may be judged. Thus, every strategic decision is forced to pass the "reality test" – something that frequently does not occur in the public context. The public sector tends to find it harder to identify automatic feedback indicators and often does a poor job of actively seeking them out.[3] Indeed, civil servants often have every reason to wish to avoid being evaluated, as bad results will adversely affect their careers, so the job is left to opposition politicians or civil society, who are forced to do the job with only limited access to financial and data resources. While it is true that the citizens of democratic states can provide feedback once every few years during elections, this is a relatively imprecise process – in representative systems a vote covers the entirety of a government's performance, rather than individual policies, so it can be hard to work out the degree to which any particular policy led to a positive or negative vote.

However, while it is difficult for public organisations to get the same level and accuracy of feedback as private entities, this does not mean that they cannot apply the same tools that have proved successful in the corporate world. This being said, these strategies cannot simply be transferred across wholesale. They must be applied using the good judgement and experience of policy practitioners. It is this that this book aims to teach its readers how to do it.

2. Defining Bureaucracy

While bureaucracy may not be a likeable term, bureaucratisation has historically been a reliable precursor of social revolution. In China, the development of a professional administrative class during the Warring States era was the harbinger of the collapse of the feudal system and its replacement by an imperial technocratic bureaucracy. In Europe, the same phenomena created the urban bourgeoisie that was to trigger the wave of democratic and republican revolutions that accompanied the Enlightenment. In Japan, the educated administrators of the Tokugawa shogunate were also the heralds of the Meiji restoration.[4]

While China already had a wide variety of theories of public administration by the time it became a unitary Empire in 221 BC, these tend to be considered by academic research as falling under the remit of political philosophy rather than public policy.[5] The majority of university courses in the history of public policy focus instead on the discipline's emergence in Europe and the United States in the 19th and early 20th centuries.

John Stuart Mill, for example, wrote that bureaucracy had much to recommend it, in the form of the technocratic expertise accumulated by public officials, but that it required some democratic component to provide checks and balances and ensure that the administration remains beholden to the public. Karl Marx, by contrast, saw public administration as being the captive of capitalist elites, and therefore necessarily an enemy of the working classes.[6]

However, the concept of public administration as we understand it today is based largely around Max Weber's analysis of bureaucracy, published in the 1920s. In this, he argues that "The fully developed bureaucratic apparatus compares with other organisations exactly as does the machine with the non-mechanical modes of production" – echoing 2000-year-old Chinese arguments for the greater efficiency produced by mechanistic standardisation in public administration. Weber observed the same phenomena in both public administration and large enterprises, many of which had adopted the radical standardisation and division of labour promoted by entrepreneurs such as Henry Ford.[7] He boiled bureaucratic administration down to a succession of key features:

- Hierarchical organisation
- Formal lines of authority
- A fixed area of activity
- Rigid division of labour
- Regular and continuous execution of assigned tasks
- All decisions and powers specified and restricted by regulations
- Officials with expert training in their fields
- Career advancement dependent on technical qualifications
- Qualifications evaluated by organisational rules, not individuals[8]

The "scientific" efficiency of these systems was attractive not just to business magnates like Ford but also to political progressives who believed in the capacity of the state to take a proactive and interventionist approach to improving citizens' lives. The greatest proponent of bureaucracy as a force for good was the US President Woodrow Wilson, who argued not only for strict separation of the political and bureaucratic sphere but also for the elevation of the latter: "Administrative questions are not political questions. Although politics sets the tasks for administration, it should not be suffered to manipulate its offices".[9] However, Wilson's wide-eyed enthusiasm for the capacity of public policy to build a better society did not survive the rise of fascism in Europe. The US progressive movement shared many of the same enthusiasms as the European fascist parties that rose in Europe throughout the 1920s and 1930s: elite technocracy, eugenics and bureaucratic government. World War II made it clear that the same techniques that could be used to produce a Model-T or implement the New Deal could also be used – as in Nazi Germany – to accelerate genocide. Mill had effectively been vindicated: bureaucracy can be a positive thing, but only when subject to checks and balances.

The question is beyond specific authors/thinkers, is there a more comprehensive framework that synthesises Public Administration/Management (PAM) theories "out there"?

3. Paradigms of Public Administration/Management (PAM): Historical Influences

Woodrow Wilson's seminal article in 1887 can be considered the first work in modern PAM before Leonard D. White's first PAM textbook in 1926 (Wilson, 1887; White, 1926, pp. 49–56). However, broad conceptual frameworks of PAM theories are sparse. The closest to achieving this distinction is by Laurence Lynn Jr.,[10] who attempted to provide a broad history of PAM from ancient times to the modern day: China invented public service entrance exams and the concept of public trust.[11] But the modern bureaucratic state was a social invention of Western Europe.[12] In Prussia, working for the civil service was a way to fulfil one's civic duty, and Frederick the Great instituted official exams and a civil service commission. Following "managerialist ideology",[13] Prussia advocated meritocracy, administrative science, standardised principles and professionalism. However, what is now traditionally known as public administration is an American invention[14] and Americans regard their own democratic governance as unique, even paradigmatic, and their methods of study – with their emphasis on theory-based quantitative analysis – as more rigorously scientific; US specialists advocated scientific managerialism with an emphasis on the dichotomy between politics and administration and management based on scientific principles.[15] However, the United States also experienced an "intellectual crisis"[16] within the field of public administration, as competing theories emerged: Simon's behaviourism, March & Simon's organisation theories; old institutional managerialism; new scientific managerialism, Minnowbrook & Blacksburg's normative manifestos; public choice theory, new economics of organisation, institutional studies in sociology, economics and political science.[17]

The 1970s saw a paradigm shift towards frugal and efficient government.[18] In the United States, this led to the development of New Public Management (NPM), with the "US academic reinvention featuring managerial deregulation, quality, entrepreneurship and is best represented by 1993 Government and Performance Act, George W. Bush's 'Management Agenda' emphasising performance-driven, Federal outsourced management and 'program assessment rating tool' in budgeting".[19] Europe also began to take an interest in NPM in the 1980s, spurred by the economic crisis of mid-1970s and the complex challenges of the post-war welfare state.[20] This was particularly notable in the United Kingdom under Margaret Thatcher, and in Australia and New Zealand's managerialist reforms[21] focusing on a "popularised mixture of management, business motivation psychology and the neo-liberal economy".[22] There was a growing consensus that private sector concepts could outperform traditional bureaucratic institutions[23] and what was required was just a "slenderised state with well-functioning competitive markets".[24]

This section discusses PAM theories of the last century within a larger historical and intellectual framework. Against this background, we reflect on three paradoxes in PAM, which we will refer to as "pendulums, practice and particularism". We then look at what's next for PAM, with a normative appraisal of the New Synthesis (Complexity Thinking) and Pragmatism[25] as the potential next paradigms.

Historical Influences on PAM

In order to build a conceptual framework of PAM, it is useful to start by embedding the evolution of PAM theories within their historical context because real-world events are exogenous factors that can influence either the theory or praxis of PAM, and ideally, theory-building should not happen in a vacuum, but rather "is always for someone and for some purpose (reaction to real events or theoretical development to influence reality)".[26] Hence, it is useful to embed PAM theories within their historical context.

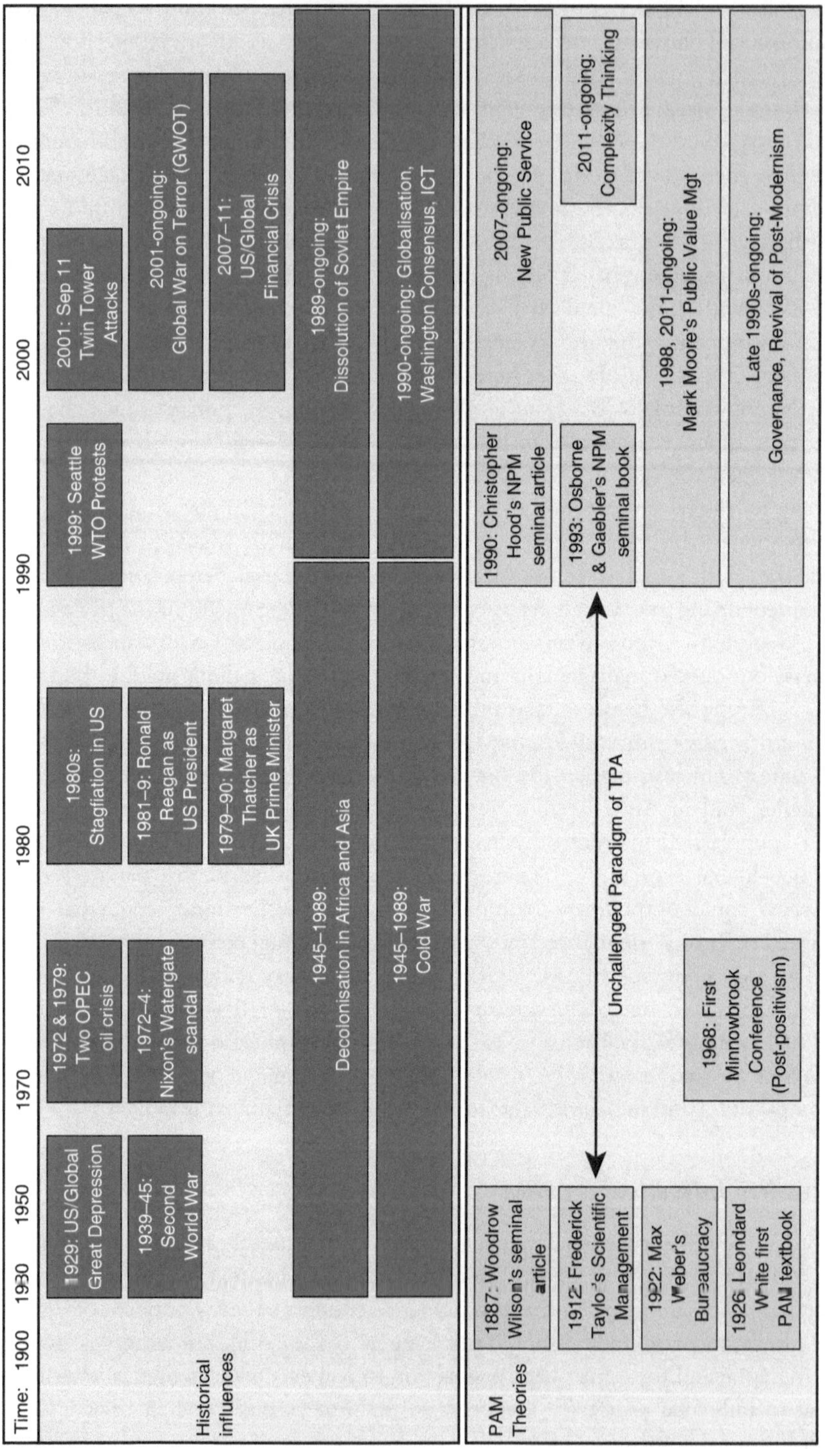

FIGURE 1.1 Historical Influence on Public Administration/Management Paradigms (Phua, 2015)

Orthodoxy – State for Market Failure

At risk of over-generalising, modern PAM theory began as an academic discipline in the last century with Woodrow Wilson's seminal 1887 article on the topic, followed by Leonard D. White's first PAM textbook in 1926.[27] From that point on, traditional PA, with its application of Taylor's scientific management principles and Weber's theories of bureaucracy,[28] was regarded as the mainstream paradigm. This revolution was crucial in transforming monarchical systems of government into modern bureaucracies.[29] Two world wars and the interwar Great Depression meant that central coordination of resources was important in the management of ravaged economies; this led to the post-1945 Keynesian Consensus and the welfare state.[30] Concomitantly, this period also witnessed the decolonisation movement and the rise of developmental states.[31] Together with the Cold War which required strong government planning of military and strategic affairs, these required the predominance of the state over other sources of power such as markets or civil society.

New Orthodoxy – Markets for State Failure

However, this paradigm was increasingly challenged by world events throughout the 1970s. The 1970s OPEC oil crisis hit the United States, which was heavily dependent on oil, leading to stagflation during the 1980s, both of which highlighted the weaknesses of Keynesian economics and ushered in its Monetarist competitors, and notably the works of Milton Friedman. Politically, the Watergate scandal involving President Nixon and the Vietnam war reduced confidence in the political system. As a reaction to this feeling of decline, Ronald Reagan and Minister Margaret Thatcher came to power in the 1980s, bringing in neo-liberal ideas to address government failure[32] by reasserting the primacy of the elected politician over the bureaucrat as well as trimming the "fat" from the bureaucracy using private sector management principles[33]; this New Public Management (NPM) was later codified as an intellectual movement in the early 1990s, best represented by Osborne & Gaebler's *Reinventing Government*.[34]

The 1990s can be considered the peak of the NPM movement. Several factors contributed to this. Globally, the end of Cold War secured the dominance of US ideas, and in the United States NPM was practised widely.[35] In the United Kingdom, NPM was adopted by successive Prime Ministers, supported by the organisational clout of the Cabinet Office, and informed by the market-oriented perceptions of private sector advisors.[36] From there, NPM wasinternationalised,[37] both as the result of post-Cold War dominance of the US-led neo-liberal model (the Washington Consensus[38]) and policy learning/transfer by other countries supported by the growth in Information and Communications Technology (ICT) and globalisation. Second, NPM was frequently forced upon non-Anglo-European countries via the World Bank, the International Monetary Fund and to some extent UNDP and bilateral donors, which required recipient countries to adopt NPM reforms in order to receive aid.[39] Although it is debatable whether NPM reforms were accepted internationally or merely or not, a certain level of piecemeal and decontextualised adoption of NPM was visible – corroborated by Cheung & Scott[40] and Manning's[41] study of piecemeal adoption of NPM in Asia and developing countries, respectively.

Globalisation, US Hegemony, Democratisation and ICT

What is seldom discussed is the historical context of the efforts to explore what will come after NPM. These PAM theories include Public Value Management (PVM)[42] and the "Governance" movement[43] of the late 1990s, the revival of postmodernism[44] (early 2000s), New Public Service (NPS) (2007)[45] and complexity thinking/the "New Synthesis" (CT/NS)[46] since 2011. These PAM theories should be seen in the context of increasing globalisation, US hegemony, democratisation and the popularisation of ICT. While these global exogenous forces are hard to measure, a few milestone events can act as proxies for their effects and they include:

(1) 50,000–100,000 anti-trade/pro-democracy protesters from all over the world congregating in Seattle against the WTO meeting there in November 1999;[47] emphasising the power of civil society, people and networks across borders;
(2) 11 Sep 2001 Al Qaeda attacks on the World Trade Centre in New York brought to light the power of transnational terrorism enabled by globalisation and ICT.

Both of these events brought an awareness that civil society (enabled by citizens and networks) was a key stakeholder to be reckoned with. Hence, PVM reasserted the primacy of the citizens and called for "inclusive management" to maximise public participation, and "active user involvement in service design and delivery" to the extent of "co-production".[48] PVM was co-developed between theorists and practitioners following a realisation on the part of the practitioners that there was a need to engage with civil society. Governance (New Public Governance), with its roots in organisational sociology and network theory,[49] was an attempt to deal with the increasingly fragmented and uncertain nature of PAM[50] and include the aspects of participative administration (with public consultation and negotiation)[51] and flexible government[52] (through e-government[53] and virtual organisations[54]). It had a focus on non-state institutions (non-profit and for-profit contractors, non-governmental organisations, inter-governmental organisations)[55] and networks[56] to "do its work",[57] as well as the primacy of citizens as "equal partners" to governments in "collaborative management"[58] that the major NPM pioneers (United States, United Kingdom, Australia and New Zealand) subsequently adopted governance-based reforms.[59] NPS's focus on serving citizens (not customers), valuing citizenship (over entrepreneurship), thinking strategically and acting democratically and valuing people (not just productivity)[60] was essentially a reassertion of the primacy of citizens as part of the democratisation process. Postmodernism can be considered an epistemological twin of PVM, Governance and NPS. PVM's focus on multiplicity (actors, goals, objectives, preferences, accountability, alternatives) and relationships[61] reflects a post-positivist viewpoint, while NPS describes itself as a postmodern project.[62] Postmodernist approaches advocate for democratisation, citizen empowerment and civil society.

"Global Wicked Problems" of Chaos, Uncertainty and Complexity

The next watershed event was probably the US/global financial crisis in 2007/2011,[63] which highlighted the complex and uncertain nature of economic reality and that there exist certain wicked problems that are hard to resolve without making trade-offs and engaging all stakeholders. A political corollary was probably the Global War on Terror (GWOT), which involved a realisation during the Obama administration[64] that toppling the Taleban and the Ba'ath regime was not sufficient to usher peace in the region and that the complex politico-strategic reality required the engagement of international and regional stakeholders. These events provide context for the development of CT/NS[65] since 2011. CT/NS sees public administration as a dynamic system with the capacity to adapt to changing circumstances and to co-evolve with society: government transforms society and is transformed by it.[66] It argues that "public results are a combination of public policy results and civic results" and public servants, as stewards, are to "mediate and leverage on collective capacity (of public, private and civic spheres) for better results".[67] It emphasises dynamism (non-linearity), adaptability, co-evolution and synergistic co-production with public. Philosophically, CT aims to move beyond dualism and embraces duality (both/and) in generating consensus, and co-production with multiple stakeholders across systems and boundaries in "one-ness". This recognition of complexity is also found in Bennington and Moore's (2011) revised vision of PVM, in which he acknowledged the changing context as a "complex adaptive system" (CAS) and the need to "make sense of this complex new pattern of polycentric networked governance".[68] For this reason, Bennington and Moore (2011) reformulated PVM to guide "networked community governance" (NCG) and focus on relationships between state, civil society and citizens.[69]

4. Paradigms of Public Administration/Management (PAM): Intellectual Influences

The previous section described how history has a direct influence on PAM, though the exact causality is hard to determine with precision even in retrospect. Just as within the sub-disciplines of social and policy sciences (SPS), there is a sub-conscious cross-learning and intellectual borrowing between sub-disciplines. For example, the broad academic paradigms that have influenced SPS have also influenced PAM theories and International Relations (IR) – see later. In this section, we will look at the various influences on interpretation of phenomena in the social sciences.

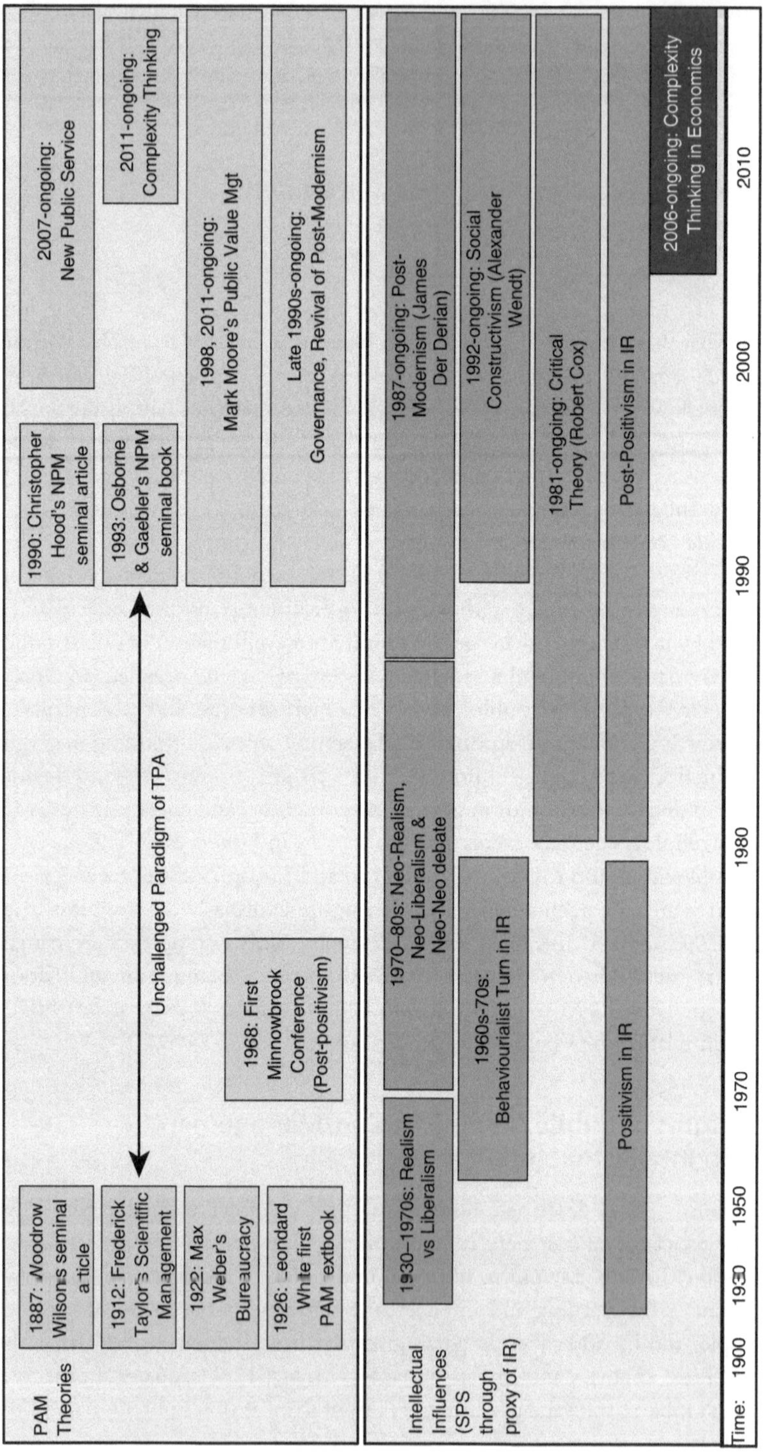

FIGURE 1.2 Intellectual Influences on PAM (Phua, 2015)

Positivism

Similar to PAM, IR has been deemed an American Social Science due to the sheer quantitative dominance of American scholars.[70] In the realism[71] versus liberalism,[72] the debate was on agency and within a positivist paradigm whereby agency will, by nature, act in a certain manner (period). Agency in the PAM context would probably refer to TPA's bureaucratic, NPM's market and Governance's civil society. There was a behaviourialist turn in Political Science which affected IR[73] where formal modelling and quantitative studies became prevalent. Neo-Realism[74] and Neo-Liberalism[75] focused on structures in international relations that drive agents to behave in a certain manner (period). Structures in the PAM context would probably refer to role of institutions in Public Policy (PP) literature and how government structures (classical institutionalism) determine policy outcomes.[76] There was an intense neo–neo debate[77] between both camps. Both these strands of thought represent the Rationalism and Positivism in IR, and there was even a structure–agency debate arguing whether structure, by itself, drives agents to behave in a certain manner or agents have self-volition to behave as they wish.[78] This structure–agency debate can also be observed within PP with the policy dynamics frameworks such as Ostrom's Institutional Analysis and Design (IAD) and Sabatier's Advocacy Coalition Framework (ACF).[79]

Post-Positivism

Positivist positions in IR were challenged by the post-positivist movement.[80] There are various post-positivist camps: critical theorists[81] argue that "theory is always for someone and for some purpose" and that research should be explicitly ideological,[82] refuting the positivist assertion that value-free research is possible. In PAM, the emphasis on civil society enabled by networks, democratisation and globalisation in PVM/Governance/NPS can be argued to be an outcome of this intellectual influence, via Jurgen Habermas's Frankfurt School[83] on SPS. Social constructivists,[84] meanwhile, argued that international politics is socially constructed, being the product of ideas,[85] interests,[86] culture[87] and norms.[88] This has much parallel in public policy (PP) literature on role of institutions,[89] interests and ideas.[90] In PAM, PVM focuses on the roles of ideas, culture and norms in the search for public value.[91] This reflects the wider intellectual influence of Lev Vygotsky's[92] social constructivism/constructionism on SPS. Moreover, PAM has its own strand of post-modernism, and hence the intellectual influence of sociolinguists and philosophers such as Foucault and Derrida has permeated through both PAM and IR.

Complexity Thinking

NPM is a child of (traditional) neo-classical economics,[93] whereas complexity economics (CE) steered away from traditional economics in the following ways:

(1) It focuses on open, dynamic, non-linear systems far from equilibrium (vs. closed, static, linear systems in equilibrium);

(2) Agents are modelled as having incomplete information and subject to errors and biases but can learn and adapt over time (vs. complete information and perfection without errors, biases and need to learn);
(3) Macro-patterns are an emergent result of micro-level interactions (vs. macro and micro being treated as separate disciplines);
(4) Evolutionary processes of differentiation, selection and amplification to provide are present (vs. no endogenous mechanism for growth).[94]

CE has strong parallels with CT/NS in PAM as both were adapted from CT and Complex Adaptive Systems (CAS), which was inspired by "various philosophical theories such as dynamical systems theory, chaos theory, biological evolution, genetics, cybernetics, game theory and science of networks".[95]

Historical and Intellectual Influences on PAM

To take stock, both real events and developments within SPS have influenced PAM (see Figure 1.3) and such influences are dynamic (moreover, PAM theories could, in theory, also potentially influence SPS and real-world events). The primacy of positivism prevalent in neo-classical economics and behaviourialist IR also had an impact on PAM, as evidenced by the positivist tendencies of TPA and NPM, where singularity, unitary, static-ness and ideological one-ness is assumed. This starkly contrasts with post-positivist IR (critical theory, constructivism and postmodernism). In PAM, to an extent, PVM's focus on multiplicity (actors, goals, objectives, preferences, accountability, alternatives) and relationships[96] reflects post-positivism; NPS is a self-defined postmodernist project;[97] governance and collaborative management are arguably postmodernist in their emphasis on democratisation, citizen empowerment and civil society.

5. Paradoxes in Public Administration/Management

Paradoxes: Pendulums

Based on the broad conceptual framework of PAM provided previously, it is possible to identify three interesting paradoxes, which we call "pendulums, practice and particularism". By "pendulums", there is an observed "two steps forward, one step backward" phenomenon whereby theories a dialectic manner, with each new development being a reaction against the previous one.[98] Per this pendulum effect, PAM started with the pro-state TPA, and then moved onto the anti-state, pro-market NPM, to the current anti-market, pro civil society governance.[99] In each of these paradigms, a new entity is championed in order to mitigate the excesses of the one that is currently dominant. Civil society was not an invention of the 2000s, but it was never entirely accounted for under the NPM paradigm; similarly, while markets existed during the TPA era but were not considered important within the

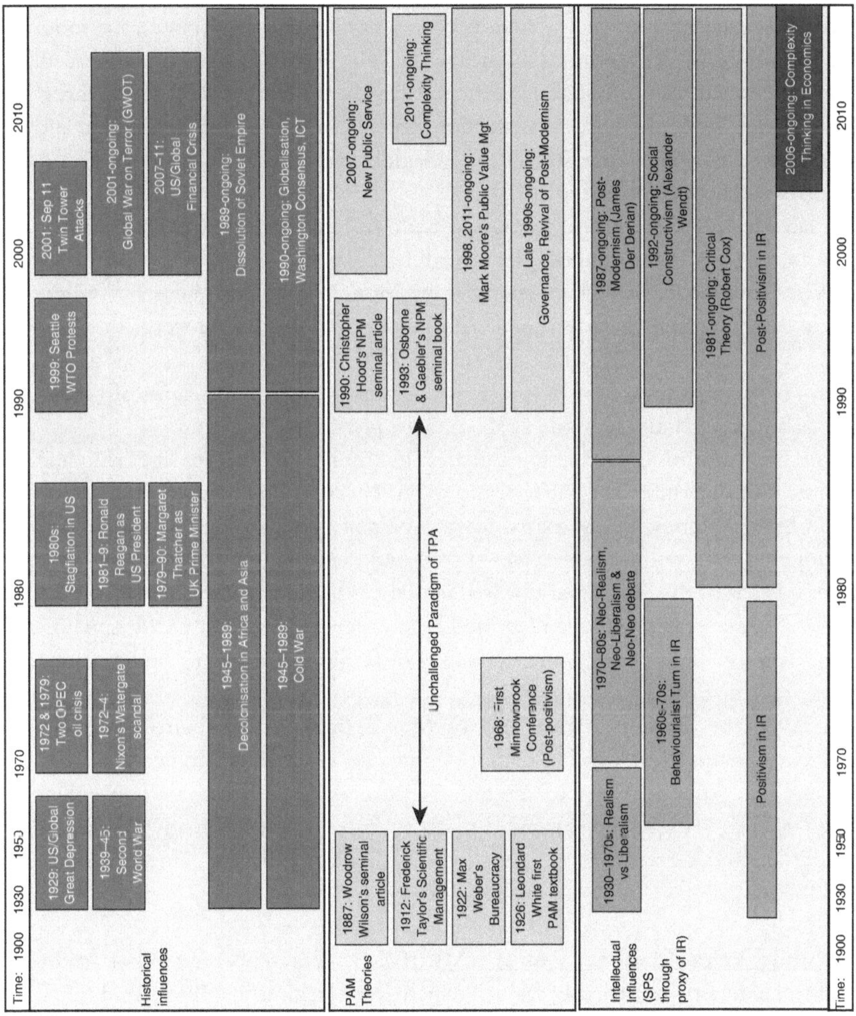

FIGURE 1.3 Historical and Intellectual Influences on PAM (Phua, 2015)

public sector context. It took almost a century before CT in the form of NS[100] emerged, asserting that state, market and civil society are equally important.

The reasons for this pendulum effect are manifold, many of which are abstract and empirically untestable, but this chapter will focus on one: the "Western Knowledge Enterprise", because PAM as a field has traditionally been dominated by western (US) academia. At the risk of over-generalising, PAM over the last century tended to be subject to philosophical reductionism, which is related to the positivism/modernism in SPS. There had to be one right answer with no room for uncertainty. In economics, this meant that Keynesian school argued that all economic reforms must be state-led lest another Great Depression (due to market failure) occur, while the monetarist school argued that state-led reform is bad and market-led reforms are better. Today, the US/global financial crisis in 2007/2011[101] was seen as a failure of monetarism.[102]

Related to this reductionist approach is philosophical dualism: the Western tendency to think in binary opposites. According to Jacques Derrida,[103] meaning in the West is defined in terms of binary oppositions, "a violent hierarchy" where "one of the two terms governs the other". Hence, in TPA, state governs the market, and vice versa in NPM. The implication is that in order to win, one has to find all ways to suppress the *other* in this zero-sum game. Hence, proponents of NPM/monetarism are inclined to argue at all costs for pro-market reforms

The implications of reductionism and philosophical dualism are real and immense. For one thing, the half-century Cold War was essentially a fight between the US Liberals and Soviet Marxists. It was a case of "both Americans and Soviets thinking that their political ideals were better and that there can be only one right answer". It has been argued that this is a natural consequence of the categorisation process.[104] Once countries have identified each other as being part of the same in-group, there will be both a natural tendency to favour the in-group and a natural tendency to mistrust the outgroup.[105]

Similarly, the TPA (pro-state) and NPM (pro-market) paradigms were self-reinforcing groups that tended to demonise the *other* in order to advance their own solution as the superior one. In the post-NPM era, NPM became a convenient target (*other*) to critique and springboard to advance diverse normative visions as *the* right answer. Currently, the various competing voices in the larger discourse are as follows:

(1) **<u>Public Value Management (PVM)</u>**. PVM[106] represents a new look at the normative aspects of public values which were lacking in NPM. Traditional Public Administration (TPA) treated citizens as clients and constituents,[107] NPM treated citizens as consumers/customers and focused on results,[108] but PVM reasserted their primacy as citizens, in the aim of seeking the public good.[109] This was essentially a critique of NPM's extreme managerialism, whereby citizens were treated as private consumers of public services, devoid of any desire to be involved in the policy process.

(2) **Governance**. Inspired by international regime theory,[110] governance is defined as the "regimes, laws, rules, judicial decisions, and administrative practices that constrain, prescribe and enable the provision of publicly supported goals and services".[111] To the extent that governance incorporates an interest in markets, competition and deregulation,[112] it can be considered an extension of NPM. However, it also includes aspects of participative administration. As Kikert said, if NPM was steering, then governance is "steering at a distance".[113]

(3) **New Public Service (NPS)**. NPS can be considered an "all-round" critique of NPM. Key tenets of NPS are (1) to serve citizens, not customers; (2) to seek the public interest; (3) to value citizenship over entrepreneurship; (4) to think strategically and act democratically; (5) to recognise that accountability isn't simple; (6) to serve, rather than steer; and (7) to value people, not just productivity.[114] This was intended to be a comprehensive critique of NPM's focus on customers, entrepreneurship, steering and productivity and a critique of NPM's extreme managerialist tendencies.[115]

(4) **Postmodernism**. From an epistemological perspective, postmodernism is a critique of the positivist paradigm represented by TPA and NPM. PVM's focus on multiplicity (actors, goals, objectives, preferences, accountability, alternatives) and relationships[116] reflects post-positivism, while NPS describes itself as a postmodernist project.[117] It critiques NPM's focus on markets, steering, productivity and results at the expense of democratisation, citizen empowerment and civil society.

(5) **CT/NS.**[118] CT/NS sees public administration as a dynamic system with the capacity to adapt to changing circumstances and to co-evolve with society: government transforms society and is transformed by it.[119] Philosophically, CT aims to move beyond dualism and embrace duality in generating consensus, and co-producing with multiple stakeholders across systems and boundaries in "one-ness".

Paradoxes: Practice

The next paradox is the theory–praxis divide (theory-led vs. practitioner-led development). In the last century, with the exception of NPM, PVM and CT, most PAM theories were developed within academia and represented the normative ideals of the theorists. NPM was unique in that it was first practised by Anglo-Saxon countries (including Australia and New Zealand) before it was codified by Christopher Hood's *A Public Management for All Seasons*[120] and later popularised by Osborne & Gaebler's *Reinventing Government*[121] a decade later. Hence, it was practiced before being codified.

PVM was initially developed out of a long process of interactive teaching and engagement with public managers. Once the book was published, the ideas were tested and developed further, mainly through debate by teachers on courses for public managers at Harvard, Melbourne and Warwick universities, and practical applications by these trained public managers in their workplaces.[122] Although the later developments (1998–2008) where "academic debate about public value has lagged behind the emerging practice" showed the limits of academia, PVM can be considered a success of iterative theorist-practitioner theory development, though the theory remained an ideal from the perspective of both theorists and practitioners.

Complexity Thinking (CT), in the form of New Synthesis (NS), can be considered a joint theorist-practitioner theory development. NS[123] was a cross-national project which started in 2009 involving close to 200 theorists and practitioners in international roundtables in the Hague, Ottawa, Singapore, Rio de Janeiro and London. It sought to establish

> an intellectual framework, that integrates past practices of enduring value, lessons learnt from 30 years of public sector reform and reality of practice in a post-industrial era, . . . to prepare government to serve the public good and collective interest in face of increasing complexity, uncertainty and volatility.[124]

The project participants argued that:[125]

- The nature of governance is changing.[126]
- Past practices will be insufficient to cope.[127]
- Virtual communities have real influence to shape public policy issues.
- Governments require the active contributions of the people, families and many other actors as public results are a shared responsibility requiring collective effort.
- New ideas, new capacities and new ways of doing things are needed to address these complex issues.[128]

NS describes itself as an "enabling framework that helps to frame questions and explore a space of possibilities".[129] It argues that "public results are a combination of public policy results and civic results" and public servants, as stewards, are to "mediate and leverage on collective capacity (of public, private and civic spheres) for better results".[130] Innovation is hence strongest when "synergistic sharing of roles and responsibilities between people, government and society" in this concept of governance.[131] This adaptive system of government would require four sub-systems[132]:

- Efficient compliance sub-systems include constitutions, conventions, rules and norms that govern how we live in society and help to "set priorities, forge societal and political consensus and conserve energy within a context of constrained actions and behaviours".
- Effective performance sub-systems transform public purpose into concrete actions. It "thinks across systems and work across boundaries, sectors and disciplines" to "reconcile hierarchical accountability with shared responsibility to achieve system-wide, government-wide and societal public results".

- Strong emergence sub-systems help build government's capacity to "anticipate and detect emerging issues and phenomena and introduces proactive interventions to mitigate the risks associated with undesirable events". It also "taps collective intelligence to shape emergent solutions and co-create responses to complex policy issues".
- Powerful resilience sub-systems provide the "reality check to adaptive capacity of government and society". It seeks to "co-produce public results, encourage active participation of citizens, families, communities as value creators and build the adaptive capacity of society to prosper and adapt in all circumstances".

NS describes itself as a "work in progress".[133] First, participant countries have fully adopted NS in practice. Second, the four sub-systems of adaptative government are ideals rather than examples of current practice.

The theory–praxis gap is real and is perhaps best described by Marysia Zalewski's article, "All these theories yet the bodies keep piling up: theory, theorists, theorising".[134] Although it was published in reference to the IR field, Zalewski's comments are relevant across the social sciences. In IR, this led to the recent "practice turn"[135] and the author's own emphasis on pragmatism as an epistemology.

While it can be helpful for practitioners to lead theory development, given their closer proximity to empirical reality, this can be difficult given the divide between academia and practice. Ideally, theory should be co-developed by both theorists and practitioners to tap the strengths of both. However, while there are incentives for academics to co-theorise with practitioners, such cooperation is not yet the norm.

Paradoxes: Particularism

The final paradox is that of particularism (as opposed to universalism). Here, PAM is plagued by the inherent desire to generalise given PAM theories, constructed from and perhaps for specific contexts, to all contexts (universalism). However, across PAM, and perhaps even across SPS broadly, the aim of many – if not most – theories is to become *the universal* theory. NPM is a case in point. At its peak, NPM was the dominant paradigm; there were even claims that NPM was growing "internationalised".[136] However, NPM is a patchwork of practices, many of which existed before the broader concept was articulated.[137] Nevertheless, translation even across Western countries[138] was difficult[139] due to differences in local political culture.

This episode is instructive in theory development terms in three aspects: First, theory development has become increasingly complex as a corollary of the persistent tensions between globalisation and nationalism. In theory, globalisation implies that theory A developed in country A should work better in country B than it may once have done. However, this has not necessarily been the case. However, while universal theorising is impossible, any given theory can still be useful when applied with caution. Hence, "near-generic" principles may be induced but their deductive application needs to be sensitive to intricacies of context. For example, NPM was derived in the US context where private sector leadership had proven to be more capable than its public sector equivalent, and the former was better regarded by citizens than the latter. Elsewhere, such as in Singapore where the public sector leadership was traditionally well-regarded, the adoption of NPM may not be appropriate.[140] Also, well-established theories are liable to be hijacked by practitioners for political reasons unanticipated during the theory development/codification process.

What's Next?

After having described the changes in PAM over the last century, juxtaposing these against historical events and SPS paradigms, and reflecting on its inherent paradoxes, it is apt to conclude with a discussion on what is next for PAM. In fact, it is not clear what will follow NPM, as we remain in the "let a hundred flowers bloom" post-NPM era, during which NPM became a convenient target to critique and a springboard to advance diverse normative visions.

6. Contextual Shift Towards Wicked Problems

However, before trying to determine which of paradigms/theories is the best. It is vital to note that the nature of problems faced has changed. The world currently faces many "wicked problems" – problems that are impossible to solve without radical innovation. Per the Austin Centre for Design – a leading source of research on the topic – a wicked problem is

> a social or cultural problem that is difficult or impossible to solve for as many as four reasons: incomplete or contradictory knowledge, the number of people and opinions involved, the large economic burden, and the interconnected nature of these problems with other problems.[141]

Of course, such problems have always existed (historically), the black death, the Huns' invasion of Europe, the South Sea bubble, etc. In the past, however, these problems were simply written off as being insoluble by human means, and people simply got on with attempting to live with them, leaving their resolution up to Providence. In the modern post-Enlightenment world, however, the belief in humanity's ability to exercise almost unlimited control of its environment is more widespread. If humanity is capable of creating a hole in the ozone layer, wiping out species and warming the planet, the reasoning goes, we must be capable of undoing all of these things if we put our minds to it. Moreover, enthusiasm for such enterprises has never been higher. As interest in traditional party politics has declined, participation in campaign groups and direct action has increased.[142] People are less and less inclined to buy wholesale into a party's full package of policies and would rather commit their time to a single cause that they genuinely believe in – animal rights, social justice, environmental protection or religion, for example. This modular approach to problem-solving is a very 21st-century phenomenon, reflecting the flexibility and specialisation valued in the world of work. It also compounds the difficulty in solving wicked problems.

Horst Rittel summed up the characteristics of wicked problems as follows:[143]

1. There is no definitive formulation of what constitutes a wicked problem. Regular problems can be defined via a simple formulation. For example, the problem of littering can be described quite easily – people tend to drop rubbish in the street rather than taking care to put it in the bin. On the other hand, the problem of poverty is hard to define. Are we talking about absolute or relative poverty, for example? The causes are similarly hard to trace. The cause of litter is either laziness or a lack of rubbish bins. The causes of poverty are far harder to identify. Is it a product of poor education systems? Inequality? Inept government? War? Because the causes cannot easily be identified and enumerated, it is not possible to simply remove them from the equation and thereby end the problem.
2. Wicked problems have no stopping rule. In other words, there is no clear point at which the problem can be said to be solved. At what point can we say that poverty has been "solved"? When absolute poverty has been eliminated? When food and water insecurity is no longer a worry? When all incomes are made equal? This is – obviously – a boon for organisations set up to solve them. The day that cancer is cured everyone involved in cancer-related NGOs will be jobless. This is not a worry for those employed by organisations campaigning for social justice or environmental protection. There will always be something more to do.
3. Solutions to wicked problems are not true-or-false but good-or-bad. It is easy to check whether a litter problem has been fixed: either there is litter in the streets or there is not. If there is no litter, then the solution you applied was correct; if there is still litter to be seen, then your solution was wrong and you will have to try again. On the other hand, it can be difficult to rank potential solutions to wicked problems. A solution that reduces poverty by 5% may seem like a positive thing, but it looks less appealing if another potential solution exists that is capable of reducing it by 10%. Also, most solutions carry concomitant risks or benefit one part of the population while harming others. A shift from a capitalist to a socialist economy may reduce poverty, or it may vastly increase it, for example. Can the change be justified? Should a cost–benefit analysis be applied, or should governments apply the precautionary principle and do nothing that is liable to cause harm? It is likely that those who benefit from any given solution will judge it to have been a success, while those who lose out will assess it to have failed. Which group should be believed?
4. There is no immediate and no ultimate test of a solution to a wicked problem. In the case of a simple problem such as littering, the success or failure of a solution can immediately be assessed once and for all. A successful solution is

one that results in no litter being present. Assuming that the solution did not involve summarily executing anyone suspected of being about to drop litter, it is unlikely to have significant second-order effects. In the case of wicked problems, by contrast, the knock-on effects can be immense and wide-reaching. One famous example of this would be Chairman Mao Zedong's "four pests" campaign, which aimed at improving public health and agricultural production. Citizens were co-opted to help wipe out the mosquitos and flies responsible for spreading disease and the rats and sparrows that were blamed for eating seed grain and fruit. The campaign was highly successful, but as it progressed the Chinese leadership gradually realised that the sparrows performed an essential function in the ecosystem, eating insects that would otherwise feed on crops. With the sparrow population decimated, locusts spread unchecked, swarming across the country and vastly reducing rice yields. This exacerbated the problems provoked by the intensive industrial agriculture promoted during the Great Leap Forward, and contributed to a famine in which between 15 million and 45 million people died. In the end, the Chinese authorities were forced to import 250,000 sparrows from the Soviet Union in an attempt to bring the locust population back under control.[144] While the campaign was successful as far as reducing the sparrow population was concerned, it was a dismal failure when it came to the indirect goal of improving agricultural production.

5. Every solution to a wicked problem is a "one-shot operation"; because there is no opportunity to learn by trial and error, every attempt counts significantly. If a local government puts up anti-littering posters and this fails to have an impact on the litter problem, then the only real cost is that of printing the posters. Once it has been recognised that this tentative solution has failed, another option (fines, additional street cleaners, more bins) can be tried. On the other hand, the cost of the Four Pests campaign was not merely that of the effort involved in wiping out the pests in question but also the rice crops eaten by locusts and the lives lost as a result. Abandoning the sparrow extermination policy and importing foreign birds could fix the problems created by the policy, but not bring back those who had died or bring economic growth back to the level at which it would have been had the policy never been implemented.
6. Wicked problems do not have an enumerable (or an exhaustively describable) set of potential solutions, nor is there a well-described set of permissible operations that may be incorporated into the plan. As described earlier, there are only a certain number of reasonable solutions to a littering problem (even if one includes the possibility of mass murder, previously laid aside). On the other hand, there are an almost infinite variety of potential solutions to the problem of poverty, and it is never entirely certain that any of them will do any good. There will usually be as many proposed solutions as there are contributors, and it will be difficult or impossible to assess which is the "best".
7. Every wicked problem is essentially unique. According to Rittel, this means that

> despite long lists of similarities between a current problem and a previous one, there always might be an additional distinguishing property that is of

> overriding importance. Part of the art of dealing with wicked problems is the art of not knowing too early which type of solution to apply". In other words, "there are no classes of wicked problems in the sense that principles of solution [sic] can be developed to fit *all* members of a class.[145]

This means that while one set of solutions may work in a particular place, time and context, they will likely be completely ineffective elsewhere. Thus, the policies that would be likely to reduce poverty in Glasgow or Alabama are unlikely to be effective in Gansu or Nairobi. While the effects are broadly similar, the causes in each case – and thus the solutions – will be different.

8. Every wicked problem can be considered to be a symptom of another problem. As Rittel puts it,

> Problems can be described as discrepancies between the state of affairs as it is and the state as it ought to be. The process of removing the problem starts with the search for causal explanation [sic] of the discrepancy. Removal of that cause poses another problem of which the original problem is a "symptom". In turn, it can be considered the symptom of still another, "higher level" problem. Thus, "crime in the streets" can be considered as a symptom of general moral decay, or permissiveness, or deficient opportunity, or wealth, or poverty, or whatever causal explanation you happen to like best. The level at which a problem is settled depends upon the self-confidence of the analyst and cannot be decided on logical grounds.

In other words, a given problem may interfere in and be subject to interference from a variety of other problems – above, below and orthogonal to the original problem. Thus, attempts to solve the problem of poverty are likely to affect personal liberties, economic growth, inequality, the environment and inflation, among others.

9. The existence of a discrepancy representing a wicked problem can be explained in numerous ways; the choice of explanation determines the nature of the problem's resolution. In other words, wicked problems are highly subject to interpretation and even to social construction. Thus, someone already inclined towards a liberal economic point of view is liable to see poverty as the result of government failure, being the product of incompetent intervention in the free market by the state. On the other hand, people with pre-existing socialist sympathies are more likely to see poverty as a result of market failure, requiring more state intervention to prevent the exploitation of the poor by large corporations. Moreover, both explanations and solution sets can potentially be correct. Often state failure goes hand in hand with market failure, and more interventions are required in certain areas and fewer in others. Similarly, it is possible – as we discussed earlier – that one interpretation will be correct in one context and another elsewhere. This, in turn, will affect the solutions applied.

10. The planner has no right to be wrong. Anyone backing an intervention to change the status quo is responsible for everything that follows. Mao Zedong was not aware that killing sparrows would create a famine, but he nevertheless remains responsible for the results of his policy. For any particular solution to be applied, a high probability of success must be demonstrated, as well as few or trivial adverse side effects. However, such is the nature of the problems in question that it is often impossible to be entirely confident in this score.

As the Austin Center for Design expressed it:

> Based on these characteristics, not all hard-to-solve problems are wicked, only those with an indeterminate scope and scale. So most social problems – such as inequality, political instability, death, disease, or famine – are wicked. They can't be "fixed". But because of the role of design in developing infrastructure, designers can play a central role in mitigating the negative consequences of wicked problems and positioning the broad trajectory of culture in new and more desirable directions. This mitigation is not an easy, quick, or solitary exercise. While traditional circles of entrepreneurship focus on speed and agility, designing for impact is about staying the course through methodical, rigorous iteration. Due to the system qualities of these large problems, knowledge of science, economics, statistics, technology, medicine, politics, and more are necessary for effective change. This demands interdisciplinary collaboration, and most importantly, perseverance.[146]

7. Complexity for Wicked Problems

The concept of wicked problems is related to the idea of complexity. It was borrowed from scientific studies on networked systems, whether in biology or information technology. However, it is important to make clear distinctions between the hard scientific concepts that underlie the idea and the various applications that have been made of it in social science and management studies. While complex systems are an object of study via modelling and other statistical methods in scientific and economic contexts, the majority of social science and management texts on the topic use terms from the field loosely to describe anecdotal information, and their arguments cannot be applied predictively. As Paul Cairney put it,

> The first difficulty with complexity theory is that it is difficult to pin down when we move from conceptual to empirical analysis. While we may find similar discussions in a wide range of texts in the literature, many accounts still highlight terminological and conceptual variation, and often link it to the novelty of complexity theory. Its appeal in the sciences may be because it means different things to different people, suggesting that initial enthusiasm and cross disciplinary cooperation (when focused on broad concepts) may be replaced by growing dissatisfaction, scepticism and uncertainty about a core subject of common study (when focused on applying those concepts).[147]

In a policy and management context, complexity theory looks at questions of uncertainty and non-linearity, as well as feedback loops and interactions.[148] It argues that organisations should not be seen as static structures, but rather as a product of all the processes that go into their functioning. They not only are unpredictable, given the vast number of interactions involved in even simple organisations, but also follow broadly predictable rules that can be isolated with enough thought and study.

Organisations are seen as complex adaptive systems, showing properties such as

- Self-organisation
- Complexity (i.e. the components of the system interact in multiple ways according to rules of their own, with no high-level instruction defining their interactions)
- Emergence (the organisation when considered as an entity on its own has properties not visible in individual components)
- Interdependence
- Co-evolution
- Chaos (small differences in initial inputs can create massive differences in results)
- Self-similarity (the properties of the whole can be extrapolated from a part and vice versa)

Obviously, some of these characteristics are mutually exclusive, so no one system will conform to all of them, but any system showing some of these properties can potentially be described as complex and adaptive. Examples of complex adaptive systems include the stock market, political parties and businesses. The precise characteristics of a given system will affect the formulation and decision-making components of its policy cycles.

For the purposes of public policymaking, there are six characteristics that are key to recognising and interpreting complex systems:

1. A complex system cannot be interpreted by looking at its various component parts, because it is not the parts but their interactions that are the key to understanding it. Moreover, by interacting with one another, the components of the system modify each other, meaning that any static interpretation is merely a one-off snapshot. Thus, for example, analysing one department within a business will not allow you to make predictions about the state of the business, as a whole.
2. The behaviour of complex systems is difficult or impossible to predict. They are subject to feedback loops and non-linear dynamics, as well as the aforementioned chaotic effects. Effect A may be nullified or multiplied when it comes into contact with Effect B, and it is extremely difficult to predict in advance which will occur. When a stock falls, for example, it is difficult or impossible to work out at any given moment whether the drop will continue or whether the market will judge that it is time to "buy the dip" and the price will begin to rise again.

3. Complex systems are particularly sensitive to initial conditions, both due to the aforementioned chaos effect and because they are highly subject to path dependency effects (i.e. they get stuck in a rut). A two-party, first-past-the-post electoral system is likely to continue as a two-party system, even if one of the parties involved collapses. The defunct party will immediately be replaced by another challenger, while the incumbents have no interest in changing rules that provide them with a significant advantage.
4. They exhibit emergence – that is to say, because their behaviour is the product of interactions between different agents, the behaviour of the whole does not necessarily reflect the characteristics of its parts. Thus, for example, while individual economic agents are not necessarily highly rational, the market as a whole displays rational behaviour.
5. They tend to demonstrate punctuated or dynamic equilibrium, being stable for a significant period of time, before going through a burst of significant changes, and then returning to a state of stability.
6. The problems that are most apt to be described using terms from complexity theory tend to be wicked problems: global warming, economic collapse, trade imbalances, etc. These problems have the characteristics described earlier and can only be tackled from an interdisciplinary perspective.

The initial ventures into the complexity arena by public policy scholars focused on the errors that were likely to arise when policymakers and analysts failed to recognise the complex nature of the systems with which they had to deal. Thus, for example, this failure to recognise the implications of complexity has been blamed for the failure of the Soviet Union and of the repeated attempts to jump-start development in Africa.[149] Scholars argued that the reason it is difficult to identify hard and fast laws that can be used to predict social phenomena is because every process is affected by multiple forces. Moreover, attempts to exercise top-down control on such systems are often doomed to failure in the face of their self-organising qualities.

Complexity-related concepts can be tied in with several key ideas from the theories of public policy described in the earlier paragraphs: path dependency, punctuated equilibrium and street-level bureaucracy, for example, all predated the idea of complexity.

8. Complexity Paradigm for Public Administration and Management

Perhaps CT/NS can break through the current deadlock between competing PAM paradigms, given its focus on wicked problems. It is a strong candidate in three aspects.

First, NS is a cumulative synthesis of past PAM theories and hence intended as a break from the aforementioned: 'pendulum effect'.[150] In this pendulum effect, PAM started from pro-state then to pro-market then to pro-civil society and reasserting the public (state). It is designed to combine several strengths of previous NPM theories. By emphasising collective capacity (of public, private and civic spheres) for better results, NS synthesises TPA's argument for a strong public sector, NPM's private sector characteristics and the governance movement's focus on people/civic spheres, while NS's acknowledgement of the influence of virtual communities is an affirmation of the networked governance concept. Its focus on public servants as stewards conceptually parallels NPS's focus on "serving instead of steering". Second, NS seeks to bridge the theory–praxis gap by involving both theorists and practitioners in this initial phase. Third, it relies on a cumulative knowledge enterprise in its attempt to strengthen external validity.

However, existing literature in this emerging field is thin. Rhodes et al. wrote about CT and public management,[151] while Morcol wrote about CT and public policy.[152] Interest in CT in PA theory likely started in 2005 with Jeffrey Weber noting that "public administration theories is drifting and no longer relevant to practitioners and proposed that theories of complexity may reinvigorate the discipline and increase coherent of theory across many perspectives".[153] Rhodes devised a Complex Adaptive System (CAS) framework comprising[154] (1) systems, (2) endogenous and exogenous environment rules and factors, (3) agents, (4) processes and (5) outcomes.[155] CAS described the following dynamics of complex systems[156]: (1) self-organisation, (2) adaptation, (3) path dependency, (4) emergence and (5) bifurcation.[157] While NS articulated a normative framework of how complexity should work to anticipate emergence, manufacture consent, work across boundaries performance and adapt resilience in face of increasingly complex policy issues and environments, CAS represents a positive conceptual framework of how CT and CAS dynamics should work in a given context.

Morcol dissected CT on the conceptual, epistemological and methodological planes, arguing that it views public policy and organisations as being similar to a biological system, being socially constructed via complex interactions with system actors; adaptive and resilient to dynamically and endogenous change in close interaction with external stimuli/environment.[158]

NS and CT are still work in progress. NS is a normative framework, but CT has yet to become a coherent paradigm with a framework, theories and "testable" propositions. Nonetheless, NS and CT have demonstrated promise as an alternative PAM paradigm.

First, from an epistemological perspective, CT changes the conversation on positivism and post-positivism, making an effort to move beyond dualism and embrace duality. NS is about manufacturing consent, co-producing, co-evolving and co-creating with multiple stakeholders across systems and boundaries.

Second, from an ontological perspective, the acknowledgement of complex, uncertain and volatile reality is a key impetus to build adaptive and resilient organisations that will act as best defence against harsh reality; this is in stark contrast to positivism's reductionist tendencies which disregards reality's inherent complexity (though it is worth noting that the goal of modelling is to make accurate predictions, not to describe reality).

Third, from a methodological perspective, CT uses mixed methods as quantitative methods and models are drastically simplified pictures of inherently complex reality and should be complemented with contextual and qualitative understandings of systems and their actors.

Lastly, as a framework/theory, CT (especially CAS) has the potential to be a dynamic framework for decision-making and policy dynamics.

9. Which Way Now? Whither Complexity + Strategic Pragmatism Hybrid Paradigm

However, there are still rooms for other theories in the field. This being so, we would like to propose a synthesis between CT/NS and the author's own work on pragmatism in international relations. Although the discourse on pragmatism in IR is still in its infancy, with pragmatism itself being under-theorised, we have argued that Pragmatism can improve IR theory through (1) empirical insight into concrete problems; (2) "stoic optimism" or the belief that a prudent and productive path towards solving global problems lies somewhere between the extremes; (3) the notion of "Collaborative culture" or that attention the social–cultural context, not simply isolated agents and their motivations, promises theorists and practitioners a more holistic understanding of the international situation.[159] These are also relevant to PAM.

In PAM, there are also faint signals of an interest in pragmatism, with Alford and Hughes (2008) alluding it under the form of "Public Value Pragmatism". Specifically, they argue, "there is no one best way, there are many possible answers . . . it all depends – on the nature of task, context, available technologies and resources". Therefore, it is useful to "be open to alternative possibilities in each situation [and do] problem-solving through pragmatic means (many possible solutions to problems)".[160]

In a previous book (*Towards Strategic Pragmatism in Foreign Policy*),[161] the author set out a definition of strategic pragmatism: "Grand strategy and pragmatism are not antithetical and can co-exist. Strategic pragmatism exists when one has a rigorously devised grand strategy (potentially guided by principles/ideology) that is realistic in its analysis and policy options, and flexibly implemented to adapt to the situation, including tactical adjustments and strategic reversals, to achieve the desired vision and goals. Without an overarching grand strategy, it is likely that feedback loops will lead to knee-jerk responses. This is the gold standard for Pragmatism". For parsimony's sake, it can be summarised in terms of five key features:

Realistic analysis: fact-based analysis of reality; reality as it is, not as one wishes.

Duality: striving for policy innovation or hybrids; breaks the either/or construct, moving towards a both/and construct (duality) where co-existence, mutual wins are possible and desired. This combines principles and pragmatism. Fitzgerald aptly surmised the essence of duality: "The test of first-rate intelligence is the ability to hold two opposed in mind at the same time and still retain the ability to function".[162]

Grand strategy: having a grand strategy to achieve desired strategic vision. Grand strategy has to demonstrate foresight (scenario planning) and insight (systems thinking) in analysis, and long-term planning to achieve long-lasting goals. This is differentiating factor between Strategic Pragmatism and Pragmatism.

Flexibility in implementation: adopting an experimental, trial-and-error approach during implementation which acknowledges that the initial plan may not be perfect. This entails tactical adjustments, operational changes, strategic policy reversals and tight feedback loops. This is a response to the dynamism inherent in complex reality.

Contextualism: having a propensity to reject universal application of particular principles/ideology regardless of context. Having a sensitivity to context allows one to better solve problems in a systemic and long-lasting manner. At the opposite end of the scale, non-pragmatism is directed by ideology: driven by wish-based analysis and with principle predominating over being realistic when the two enter into conflict.

While both appear to be rooted in different academic disciplines (CT from biology and pragmatism from philosophy), a CT–pragmatism hybrid is a possibility. Epistemologically, CT works towards one-ness through philosophical holism, while Pragmatism embraces eclecticism insofar as that it assumes that "there are many possible answers". Ontologically, CT is concerned about the complexity of reality and pragmatism implicitly presupposes such a complex reality when it states that "there is no one best way [to deal with this complex reality]". Methodologically, CT aims to use mixed methods, as does pragmatism.

However, this – for the time being – is where the story ends. It is, of course, up to you to decide which of these theories appeals most to you. The important thing is to understand the history of their development and the reasons behind the changes in fashion from one theory to another. At the time of writing, academics and practitioners were in thrall to complexity, though this will almost certainly have changed by the time you read this. If you know that public servants in a particular department within your area are proponents of a particular theory of public administration, then you can begin to understand why they follow this approach and what it implies for their behaviour and approaches. By understanding the various theories that guide their actions, you will have a greater chance of structuring arguments for your own preferred policies that are likely to appeal to them, and of fitting your own plans in with the plans that they already have. Certainly, most of these approaches have been subject to criticism from those in the field, but they have also been subject to much praise. It is up to the reader to decide in each case whether the former should outweigh the latter. The authors' aim is simply to give the reader access to the best that the public and private sectors have to offer, and thus provide the means, by which they may make their own decisions.

Strategy and innovation are panaceas for all of life's problems, and it is the youngest in society who are often best equipped to innovate, not being bogged down by old theories and the cynicism of age. This is important, because the world currently faces many "wicked problems" – problems that are impossible to solve without radical innovation. These have radically changed the agenda-setting stage of the policy process.

The ensuing chapters will build on the possibility of CT-strategic pragmatism hybrid from scratch – a brick at a time.

Chapter 2 intends to familiarise the reader with the policy process (agenda setting/problem-finding, policy formulation, decision-making, policy implementation and evaluation). Chapter 3 looks at analysis of the macro-situation (environment and organisation) in a pre-problem-finding stage. Chapter 4 is devoted to organisational factors and Chapter 5 to environment–organisation interaction. Chapter 6 starts with the policy lifecycle and enters into the agenda-setting phase with problem re/definition, data collection with stakeholders and analysis tools such as scenarios and systems thinking. Chapter 7 addresses the idea-generation problem using the blue ocean strategy approach and clarity of needs to break through inertia.

Notes

1 Izre'El, Shlomo. "The Amarna letters from Canaan." *Civilizations of the Ancient Near East* 4 (1995): 2411–2419.
2 Linhu, Guo. "Thoughts on criminal law in Shang Shu, or book of documents." *Journal of Beijing College of Politics and Law* 4 (2012): 11.
3 Howlett, Michael. "Policy design: What, who, how and why." *L'instrumentation de l'action publique: Controverses, résistances, effets* (2014): 281–316.
4 Tibebu, Teshale. "On the question of feudalism, absolutism, and the bourgeois revolution." *Review Fernand Braudel Center* (1990): 49–152.
5 Phua, Charles Chao Rong. "From the gulf war to global war on terror-a distorted Sun Tzu in US strategic thinking?" *The RUSI Journal* 152, no. 6 (2007): 46–52.
6 Jackson, Michael W. "Marx's 'critique of Hegel's philosophy of right'." *History of European Ideas* 12, no. 6 (1990): 799–811.
7 Waring, Stephen P. *Taylorism transformed: Scientific management theory since 1945*. New York: UNC Press Books, 2016.
8 Swedberg, Richard, and Ola Agevall. *The Max Weber dictionary: Key words and central concepts*. Redwood City, CA: Stanford University Press, 2016.
9 Walker, Larry. "Woodrow Wilson, progressive reform, and public administration." *Political Science Quarterly* 104, no. 3 (1989): 509–525.
10 Lynn, Laurence. "Public management: A concise history of the field.' In Ewan Ferlie, Laurence E. Lynn Jr, and Christopher Pollitt (Eds.), *The Oxford handbook of public management*, pp. 27–50. New York: Oxford University Press, 2005.
11 Creel, H.G. "The beginnings of bureaucracy in China: The origin of the Hsien." *Journal of Asian Studies* 23 (1964): 155–184.
12 Rosenberg, Hans. *Bureaucracy, aristocracy and autocracy: The Prussian experience 1660–1815*, p. 2. Boston: Beacon Press, 1958.
13 Pollitt, Christopher. *Managerialism and the public services: The Anglo-American experience*. Oxford: Basil Blackwell, 1990.
14 Mosher, F.C. "Introduction." In F.C. Mosher (Ed.), *American public administration: Past present, future*. Alabama: Alabama University Press, 1975.

15 A. Dunsire, *Administration: The word and the science*, p. 94. New York: John Wiley & Sons, 1973.
16 Ostrom, V. *The intellectual crisis in public administration*. Alabama: Alabama University Press, 1973.
17 Lynn, Laurence, *op cit*, 2005, pp. 40–41.
18 *Ibid.*, p. 41.
19 *Ibid.*, p. 42.
20 *Ibid.*
21 Hood, Christopher. "Public management for all seasons." In Jay M. Shafritz, Albert C. Hyde, and Sandra J. Parkes (Eds.), *Classics of public administration*, p. 496. Belmont, CA: Wadsworth, 2008 (1990).
22 Konig, K. "Entrepreneurial management or executive administration: The perspective of classical public administration." In W.J.M. Kickert (Ed.), *Public management and administrative reform in Western Europe*, p. 219. Cheltenham: Edward Elgar, 1997.
23 Minogue, Martin, Chris Polidano, and David Hulme, eds. *Beyond the new public management: Changing ideas and practices in governance*. Cheltenham: Edward Elgar, 1998.
24 Konig, K. *op cit*, 1997, pp. 213.
25 Alford, John, and Owen Hughes. "Public value pragmatism as the next phase of public management." *The American Review of Public Administration* 38, no. 2 (2008): 130.148.
26 Cox, Robert W. "Social forces, states and world orders: Beyond international theory." *Millennium Journal of International Studies* 10, no. 2 (1981): 128.
27 Wilson, Woodrow. (1887). "The study of administration." pp. 16–27 and White, Leonard D. (1926). "Introduction to the study of public administration." pp. 49–56 In Jay M. Shafritz, Albert C. Hyde, and Sandra J. Parkes (Eds.), *op cit*, 2008.
28 Taylor, Frederick. (1912). "Scientific management." pp. 36–8 and Weber, Max. (1922). "Bureaucracy." pp. 43–48 In Jay M. Shafritz, Albert C. Hyde, and Sandra J. Parkes (Eds.), *op cit*, 2008.
29 Minogue, Martin. "The internationalisation of new public management." In Willy McCourt and Martin Minogue (Eds.), *The internationalisation of public management*. Cheltenham: Edward Elgar, 2001, p. 4.
30 *Ibid.*
31 *Ibid.*
32 *Ibid.*, p. 5.
33 NPM had two constituent theoretical paradigms. The former emphasis represented Public Choice Theory and the latter represented Managerialism. As cited in Aucoin, Peter. "Administrative reform in public management: Paradigms, principles, paradoxes and pendulums." *Governance: An International Journal of Policy and Administration* 3, no. 2 (April 1990): 117–118.
34 Osborne, David, and Ted Gaebler, *Reinventing government: How the entrepreneurial spirit is transforming the public sector*. New York: Plume, 1993.
35 Lynn, Laurence, *op cit*, 2005, p. 42.
36 Minogue, Martin, *op cit*, 2001, p. 10.
37 *Ibid.*
38 Gray, J. *False dawn: The delusions of global capitalism*. London: Grata, 1998, as cited in Minogue, Martin, *op cit*, 2001, pp. 1–2.
39 Mathiasen, David. "International public management." In Ewan Ferlie, Laurence E. Lynn Jr, and Christopher Pollitt (Eds.), *The Oxford handbook of public management*. New York: Oxford University Press, 2005, pp. 659–664. See also Minogue, Martin, *op cit*, 2001, p. 7.
40 Cheung, Anthony B.L., and Ian Scott. "Governance and public sector reforms in Asia: Paradigms, paradoxes and dilemmas." In Anthony B.L. Cheung and Ian Scott (Eds.), *Governance and public sector reform in Asia: Paradigm shifts or business as usual?* pp. 1–24. London: RoutledgeCurzon, 2003.
41 Manning, Nick. "The legacy of the new public management in developing countries." *International Review of Administrative Sciences* 67 (2001): 297–312.

42 See Moore, Mark H. *Creating public value: Strategic management in government.* Cambridge, MA: Harvard University Press, 1998. See also Bennington, John, and Mark H. Moore, *Public value: Theory and practice.* Basingstoke: MacMillan Palgrave, 2011.
43 See Kjaer, Anne Mette. *Governance.* Cambridge: Polity Press, 2004. See also Ingraham, Patricia W., and Laurence E. Lynn. *The art of governance.* Washington: Georgetown University Press, 2004.
44 Frederickson, George, and Kevin B. Smith. *The public administration theory primer.* Boulder, CO: Westview Press, 2003, pp. 127–159.
45 Denhardt, Robert B., and Janet Vinzant Denhardt. *The new public service: Serving not steering.* New York: M.E. Sharpe, 2007.
46 Bourgon, Jocelyne. *A new synthesis of public administration: Serving the 21st century.* Montreal: McGill-Queen's University Press, 2011. See also Rhodes, Mary Lee, Joanne Murphy, Jenny Muir, and John A. Murray, *Public management and complexity theory: Richer decision-making in public service.* New York: Routledge, 2011; Morcol, Goktug. *A complexity theory for public policy.* New York: Routledge, 2012.
47 Accessed from: www.globalissues.org/article/46/wto-protests-in-seattle-1999. Accessed on 1 November 2013.
48 Bennington, John, and Mark H. Moore, *op cit*, 2011, p. 25.
49 Osborne, Stephen P. "The new public governance." *Public Management Review* 8, no. 3 (2006): 377–387.
50 Haveri, A. "Complexity in local government change: Limits to rational reforming." *Public Management Review* 8, no. 10 (2006): 31–46.
51 Peters, Guy. *The future of governing.* Lawrence: University Press of Kansas, 2001 as cited in Frederickson, H. George. "Whatever happened to public administration? Governance governance everywhere." In Ewan Ferlie, Laurence E. Lynn Jr, and Christopher Pollitt (Eds.), *op cit*, 2005, p. 288.
52 *Ibid*, p. 288.
53 Snellen, Ignance. "E-Government: A challenge for public management." In Ewan Ferlie, Laurence E. Lynn Jr, and Christopher Pollitt (Eds.), *op cit*, 2005, pp. 398–421.
54 Margetts, Helen. "Virtual organisations." In Ewan Ferlie, Laurence E. Lynn Jr, and Christopher Pollitt (Eds.), *op cit*, 2005, pp. 305–325.
55 Frederickson, H. George., *op cit*, 2005, p. 290.
56 Rhodes, R.A.W. "Governance and public administration." In J. Pierre (Ed.), *Debating governance: Authority, steering and democracy*, pp. 54–60. Oxford: Oxford University Press as cited in Frederickson, H. George., *op cit*, 2005, p. 286.
57 Kettl, D. *Sharing power: Public governance and private markets*, p. xxi. Washington, DC: Brookings Institution, 1993 as cited in Frederickson, H. George., *op cit*, 2005, p. 286.
58 Vigoda, Eran, "From responsiveness to collaboration: Governance, citizens, and the next generation of public administration." *Public Administration Review* 62, no. 5 (September–October 2002): 527–540.
59 Peters, Guy, *op cit*, 2005, p. 287.
60 Denhardt, Janet V., and Robert B. Denhardt, *op cit*, 2007.
61 O'Flynn, Janine. "From new public management to public value: Paradigmatic change and managerial implications." *The Australian Journal of Public Administration* 66, no. 3 (2007): 361.
62 Denhardt, Janet V., and Robert B. Denhardt, *op cit*, 2007, pp. 39–42.
63 Accessed from: www.theguardian.com/business/2011/aug/07/global-financial-crisis-key-stages. Accessed on 1 November 2013.
64 This is evident in 2010 National Security Strategy which steered away from George W. Bush's unilateral military might and emphasised on engaging US's allies and partners in GWOT. Accessed from: www.washingtonpost.com/wp-dyn/content/article/2010/05/27/AR2010052701044.html. Accessed on 1 November 2013.
65 Bourgon, Jocelyne, *op cit*, 2011. See also Rhodes, Mary Lee, Joanne Murphy, Jenny Muir, and John A. Murray, *op cit*, 2011; Morcol, Goktug, *op cit*, 2012.

66 Bourgon, Jocelyne. "Reclaiming public administration." *Ethos*, no. 4 (April 2008). See also Bourgon, Jocelyne. "Serving beyond the predictable." *Ethos*, no. 7 (January 2010).

67 Bourgon, Jocelyne. "The new synthesis: Preparing government for challenges of the 21st century." *Ethos*, no. 10 (October 2011).

68 Bennington, John, and Mark H. Moore, *op cit*, 2011, p. 15.

69 *Ibid*, p. 35.

70 Hoffmann, Stanley. "An American social science: International relations." *Daedalus* 106, no. 3, *Discoveries and Interpretations: Studies in Contemporary Scholarship* I (Summer 1977): 41–60.

71 Morgenthau, Hans. *Politics among nations: The struggle for power and peace* (6th ed.), pp. 1–51. New York: Knopf, 1985; E.H. Carr, *The twenty years crisis*. London: Macmillan, 1946; Waltz, Kenneth. *Man, the state and war*. New York: Columbia University Press, 1959. For Classical Realism, see Thucydides. *The Peloponnesian War*, Book 1, paras 1–23, 66–88, 118–124, 140–146; Book 4, paras 37–51; Book V, Melian dialogue; Book 6, paras 84–116.

72 Axelrod, Robert. *The evolution of cooperation*. New York: Basic Books, 1984, pp. 3–105, 145–191; Doyle, Michael. "Liberalism in world politics." *American Political Science Review* 80, no. 4 (1986): 1151–1169.

73 Frieden, Jeffry A., and David A. Lake. "International relations as a social science: Rigor and relevance." 23 March 2005. Accessed from: www.rochelleterman.com/ir/sites/default/files/Frieden%20Lake%202005.pdf. Accessed on 1 December 2013.

74 Waltz, Kenneth. *Theory of international politics*. New York: McGraw Hill, 1979; Jervis, Robert. "Realism, game theory, and cooperation." *World Politics* 40 (1988): 317–349.

75 Keohane, Robert, ed. *Neorealism and its critics*. New York: Columbia University Press, 1986.

76 Weaver, R. Kent, and Bert A. Rockman. "When and how do institutions matter?" In R. Kent Weaver and Bert A. Rockman (Eds.), *Do institutions matter? Government capabilities in the United States and abroad*, pp. 445–461. Washington, DC: Brookings Institution, 1993.

77 Powell, Robert. "Anarchy in international relations theory: The neorealist-neoliberal debate." *International Organization* 48 (Spring 1994): 313–344.

78 Dessler, David. 'What's at stake in the agent-structure debate?" *International Organization* 43, no. 3 (1989): 441–473; Wendt, Alexander. "The agent-structure problem in international relations theory." *International Organization* 41 (Summer 1987): 35–73.

79 Morcol, Goktug, *op cit*, 2012, p. xii.

80 Smith, Steve, Ken Booth, and Marysia Zalewski, *International theory: Positivism and beyond*. Cambridge: Cambridge University Press, 1996.

81 Cox, Robert W., *op cit*, 1981, p. 128.

82 Cox, Robert W. "Gramsci, hegemony, and international relations: An essay in method." *Millennium Journal of International Studies* 12 (1983): 162–175.

83 Gottlieb, Roger S. "The contemporary critical theory of Jürgen Habermas." *Ethics* 91, no. 2 (January 1981): 280–295.

84 Wendt, Alexander. "Anarchy is what states make of it: The social construction of power politics." *International Organization* 46 (Spring 1992): 391–425; Wendt, Alexander. *Social theory of international politics*. Cambridge: Cambridge University Press, 1999; Adler, Emanuel. "Seizing the middle ground: Constructivism in world politics." *European Journal of International Relations* 3, no. 3 (1997): 319–363; Ruggie, John Gerard. "What makes the world hang together: Neo-utilitarianism and the social constructivist challenge." *International Organization* 52, no. 4 (1998): 855–885.

85 Goldstein, Judith, and Robert Keohane. "Ideas and foreign policy: An analytical framework." In Judith Goldstein and Robert O. Keohane (Eds.), *Ideas and foreign policy: Beliefs, institutions and political change*, pp. 3–30. Ithaca: Cornell University Press, 1993.

86 Finnemore, Martha. *National interest in international society*. Ithaca: Cornell University Press, 1996.

87 Katzenstein, Peter, ed. *The culture of national security*. New York: Columbia University Press, 1996.
88 Barkin, Samuel, and Bruce Cronin. "The state and the nation: Changing norms and the rules of sovereignty in international relations." *International Organization* 48 (1994): 107–130.
89 Hall, P.A., and R.C.R. Taylor. "Political science and the three new institutionalisms." *Political Studies* 44 (1996): 936–57.
90 Braun, D. "Interests or ideas? An overview of ideational concepts in public policy research." In D. Braun and A. Busch (Eds.), *Public policy and political ideas*, pp. 11–29. Cheltenham: Edward Elgar, 1999.
91 Bennington, John, and Mark H. Moore, *op cit*, 2011, p. 24.
92 Vygotsky, Lev. *Social development theory*, 1978. As cited in www.k-state.edu/musiceducation/eportfolio/cexum/images/Images%20File%20for%20Eportfolio/Lev%20Vygotsky%20Social%20Development%20Theory%20Class%20Hand%20Out.pdf. Accessed on 1 November 2013.
93 Osborne, Stephen P. "The new public governance?" *Public Management Review* 8, no. 3 (2006): 382.
94 Beinhocker, Eric, *The origin of wealth: Evolution, complexity and the radical remaking of economics*, p. 97. Boston, MA: Harvard Business School Press, 2006.
95 Morcol, Goktug, *op cit*, 2012, p. 2.
96 O'Flynn, Janine, *op cit*, 2007, pp. 353–366.
97 Denhardt, Janet V., and Robert B. Denhardt, *The new public service: Serving not steering*. New York: M.E. Sharpe, 2007.
98 Pendulum effect is creatively adapted from Light, P.C. *The tides of reform, making government work 1945–199*5. New Haven, CT: Yale University Press, 1998.
99 Ramesh, M., Eduardo Araral Jr, and Xun Wu, eds. *Reasserting the public in public services: New public management reform*. Oxon: Routledge, 2010.
100 Bourgon, Jocelyne, *op cit*, 2011. See also Rhodes, Mary Lee, Joanne Murphy, Jenny Muir, and John A. Murray, *op cit*, 2011; Morcol, Goktug, *op cit*, 2012.
101 Accessed from: www.theguardian.com/business/2011/aug/07/global-financial-crisis-key-stages. Accessed on 1 November 2013.
102 Accessed from: www.nytimes.com/2008/04/13/weekinreview/13goodman.html?pagewanted=all&_r=0. Accessed on 1 December 2013.
103 Derrida, Jacques. *Positions*, p. 41. Chicago: University of Chicago Press, 1981.
104 Chen-Bo, Zhong, Katherine W. Phillips, Geoffrey J. Leonardelli, and Adam D. Galinsky. "Negational categorization and intergroup behavior." *Personality and Social Psychology Bulletin* 34, no. 6 (2008): 793–806. Accessed from: www.ncbi.nlm.nih.gov/pubmed/1839102.5 Accessed on 1 December 2013.
105 "You are either with us or against us." *CNN*, 6 November 2001. Accessed from: http://edition.cnn.com/2001/US/11/06/gen.attack.on.terror/. Accessed on 1 December 2013.
106 Moore, Mark H., *op cit*, 1998, pp. 1–26.
107 Denhardt, Janet V., and Robert B. Denhardt, *op cit*, 2007, p. 28.
108 O'Flynn, Janine, *op cit*, 2007, p. 361.
109 *Ibid*, p. 361.
110 Frederickson, H. George, *op cit*, 2005, pp. 283, 293–294.
111 Lynn, Laurence E. Jr., Carolyn J. Heinrich, and Carolyn J. Hill. *Improving governance: A new logic for empirical research*, p. 7. Washington, DC: Georgetown University Press, 2001.
112 Peters, Guy, *op cit*, 2001 as cited in Frederickson, H. George, *op cit*, 2005, p. 288.
113 Kikert, Walter. "Public governance in the Netherlands: An alternative to Anglo-American 'managerialism'." *Public Administration* 75 (1997): 731–752 as cited in Frederickson, H. George, *op cit*, 2005, p. 287.
114 Denhardt, Janet V., and Robert B. Denhardt, *op cit*, 2007.
115 The latest rendition is perhaps Ramesh, M., Eduardo Araral, and Xun Wu, *op cit*, 2010.

116 O'Flynn, Janine, *op cit*, p. 361.
117 Denhardt, Janet V., and Robert B. Denhardt, *op cit*, 2007, pp. 39–42.
118 Bourgon, Jocelyne, *op cit*, 2011. See also Rhodes, Mary Lee, Joanne Murphy, Jenny Muir, and John A. Murray, *op cit*, 2011; Morcol, Goktug, *op cit*, 2012.
119 Bourgon, Jocelyne, *op cit*, April 2008. See also Bourgon, Jocelyne, *op cit*, January 2010.
120 Hood, Christopher, *op cit*, 1990, pp. 495–507.
121 Osborne, David, and Ted Gaebler, *op cit*, 1993.
122 Bennington, John, and Mark H. Moore, *op cit*, 2011, p. 16.
123 Bourgon, Jocelyne, *op cit*, October 2011.
124 *Ibid.*
125 *Ibid.*
126 These differences will transform the role of government, public servants and relationship between public institutions, public organisations and citizens.
127 Past practices will be insufficient to cope with increasing number of complex public policy issues and an environment characterised by uncertainties, volatility and cascading global crises.
128 This entails multiple integrations, interactions and relationships to forge emergent solutions to daunting challenges.
129 Bourgon, Jocelyne. "Exploring new frontiers of public administration: The new synthesis project." *Canadian Government Executive* 17, no. 3 (March 2011): 16–18.
130 Bourgon, Jocelyne, *op cit*, October 2011.
131 *Ibid.*
132 *Ibid.* See also Bourgon, Jocelyne, *op cit*, 2011, pp. 59–61.
133 Bourgon, Jocelyne, *op cit*, October 2011.
134 Zalewski, Marysia. "'All these theories yet the bodies keep piling up': Theory, theorists, theorising." In Steve Smith, Booth Ken, and Marysia Zalewski (Eds.), *International theory: Positivism and beyond*, pp. 340–353. Cambridge: Cambridge University Press, 1996.
135 See Millennium Journal Vol 40, 2012 on "Weaving the Theories and Practices in International Relations."
136 Hood, Christopher, *op cit*, 2008 (1990). See also Peter Aucoin, *op cit*, April 1990, pp. 115–137. See also Pollitt, Christopher, *op cit*, 1990.
137 David Mathiasen, *op cit*, 2005, pp. 645.
138 *Ibid.*, p. 10.
139 Dolowitz, D., and D. Marsh. "Policy transfer: A framework for comparative analysis." In Martin Minogue, C. Polidano, and D. Hulme (Eds.), *Beyond the new public management: Ideas and practices in governance*. Cheltenham: Edward Elgar, 1998.
140 Ramesh, M., Eduardo Araral, and Xun Wu, *op cit*, 2010.
141 Austin Center for Design. "An introduction to wicked problems." Accessed from: www.wickedproblems.com/1_wicked_problems.php#:~:text=A%20wicked%20problem%20is%20a,these%20problems%20with%20other%20problems. Accessed on 29 November 2020.
142 Grant, Wyn. "Pressure politics: From 'insider' politics to direct action?" *Parliamentary Affairs* 54, no. 2 (2001): 337–348.
143 Rittel, Horst W.J., and Melvin M. Webber. "Dilemmas in a general theory of planning." *Policy Sciences* 4, no. 2 (1973): 155–169.
144 Pantsov, Alexander V., and Steven I. Levine. *Mao: The real story*. New York: Simon and Schuster, 2013.
145 Rittel, Horst W.J., and Melvin M. Webber, *op cit*, pp. 155–169.
146 Austin Center for Design, *op cit*.
147 Cairney, Paul. "Complexity theory in political science and public policy." *Political Studies Review* 10, no. 3 (2012): 346–358.
148 Grobman, Gary M. "Complexity theory: A new way to look at organizational change." *Public Administration Quarterly* (2005): 350–382.
149 Geyer, Robert, and Samir Rihani. *Complexity and public policy: A new approach to twenty-first century politics, policy and society*. London: Routledge, 2010.

150 Pendulum effect is creatively adapted from Light, P.C., *op cit*, 1998.
151 Rhodes, Mary Lee, Joanne Murphy, Jenny Muir, and John A. Murray, *op cit*, 2011.
152 Morcol, Goktug, *op cit*, 2012.
153 Weber, Jeffrey. 'Introduction to chaos, complexity, uncertainty and public administration: A symposium." *Public Administration Quarterly* 29, no. 3 (2005): 262–267.
154 Rhodes, Mary Lee, Joanne Murphy, Jenny Muir, and John A. Murray, *op cit*, pp. 10–13.
155 (1) System refers to the boundaries that separate system from its environment; (2) Endogenous and exogenous environment rules and factors that will affect behaviour of agents and outcomes; (3) Agents who are individuals engaging in processes within the system to accomplish objectives; (4) Processes which are actions and interactions among agents to connect behaviour (constrained/facilitated by system) with outcomes; (5) Outcomes which are results or impacts of system.
156 Rhodes, Mary Lee, Joanne Murphy, Jenny Muir, and John A. Murray, *op cit*, pp. 14–15.
157 (1) Self-organisation (natural consequence of interaction between simple agents); (2) adaptation (changes made by agents in response to other participants, environmental conditions or emergent system characteristics); (3) path-dependency (tendency for systems to lock into particular behaviours early due to environmental conditions, nature of agents and early interactions); (4) emergence (creation of new properties at higher level of abstraction that cannot be predicted based on antecedent actions or component elements of phenomena); (5) bifurcation (dynamic to illustrate structures in semi-equilibrium which collapsed into disorder before adopting a new form and equilibrium state from spontaneous self-organisation).
158 Morcol, Goktug, *op cit*, pp. 1–44; 143–162; 262–275.
159 Weber, Eric Thomas, *op cit*, 2013, pp. 36–43.
160 *Ibid.*, pp. 143, 145.
161 Phua, Charles Chao Rong, *op cit*, 2021.
162 Fitzgerald, F. Scott. *Great Gatsby*. New York: Charles Scribner's Sons, 1925.

Bibliography

Adler, E. (1997). "Seizing the middle ground: Constructivism in world politics." *European Journal of International Relations* 3(3): 319–363.

Agranoff, R., M. McGuire, and S. Silivia. (2013). "Governance, networks and intergovernmental systems." In E. Araral, S. Fritzen, M. Howlett, M. Ramesh, and X. Wu (Eds.), *Routledge handbook of public policy*, pp. 361–373. New York: Routledge.

Aligica, P.D., and P.J. Boettke. (2009). *Challenging institutional analysis and development: The Bloomington School*. London: Routledge.

Anderson, T.L., and F.S. McChesney (Eds.). (2003). *Property rights: Cooperation, conflict and law*. Princeton, NJ: Princeton University Press.

Andrews, C.J. (2007). "Rationality in policy decision making." In F. Fischer, G.J. Miller, and M.S. Sidney (Eds.), *Handbook of public policy analysis: Theory, politics and methods*, pp. 43–62. Boca Raton: CRC Press.

Anonymous. (2011). "The future of public administration in 2020: The spirit of Minnowbrook 2011." *Journal of Public Administration Research and Theory (JPART)*, Special Issue III.

Aucoin, P. (1990). "Administrative reform in public management: Paradigms, principles, paradoxes and pendulums." *Governance: An International Journal of Policy and Administration* 3(2): 117–118.

Austin Center for Design. (2020). "An introduction to wicked problems." Accessed from: www.wickedproblems.com/1_wicked_problems.php#:~:text=A%20wicked%20problem%20is%20a,these%20problems%20with%20other%20problems. Accessed on 29 November 2020.

Axelrod, R. (1984). *The evolution of cooperation*. New York: Basic Books.

Bajorek, Zofia M., and Stephen M. Bevan. (2015). "Performance-related-pay in the UK public sector." *Journal of Organizational Effectiveness: People and Performance* 2(2): 94–109.

Barkin, S., and B. Cronin. (1994). "The state and the nation: Changing norms and the rules of sovereignty in international relations." *International Organization* 48: 107–130.

Barnett, M., and K. Sikkink. (2008). "From international relations to global society." In C. Reus-Smit and D. Snidal (Eds.), *The Oxford handbook of international relations*, p. 65. Oxford: Oxford University Press.

Bathlet, H., and J. Gluckler. (2011). *The relational economy: Geographies of knowing and learning*. Oxford: Oxford University Press.

Bauer, H., and E. Brighi (Eds.). (2009). *Pragmatism in international relations*. Oxon: Routledge.

Bennett, C.J., and M. Howlett. (1992). "The lessons of learning: Reconciling theories of policy learning and policy change." *Policy Sciences* 25(3): 275–294.

Bennington, J., and M.H. Moore. (2011). *Public value: Theory and practice*. Basingstoke: MacMillan Palgrave.

Birdsall, N., and F. Fukuyama. (2011). "The post-Washington Consensus: Development after the crisis." *Foreign Affairs* 90(2). Accessed from: www.foreignaffairs.com/articles/67456/nancy-birdsall-and-francis-fukuyama/the-post-washington-consensus.

Birkland, T.A. (1998). "Focusing events, mobilization, and agenda setting." *Journal of Public Policy* 18(1): 53–74.

Bourgon, J. (2008). "Reclaiming public administration." *Ethos* 4: 5–9.

Bourgon, J. (2010). "Serving beyond the predictable." *Ethos* 7: 5–11.

Bourgon, J. (2011a). "The new synthesis: Preparing government for challenges of the 21st century." *Ethos* 10: 14–20.

Bourgon, J. (2011b). *A new synthesis of public administration: Serving the 21st century*. Montreal: McGill-Queen's University Press.

Braun, D. (1999). "Interests or Ideas? An overview of ideational concepts in public policy research." In D. Braun and A. Busch (Eds.), *Public policy and political ideas* (pp. 11–29). Cheltenham: Edward Elgar.

Buchanan, J.M., and G. Tullock. (1962). *The Calculus of consent*. Ann Arbor: University of Michigan Press.

Butler, B.E. (2013). "Obama pragmatism in international relations: Appropriate or appropriation?" In S.J. Ralston (Ed.), *Philosophical pragmatism and international relations: Essays for a bold new world*, pp. 159–176. Lanham, MD: Lexington Books.

Cairney, Paul. (2012). "Complexity theory in political science and public policy." *Political Studies Review* 10(3): 346–358.

Carlsnaes, W. (2002). "Foreign policy." In W. Carlsnaes, T. Risse, and B.A. Simmons (Eds.), *Handbook of international relations*, pp. 331–349. London: Sage Publications.

Carr, E.H. (1946). *The twenty years crisis*. London: Macmillan.

Chhotray, V., and G. Stoker. (2009). *Governance theory and practice: A cross disciplinary approach*. Basingstoke: Palgrave MacMillan.

Choi, Y.J., and J.A. Caporaso. (2002). "Comparative regional integration." In W. Carlsnaes, T. Risse, and B.A. Simmons (Eds.), *Handbook of international relations*, pp. 480–499. London: Sage Publications.

Clark, I. (1999). *Globalization and international relations theory*. Oxford: Oxford University Press.

Clemens, E.S., and J.M. Cook. (1999). "Politics and institutionalism: Explaining durability and change." *Annual Review of Sociology* 25: 441–466.

Clemons, Randy S., and Mark K. McBeth. (2020). *Public policy praxis: A case approach for understanding policy and analysis*. Oxon: Routledge.

Coase, R. (1997). "Nature of the firm." *Economica* 4(16): 386–405.

Coase, R. (2013). "The institutional structure of production." In C. Menard and M.M. Shirley (Eds.), *Handbook of new institutional economics*, pp. 31–40. Heidelberg: Springer.
Cohen, B.J. (2002). "International finance." In W. Carlsnaes, T. Risse, and B.A. Simmons (Eds.), *Handbook of international relations*, pp. 429–447. London: Sage Publications.
Cohen, M., J. March, and J. Olsen. (1972). "A garbage can model of organizational choice." *Administrative Science Quarterly* 17(1): 1–25.
Cooper, H. (2010). *Research synthesis and meta-analysis*. Thousand Oaks, CA: Sage.
Cox, R.W. (1981). "Social forces, states and world orders: Beyond international theory." *Millennium Journal of International Studies* 10(2): 126–155.
Cox, R.W. (1983). "Gramsci, hegemony, and international relations: An essay in method." *Millennium Journal of International Studies* 12: 162–175.
Crabb, C.V Jr. (1989). *American diplomacy and the pragmatic tradition*. London: Louisiana State University Press.
Dahlberg, Lincoln. (2004). "The Habermasian public sphere: A specification of the idealized conditions of democratic communication." *Studies in Social and Political Thought* 10(10): 2–18.
Dator, J., D. Pratt, and Y. Seo. (2006). *Fairness, globalization and public institutions: East Asia and beyond*. Hawaii: University of Hawaii Press.
de Felice, D., and F. Obino. (2012). "Editors' introduction: Weaving the theories and practices in international relations." *Millennium: Journal of International Studies* 40(3): 431–437.
De Soto, H. (2001). *The mystery of capital: Why capitalism triumphs in the west and fails everywhere else*. New York: Basic Books.
Denhardt, R.B., and J.V. Denhardt. (2007). *The new public service: Serving not steering*. New York: M.E. Sharpe.
Dennard, F.L., K.A. Richardson, and G. Morçöl (Eds.). (2008). *Complexity and policy analysis: Tools and concepts for designing robust policies in a complex world*. Goodyear, Ariz: ISCE.
Der Derian, J. (1987). *On diplomacy: The genealogy of western estrangement*. London: Blackwell.
Dessler, D. (1989). "What's at stake in the agent-structure debate?" *International Organization* 43(3): 441–473.
Doyle, M. (1986). "Liberalism in world politics." *American Political Science Review* 80(4): 1151–1169.
Duffield, J.S. (2006). "International security institutions: Rules, tools, schools or fools?" In R.A.W. Rhodes, Sarah A. Binder, and Bert A. Rockman (Eds.), *The Oxford handbook of political institutions*, pp. 633–653. Oxford: Oxford University Press.
Dunleavy, P. (1994). "The globalization of public services production: Can government be 'best in world'?" *Public Policy and Administration* 9(2): 36–64.
Dunleavy, P., and Christopher Hood. (1994). "From old public administration to new public management." *Public Money & Management* 14(3): 9–16.
Dunlop, C. (2013). "Epistemic communities." In E. Araral, S. Fritzen, M. Howlett, M. Ramesh, and X. Wu (Eds.), *Routledge handbook of public policy*, pp. 229–243. New York: Routledge.
Edkins, J. (1999). *Post-structuralism and international relations: Bringing the political back in*. Colorado: Lynne Rienner.
Epstein, D., and S. O'Halloran. (1999). *Delegating powers*. New York: Cambridge University Press.
Evans, M., and J. Davies. (1999). "Understanding policy transfer: A multi-level, multi-disciplinary perspective." *Public Administration* 77(2): 361–385.
Farazmand, A. (1999). "Globalization and public administration." *Public Administration Review* 59(6): 509–522.

Ferlie, Ewan, and Edoardo Ongaro. (2015). *Strategic management in public services organizations: Concepts, schools and contemporary issues*. New York: Routledge.

Finkelstein, L.S. (1995). "What is global governance." *Global Governance* 1(3): 367–372.

Finnemore, M. (1996). *National interest in international society*. Ithaca: Cornell University Press.

Florini, A. (2006). "International NGOs." In R.A.W. Rhodes, S.A. Binder, and B.A. Rockman (Eds.), *The Oxford handbook of political institutions*, pp. 673–692. Oxford: Oxford University Press.

Forester, John. (1993). *Critical theory, public policy, and planning practice*. New York: SUNY Press.

Frederickson, G.H., and K.B. Smith. (2003). *The public administration theory primer*. Boulder, CO: Westview Press.

Frederickson, H.G. (1980). *New public administration*. Alabama: University Alabama Press.

Frederickson, H.G. (2005). "Whatever happened to public administration? Governance, governance everywhere." In E. Ferlie, L.E. Lynn Jr., and C. Pollitt (Eds.), *The Oxford handbook of public management*, p. 288. New York: Oxford University Press.

George, J. (1994). *Discourses of global politics: A critical (re)introduction to international relations*. Boulder, CO: Lynne Rienner.

Geva-May, I. (2001). "When the motto is 'till death do us part': The conceptualization and the craft of termination in the public policy cycle." *International Journal of Public Administration* 24(3): 263–288.

Geyer, Robert, and Samir Rihani. (2010). *Complexity and public policy: A new approach to twenty-first century politics, policy and society*. New York: Routledge.

Giddens, A. (1984). *The constitution of society: Outline of the theory of structuration*. Cambridge: Polity Press.

Gilady, L., and B. Russett. (2002). "Peace-making and conflict resolution." In W. Carlsnaes, T. Risse and B.A. Simmons (Eds.), *Handbook of international relations*, pp. 392–408. London: Sage Publications.

Goldman, L. (2013). "Getting beyond international relations theory." In S.J. Ralston (Ed.), *Philosophical pragmatism and international relations: Essays for a bold new world*, pp. 15, 65. Lanham, MD: Lexington Books.

Goldstein, J., and R. Keohane. (1993). "Ideas and FP: An analytical framework." In J. Goldstein and R.O. Keohane (Eds.), *Ideas & foreign policy: Beliefs, institutions, and political change*, pp. 3–30. Ithaca: Cornell University.

Gottlieb, R.S. (1981). "The contemporary critical theory of Jürgen Habermas." *Ethics* 91(2): 280–295.

Grant, Wyn. (2001). "Pressure politics: From 'insider' politics to direct action?" *Parliamentary Affairs* 54(2): 337–348.

Gray, J. (1998). *False dawn: The delusions of global capitalism*. London: Grata.

Grobman, Gary M. (2005). "Complexity theory: A new way to look at organizational change." *Public Administration Quarterly*: 350–382.

Guo, Linhu. (2012). "Thoughts on criminal law in Shang Shu, or book of documents." *Journal of Beijing College of Politics and Law* 4: 11.

Haas, P.M. (1992). "Epistemic communities and international policy coordination." *International Organization* 46(1): 1–35.

Hall, P.A., and R.C.R. Taylor. (1996). "Political science and the three new institutionalisms." *Political Studies* 44: 936–957.

Harris, C. (2010). *Research synthesis and meta-analysis*. Thousand Oaks, CA: Sage.

Haveri, A. (2006). "Complexity in local government change: Limits to rational reforming." *Public Management Review* 8(10): 31–46.

Hawkins, K., and J.M. Thomas. (1989). "Making policy in regulatory bureaucracies." In K. Hawkins and J.M. Thomas (Eds.), *Making regulatory policy*, pp. 3–30. Pittsburgh: University of Pittsburgh Press.

Hayes, M. (2013). "Incrementalism." In E. Araral, S. Fritzen, M. Howlett, M. Ramesh, and X. Wu (Eds.), *Routledge handbook of public policy*, pp. 287–298. New York: Routledge.

He, Baogang, and Stig Thøgersen. (2010). "Giving the people a voice? Experiments with consultative authoritarian institutions in China." *Journal of Contemporary China* 19(66): 675–692.

Heclo, H. (1978). "Issue networks and the executive establishment." In A. King (Ed.), *The new American political system*, pp. 87–124. Washington, DC: American Enterprise Institute for Public Policy Research.

Held, D. (1995). *Democracy and the global order: From the modern state to cosmopolitan governance*. Cambridge: Cambridge University Press.

Hendriks, C. (2013). "Policy evaluation and public participation." In K. Hawkins and J.M. Thomas (Eds.), *Making regulatory policy*, pp. 3–30. Pittsburgh: University of Pittsburgh Press.

Héritier, A. (2003). "New modes of governance in Europe: Increasing political capacity and policy effectiveness?" In T.A. Börzel and R. Cichowski (Eds.), *The state of the European Union: Law, politics, and society*, pp. 105–126. New York: Oxford University Press.

Higgott, R. (2006). "International political institutions." In R.A.W. Rhodes, S.A. Binder, and B.A. Rockman (Eds.), *The Oxford handbook of political institutions*, pp. 611–632. Oxford: Oxford University Press.

Holcombe, R.G. (2005). *Public sector economics: The role of government in the American economy*. New York: Prentice Hall.

Howlett, M. (2007). "Analyzing multi-actor, multi-round public policy decision-making processes in government: Findings from five Canadian cases." *Canadian Journal of Political Science* 40(3): 659–684.

Howlett, M. (2009). "Policy analytical capacity and evidence-based policy-making: Lessons from Canada." *Canadian Public Administration* 52(2): 153–175.

Howlett, M. (2014). "Policy design: What, who, how and why." *L'instrumentation de l'action publique: Controverses, résistances*, effets: 281–316.

Howlett, M., A. Perl, and M. Ramesh. (2009). *Studying public policy: Policy cycles and policy subsystem*. Toronto: Oxford University Press.

Ingraham, P.W., and L.E. Lynn. (2004). *The art of governance*. Washington: Georgetown University Press.

Izre'El, Shlomo. (1995). "The Amarna letters from Canaan." *Civilizations of the Ancient Near East* 4: 2411–2419.

Jackson, Michael W. (1990). "Marx's 'critique of Hegel's philosophy of right'." *History of European Ideas* 12(6): 799–811.

Jones, B., and H. Thomas. (2013). "Bounded rationality and public policy decision-making." In E. Araral, S. Fritzen, M. Howlett, M. Ramesh, and X. Wu (Eds.), *Routledge handbook of public policy*, pp. 273–286. New York: Routledge.

Joyce, Paul. (2016). *Strategic leadership in the public sector*. New York: Routledge.

Jupille, J., and J.A. Caporaso. (1999). "Institutionalism and the European Union: Beyond international relations and comparative politics." *Annual Review of Political Science* 2(9): 429–444.

Kadelbach, S. (2009). "From public international law to international public law: A comment on the 'public authority' of international institutions and the 'publicness' of their law'." In A. von Bogdandy, R. Wolfrum, J. von Bernstorff, P. Dann, and M. Goldmann

(Eds.), *The exercise of public authority by international institutions: Advancing international institutional law*, pp. 33–49. Heidelberg: Springer.

Katzenstein, P. (Ed.). (1996). *The culture of national security*. New York: Columbia University Press.

Kay, A. (2013). "Policy trajectories and legacies: Path dependency revisited." In E. Araral, S. Fritzen, M. Howlett, M. Ramesh, and X. Wu (Eds.), *Routledge handbook of public policy*, pp. 462–472. New York: Routledge.

Keohane, R. (Ed.). (1986). *Neorealism and its critics*. New York: Columbia University Press.

Kettl, D. (1993). *Sharing power: Public governance and private markets*. Washington, DC: Brookings Institution.

Kingdon, J.W. (1995). *Agendas, alternatives and public policies*. Boston: HarperCollins College Publishers.

Kjaer, A.M. (2004). *Governance*. Cambridge: Polity Press.

Klinger, D.E. (2004). "Globalization, governance and the future of public administration: Can we make sense out of the fog of rhetoric surrounding the terminology?" *Public Administration Review* 64(6): 737–743.

Krasner, S.D. (1983). "Structural causes and regime consequences: Regimes as intervening variables." In S.D. Krasner (Ed.), *International regimes*, pp. 1–22. New York: Cornell University Press.

Lasswell, Harold D. (1970). "The emerging conception of the policy sciences." *Policy Sciences* 1(1): 3–14.

Lejano, R.P. (2013). "Post-positivism and the policy process." In E. Araral Jr., M. Howlett, M. Ramesh, and X. Wu (Eds.), *Routledge handbook of public policy*, pp. 98–112. New York: Routledge.

Lindblom, C.E. (1959). "The science of muddling through." *Public Administration Review* 19(2): 79–88.

Lipsky, Michael. (2010). *Street-level bureaucracy: Dilemmas of the individual in public service*. New York: Russell Sage Foundation.

Little, R. (2009). "Preface." In H. Bauer and E. Brighi (Eds.), *Pragmatism in international relations*, pp. xii–xiii. Oxon: Routledge.

Margetts, H. (2005). "Virtual organisations." In E. Ferlie, L.E. Lynn Jr., and C. Pollitt (Eds.), *The Oxford handbook of public management*, pp. 305–325. New York: Oxford University Press.

Marsh, D., and M. Smith. (2000). "Understanding policy networks: Towards a dialectical approach." *Political Studies* 48: 4–21.

Martin, L.L. (2006). International economic institutions. In R.A.W. Rhodes, S.A. Binder, and B.A. Rockman (Eds.), *The Oxford handbook of political institutions*, pp. 654–72. Oxford: Oxford University Press.

Maskin, E. (2010). "Mechanism design: How to implement social goals." Accessed from: www.nobelprize.org/nobel_prizes/economic-sciences/laureates/2007/maskin_lecture.pdf. Accessed on 20 April 2014.

Maxfield, S. (2002). "International development." In W. Carlsnaes, T. Risse, and B.A. Simmons (Eds.), *Handbook of international relations*, pp. 462–479. London: Sage Publications.

McConnell, A. (2013). "Learning from success and failure?" In K. Hawkins and J.M. Thomas (Eds.), *Making regulatory policy*, pp. 3–30. Pittsburgh: University of Pittsburgh Press.

McGinnis, M. (Ed.). (1999). *Poly centricity and local public economies: Readings from workshop in political theory and policy analysis*. Ann Arbour: University of Michigan Press.

McGinnis, M. (2011). "An introduction to IAD and the language of the Ostrom workshop: A simple guide to a complex framework." *Policy Studies Journal* 39(1): 169–183.

McNabb, David E., and Chung-Shing Lee. (2020). *Public sector strategy design: Theory and practice for government and nonprofit organizations*. Oxon: Routledge.

Mendez, R.P. (1992). *International public finance: A new perspective on global relations*. Oxford: Oxford University Press.

Milner, H.V. (2002). "International trade." In W. Carlsnaes, T. Risse, and B.A. Simmons (Eds.), *Handbook of international relations*, pp. 480–499. London: Sage Publications.

Minogue, M. (2001). "The internationalization of new public management." In W. McCourt and M. Minogue (Eds.), *The internationalization of public management: Reinventing the third world state*, pp. 1–19. Cheltenham: Edwin Elgar.

Mitchell, R.B. (2002). "International environment." In W. Carlsnaes, T. Risse, and B.A. Simmons (Eds.), *Handbook of international relations*, pp. 500–516. London: Sage Publications.

Mitleton-Kelly, Eve, Alexandros Paraskevas, and Christopher Day (Eds.). (2018). *Handbook of research methods in complexity science: Theory and applications*. Oxon: Edward Elgar Publishing.

Moore, M.H. (1998). *Creating public value: Strategic management in government*. Cambridge, MA: Harvard University Press.

Morçöl, G. (2002). *A new mind for policy analysis: Toward a post-newtonian and post-positivist epistemology and methodology*. London: Praeger.

Morcol, G. (2012). *A complexity theory for public policy*. New York: Routledge.

Morgenthau, H. (1985). *Politics among nations: The struggle for power and peace* (6th ed.). New York: Knopf.

Mukherjee, Ishani, and Michael P. Howlett. (2015). "Who is a stream? Epistemic communities, instrument constituencies and advocacy coalitions in multiple streams subsystems." (April 10, 2015). *Lee Kuan Yew School of Public Policy Research Paper*: 15–18.

Muller, H. (2002). "Security cooperation." In W. Carlsnaes, T. Risse, and B.A. Simmons (Eds.), *Handbook of international relations*, pp. 369–391. London: Sage Publications.

Nagel, S.S. (Ed.). (2000). *Handbook of global international policy*. New York: Marcel Dekker.

Nye, J. (2009). "Get smart: Combining hard and soft power." *Foreign Affairs*, July/August.

O'Flynn, J. (2007). "From new public management to public value: Paradigmatic change and managerial implications." *The Australian Journal of Public Administration* 66(3): 353–366.

O'Toole, L.J. (2000). "Research on policy implementation: Assessment and prospects." *Journal of Public Administration Research and Theory* 10(2): 263–288.

Osborne, D., and T. Gaebler. (1993). *Reinventing government: How the entrepreneurial spirit is transforming the public sector*. New York: Plume.

Osborne, S.P. (2006). "The new public governance." *Public Management Review* 8(3): 377–387.

Ostrom, E. (1990). *Governing the commons: The evolution of institutions for collective action*. New York: Cambridge University Press.

Ostrom, E., L. Schroeder, and S. Wynne. (1993). *Institutional incentives and sustainable development: Infrastructure policies in perspective*. Boulder, CO: Westview Press.

Palumbo, D.J. (1987). *The politics of program evaluation*. Beverly Hills: Sage.

Pantsov, Alexander V., and Steven I. Levine. (2013). *Mao: The real story*. New York: Simon and Schuster.

Perry, James L., and Robert K. Christensen. (2015). *Handbook of public administration*. New York: John Wiley & Sons.

Peters, B. Guy, and Jon Pierre. (2017). *The next public administration: Debates and dilemmas*. London: Sage.

Peters, G. (1996). *The future of governing: Four emerging models*. Lawrence: University Press of Kansas.

Peters, G. (1998). "Policy networks: Myth, metaphor and reality." In D. Marsh (Ed.), *Comparing policy networks*, pp. 21–32. Buckingham: Open University Press.

Phua, Charles Chao Rong. (2007). "From the gulf war to global war on terror-a distorted Sun Zi in US strategic thinking?" *The RUSI Journal* 152(6): 46–52.

Phua, Charles Chao Rong. (2015). "Value of public administration management to international relations: Scaffolding an inter-disciplinary research agenda." *International Relations and Diplomacy* 3(12): 843–862.

Phua, Charles Chao Rong. (2021). *Towards strategic pragmatism in foreign policy: Cases of United States of America, China and Singapore.* Oxon: Routledge.

Pines, Yuri. (2008). *Envisioning eternal empire: Chinese political thought of the Warring States era.* Hawaii: University of Hawaii Press.

Pollitt, Christopher, Sandra Van Thiel, and Vincent Homburg (Eds.). (2007). *New public management in Europe.* Basingstoke: Palgrave Macmillan.

Powell, R. (1994). "Anarchy in international relations theory: The neorealist-neoliberal debate." *International Organization* 48(2): 313–344.

Raab, J., and P. Kenis. (2007). "Taking stock of policy networks: Do they matter?" In F. Fischer, G.J. Miller, and M.S. Sidney (Eds.), *Handbook of public policy analysis: Theory, politics and methods*, pp. 187–200. Boca Raton: CRC Press.

Ralston, S.J. (Ed.). (2013). *Philosophical pragmatism and international relations: Essays for a bold new world.* Plymouth: Lexington Books.

Raustiala, K., and A.M. Slaughter. (2002). "International law, international relations and compliance." In W. Carlsnaes, T. Risse, and B.A. Simmons (Eds.), *Handbook of international relations*, pp. 538–558. London: Sage.

Rhodes, M.L., J. Murphy, J. Muir, and J.A. Murray. (2010). *Public management and complexity theory: Richer decision-making in public services* (Vol. 6). Oxon: Routledge.

Rhodes, M.L., J. Murphy, J. Muir, and J.A. Murray. (2011). *Public management and complexity theory: Richer decision-making in public service.* New York: Routledge.

Rhodes, R.A.W. (2000). "Governance and public administration." In J. Pierre (Ed.), *Debating governance: Authority, steering and democracy*, pp. 54–56. Oxford: Oxford University Press.

Rittel, Horst W.J., and Melvin M. Webber. (1973). "Dilemmas in a general theory of planning." *Policy Sciences* 4(2): 155–169.

Roberts, Alasdair. (2020). *Strategies for governing: Reinventing public administration for a dangerous century.* New York: Cornell University Press.

Ruggie, J.G. (1998). "What makes the world hang together: Neo-utilitarianism and the social constructivist challenge." *International Organization* 52(4): 855–885.

Sabatier, P.A. (1986). "Top-down and bottom-up approaches to implementation research: A critical analysis and suggested synthesis." *Journal of Public Policy* 6: 21–48.

Sabatier, P.A. (1988). "An advocacy coalition framework of policy change and the role of policy-oriented learning therein." *Policy Sciences* 21(2/3): 129–168.

Sabatier, P.A., and C.M. Weible. (2007). "The advocacy coalition framework." *Theories of the Policy Process* 2: 189–220.

Satz, Debra, and John Ferejohn. (1994). "Rational choice and social theory." *The Journal of philosophy* 91(2): 71–87.

Saurugger, Sabine. (2013). "Constructivism and public policy approaches in the EU: From ideas to power games." *Journal of European Public Policy* 20(6): 888–906.

Savoie, Donald J. (2006). "What is wrong with the new public management?" In *Comparative public administration.* Oxon: Emerald Group Publishing Limited.

Schaferhoff, M., S. Campe, and C. Kaan. (2009). "Transnational public-private partnership in international relations: Making sense of concepts, research frameworks and results." *International Studies Review* 11(3): 451–474.

Schmidt, V. (2008). "Discursive institutionalism: The explanatory power of ideas and discourse." *Annual Review of Political Science* 11: 303–326.

Schmitz, H.P., and K. Sikkink. (2002). "International human rights." In W. Carlsnaes, T. Risse, and B.A. Simmons (Eds.), *Handbook of international relations*, pp. 517–537. London: Sage Publications.

Schneider, A. (2013). "Policy design and transfer." In E. Araral, S. Fritzen, M. Howlett, M. Ramesh, and X. Wu (Eds.), *Routledge handbook of public policy*, pp. 217–228. New York: Routledge.

Sen, A. (1977). "Rational fools." *Philosophy and Public Affairs* 6(4): 317–344.

Shafritz, J.M., A.C. Hyde, and S.J. Parkes. (2008). *Classics of public administration*. Belmont, CA: Wadsworth.

Smith, S., K. Booth, and M. Zalewski. (1996). *International theory: Positivism and beyond*. Cambridge: Cambridge University Press.

Smouts, M.C. (1998). "The proper use of governance in international relations." *International Social Science* 50.

Snellen, I. (2005). "E-government: A challenge for public management." In E. Ferlie, L.E. Lynn Jr., and C. Pollitt (Eds.), *The Oxford handbook of public management*, pp. 398–421. New York: Oxford University Press.

Stigler, G. (1962). "The economic theory of regulation." *Bell Journal of Economics and Management Science* 3: 3–18.

Stigliz, J. (2014). *Post Washington Consensus Consensus*. The Institute for Policy Dialogue. Accessed from: http://policydialogue.org/files/events/Stiglitz_Post_Washington_Consensus_Paper.pdf. Accessed on 20 February 2014.

Stoker, G. (1998). *Governance as theory: Five propositions*. Geneva: UNESCO.

Swedberg, Richard, and Ola Agevall. (2016). *The Max Weber dictionary: Key words and central concepts*. Redwood City, CA: Stanford University Press.

Taylor, F. (1912). "Scientific management." In J.M. Shafritz and A.C. Hyde (Eds.), *Classics of public administration* (6th ed.), pp. 36–38. Boston: Thomson Wadsworth.

Thucydides. (1910). *The Peloponnesian war*. London: J.M. Dent; New York: E.P. Dutton.

Tibebu, Teshale. (1990). "On the question of feudalism, absolutism, and the bourgeois revolution." *Review Fernand Braudel Center*: 49–152.

True, J.L., B.D. Jones, and F.R. Baumgartner. (1999). "Punctuated-equilibrium theory: Explaining stability and change in American policymaking." In P.A. Sabatier (Ed.), *Theories of the policy process*, pp. 97–115. Boulder: Westview Press.

Vezke, I. (2010). "International Bureaucracies from a political science perspective – Agency, authority and international institutional law." In A. von Bogdandy, R. Wolfrum, J. von Bernstorff, P. Dann, and M. Goldmann (Eds.), *Developing the publicness of public international law: Towards a legal framework for global governance activities*, pp. 3–32, 33–49, 67–98.

Vigoda, E. (2002). "From responsiveness to collaboration: Governance, citizens, and the next generation of public administration." *Public Administration Review* 62(5): 527–540.

von Bogdandy, A., P. Dann, and M. Goldmann. (2008). "Developing the publicness of public international law: Towards a legal framework for global governance activities." *German Law Journal* 9(11): 1375–1400.

Vygotsky, L. (1978). "Social development theory." Accessed from: www.k-state.edu/musiceducation/eportfolio/cexum/images/Images%20File%20for%20Eportfolio/Lev%20Vygotsky%20Social%20Development%20Theory%20Class%20Hand%20Out.pdf. Accessed on 1 November 2013.

Walker, Larry. (1989). "Woodrow Wilson, progressive reform, and public administration." *Political Science Quarterly* 104(3): 509–525.

Walker, R.B.J. (1992). *Inside/outside: International relations as political theory*. Cambridge: Cambridge University Press.

Waltz, K. (1959). *Man, the state and war*. New York: Columbia University Press.

Waltz, K. (1979). *Theory of international politics*. New York: McGraw Hill.

Waring, Stephen P. (2016). *Taylorism transformed: Scientific management theory since 1945*. New York: UNC Press Books.

Weaver, R.K., and B.A. Rockman. (1993). "When and how do institutions matter?" In R.K. Weaver and B.A. Rockman (Eds.), *Do institutions matter? Government capabilities in the United States and abroad*, pp. 445–461. Washington, DC: Brookings Institutions.

Weber, E.T. (2013). "On pragmatism and international relations." In S.J. Ralston (Ed.), *Philosophical pragmatism and international relations*, pp. 36–43. Lanham, MD: Lexington Books.

Weber, Jeffrey A. (2005). "Introduction to chaos, complexity, uncertainty and public administration: A symposium." *Public Administration Quarterly*: 262–267.

Weber, M. (1922). "Bureaucracy." In J.M. Shafritz and A.C. Hyde (Eds.), *Classics of public administration* (6th ed.), pp. 43–48. Boston: Thomson Wadsworth.

Wendt, A. (1987). "The agent-structure problem in international relations theory." *International Organization* 41(Summer): 35–73.

Wendt, A. (1992). "Anarchy is what states make of it: The social construction of power politics." *International Organization* 46: 391–425.

Wendt, A. (1999). *Social theory of international politics*. Cambridge: Cambridge University Press.

White, L.D. (1926). *Introduction to the study of public administration*. New York: Macmillan.

Wiesel, Fredrika, and Sven Modell. (2014). "From new public management to new public governance? Hybridization and implications for public sector consumerism." *Financial Accountability & Management* 30(2): 175–205.

Williamson, O. (2013). *The transaction cost economics project: The theory and practice of the governance of contractual relations*. London: Edward Elgar Pub.

Wilson, W. (1887). "The study of administration." In J.M. Shafritz and A.C. Hyde (Eds.), *Classics of public administration* (6th ed.), pp. 16–27. Boston: Thomson Wadsworth.

2

BRINGING THE PUBLIC AND PROCESS BACK INTO PUBLIC POLICY

A Citizen's Guide to Public Policy Process

Why do most people prefer sales taxes to income taxes, even though the former is more regressive? If rehabilitation of prisoners saves money in the long run, why do we not do more of it? What level of false positive results are acceptable in a public cancer screening initiative?

If you have ever wondered about these things, then you were thinking about public policy. So, what is public policy?

Introductory public policy textbooks are often so enthusiastic about their topic that they define almost everything as public policy. Indeed, Thomas Dye, in what it probably the most frequently cited definition, describes it as "anything a government chooses to do or not to do".[1] For practical purposes, however, the field is far more restrictive, and in fact refers principally to day-to-day decisions made by the executive branch of government and the administrators working under it. While parliamentary and party politics, voting behaviour, political philosophy and constitutional law do affect public policy, public policy as a discipline treats these as outside factors, rather than as the central objects of its study. Whether a constitutional assembly favours a common law system or a Napoleonic code will have an effect on much public policymaking, but it is not the central focus of public policy as a domain. Rather, public policy experts are much more interested in how a government decides to regulate tobacco, or how a local council's traffic enforcement department applies parking regulations. Public policy, in other words, refers to the nitty gritty of government: the day-to-day management of the state, rather than the deep, existential decisions that underlie its existence.

However, just because these decisions are often taken at a relatively low level, this does not necessarily mean that they are trivial. The average citizen will probably never need the protection of his constitution (though his life may indirectly be improved immeasurably by their existence), but the decision to ban parking on his

DOI: 10.4324/9781003307228-2

street may bankrupt his business or bolster the value of his home, thus changing his status in significant and dramatic ways.

Unfortunately, the systems by which such decisions are made are often so opaque and convoluted that they tend to be neglected by ordinary citizens. It is easy to have an opinion about defence, education or economic policy, but difficult and time-consuming to follow the technical bureaucratic processes by which political decisions are translated into practical measures. More often than not, citizens simply vote for the candidate or party that seems to broadly fit in with their own beliefs and preferences, and then assume that his policy proposals will percolate through the system eventually, with no need for them to track or intervene in the fine details.

On the one hand, this can be seen as reassuring: the fact that people have the freedom not to worry about day-to-day political decisions is the sign of a system that is working well. When every minor administrative choice is treated as a matter of life or death by citizens, this is the sign of a polity on the verge of collapse. Apathy is often a sign of contentment rather than despair. However, this tendency can also be the beginning of a slippery slope leading to corruption and arbitrary decision-making. If very few people are interested enough to participate in the making and application of bureaucratic decisions, those who make the effort gain a disproportionate weight within the system. In the United Kingdom, for example, relatively few people take an interest in local politics, even among those who express a high degree of interest in national politics. This has led to the "capture" of local authorities by organised interest groups, which then use their power to engage in election fraud, make regulatory and spending decisions in their own favour, and enrich themselves through corruption.[2] The phenomenon is not just present at the local level. While many of the Scottish National Party's policies are intensely unpopular among ordinary citizens, it is regularly returned to power by a voting bloc that wishes to show support for its core policy of greater independence. The result is that control over the day-to-day running of politics is surrendered in favour of a higher ideal. The principle of independence is easy to understand and stirs up intense emotions, while policies such as regulating alcohol prices and laws surrounding free speech are complicated and difficult to influence, though the latter arguably have far greater influence on individuals' daily lives.[3]

The goal of this book is to make the policymaking process more transparent, and to give readers – whether they are politicians, bureaucrats or simply concerned citizens – the tools they need to participate. However, to participate in the process it is first necessary to understand how it works.

Conventionally, public policymaking is broken down into five stages:

- Agenda setting
- Formulation
- Adoption
- Implementation
- Evaluation

Different political and civil society actors may intervene at different stages in this process, but the stage that most people are most familiar with is definitely the agenda-setting component, since this often passes via the media and party politics. Nevertheless, while many people may feel that they are locked out of the following stages, it is possible for anyone to play a role in all of them, as long as he or she understands the process.

1. Agenda Setting

The *Handbook of Public Policy Analysis* defines an agenda somewhat tautologically as "a collection of problems, understandings of causes, symbols, solutions, and other elements of public problems that come to the attention of members of the public and their governmental officials".[4] In other words, a public policy agenda includes anything that anyone feels that the authorities need to change. Obviously, not everyone's agenda is the same. Some people are highly invested in the idea of declassifying secret information about UFO encounters, and others want a return to the gold standard or an end to daylight savings time. While these may be minority interests within the body politic as a whole, they are nevertheless interests, and may be of extreme importance to the small number of people devoted to them. However, most of the time when people talk about "the political agenda", they mean those issues that are prioritised by the polity in question: crime, healthcare, defence, the economy, etc. These are the issues that feature most frequently in the media, tend to provoke strong feelings and take up the majority of government's bandwidth. It is for this reason that interest groups are so keen to get their own specific issues "on the agenda". Thus, Peta spends member donations on eye-catching publicity initiatives aimed at making people feel uneasy about their treatment of animals, while Oxfam deploys its donors' cash to lobby governments to spend more on foreign aid. While the methods used may be different, the goal is always the same: to raise a particular issue's position on the political agenda. This is often expressed using a circular diagram:

The agenda universe covers every political issue or perceived political issue in existence at a given moment. The systemic agenda, by contrast, includes those that are subject to consideration by those with political power. Thus, while declassifying all of Area 51's documents may be on the agenda of some US citizens, it is not on that of those in control of those documents, and so does not form a part of the systemic agenda. If those who support this move wish to see it implemented, they will need to use lobbying or campaigning strategies to force political deciders to pay attention to it. However, merely obliging a politician to consider a topic is not enough. Even if a politician was sympathetic to the idea of declassifying Area 51's documents, the likelihood is that he would not wish to risk the embarrassment inherent in saying as much, or prioritise it above issues such as the economy. It would thus not be on the institutional agenda – "that list of items explicitly up for the active and serious consideration of authoritative decision makers". Finally,

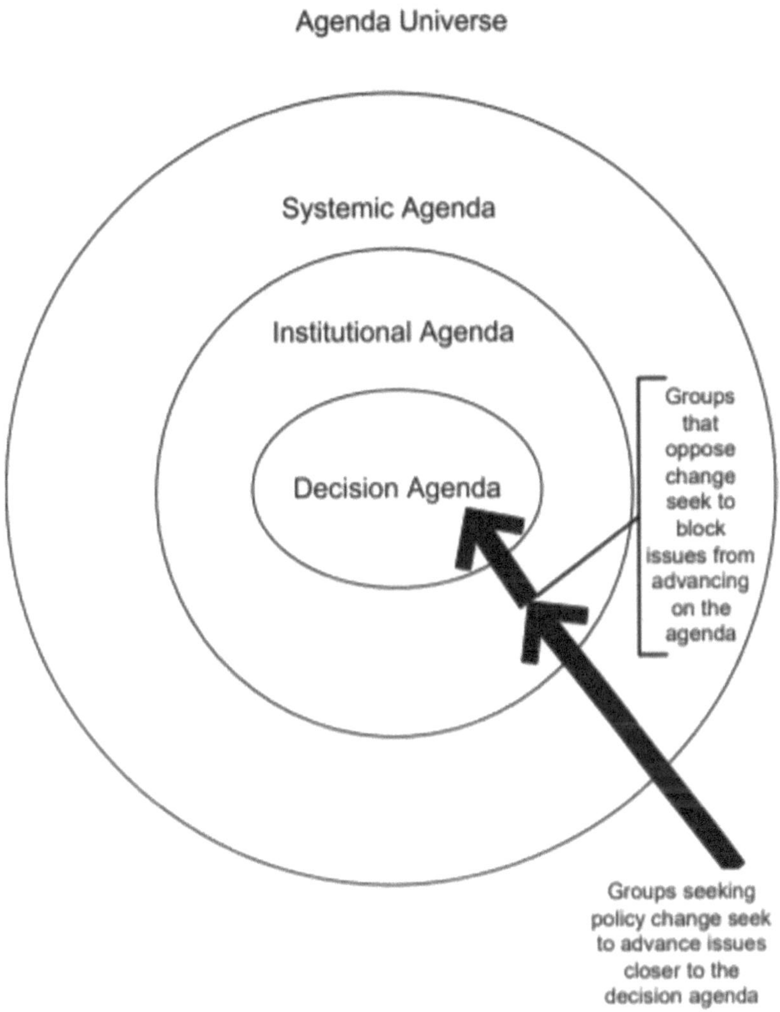

FIGURE 2.1 Agenda Universe (Adapted from Fischer et al., 2007)

there is the decision agenda: issues wherein policy change is immanent, whether via laws, regulations, policy documents or other means.

The policy agenda is very much a matter of social construction. Issues that primarily affect disenfranchised groups are likely to be pushed down the agenda, while those that touch upon the interests of powerful groups will seldom be far from the top. Thus, for example, prescription painkiller addiction is primarily a problem among poor communities (while it exists among wealthy groups, they are less likely to suffer overdose or arrest as a result; thus, it does not appear as a "problem"), meaning that it was largely ignored by US political actors for many years.[5] On the other hand, financial regulation is a major concern among the upper middle classes, so this is rarely far from the agenda.

2. Formulation

Policy formulation is the pre-decision stage of policymaking. It involves research and debate to identify or craft a set of possible solutions to a particular problem as raised during the agenda-setting stage. It involves considering the various facets of the problem, the assets possessed that could be of help in dealing with it, and the benefits and risks of each potential solution.

While it was traditionally perceived as a technocratic process, being dominated by civil servants acting under political orders, other actors do regularly participate in this stage. Lobbyists, whether for corporations or non-profit organisations, regularly submit pre-written bills to legislators in the hope of getting their agenda through parliament. Moreover, government and administrative authorities have increasingly begun carrying out consultations before making policy changes. While it must be admitted that these are very often contrived to highlight contributions that favour the solution that the government prefers and play down others, skilful lobbyists can nevertheless use them to gain publicity for their causes. In some places, government has gone a step further, employing direct democracy as in Switzerland,[6] participatory budgeting processes as in Brazil,[7] or online crowdsourcing as in China.[8]

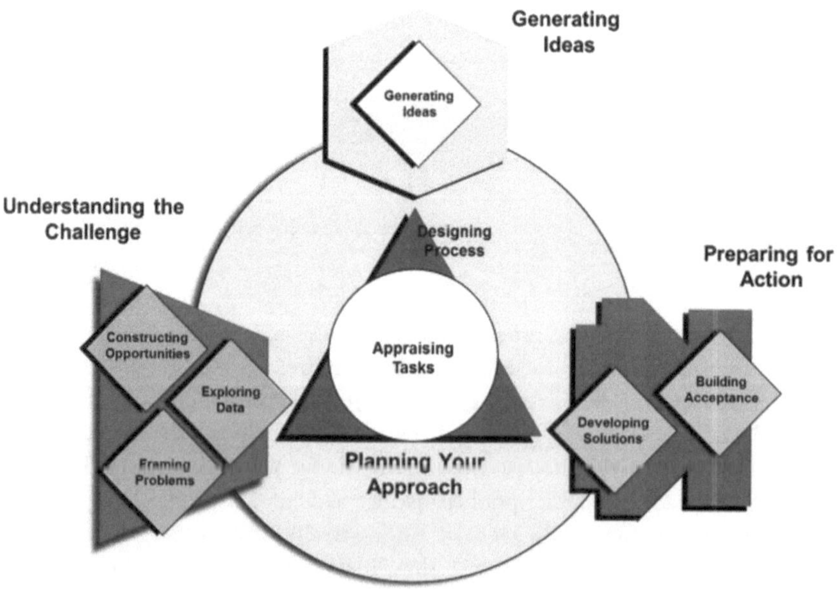

FIGURE 2.2 CPS Framework (Adapted from Dorval, Isaksen et al., 2000)

The policy design process is key to everything that follows and has been the object of much study.[9] This will also be the focus of the present book. The aim is to provide a reference for both professional policymakers, students and concerned citizens, to help all three groups understand the latest theories on the policymaking process. While this process can be approached via multiple methodologies (as will be described later), these all tend to follow the basic stages laid out by the CPS framework developed by Isaksen, Doval et al.[10]

This involves diverging at first, in order to generate as many ideas as possible, before converging to focus on the best among them.

3. Decision-Making

The decision-making stage of policymaking is both easy and difficult to analyse. It is easy because it is a simple binary: either a policy is adopted or it isn't. It is difficult because policy adoption processes vary widely by time, place and level of government. To return to the examples mentioned earlier, in the Swiss direct democracy, initiatives are proposed and adopted by residents at the local level. Brazil has a multilevel representative democratic system with a separation between political and civil service roles; however, participatory budgeting was introduced by the Worker's Party in certain cities as an effort to reduce corruption on the part of local officials and politicians. China, meanwhile, is a one-party state with no separation between political and bureaucratic functions. Decisions are made at the national, provincial or local levels by the party in collaboration with the bureaucracy.

Policy decision-making in your area will happen according to whatever rules you have in place. While a certain amount of work has been done on the creation of policy and voting coalitions, the decision-making component of the policy process is often covered to a great degree by political science.

4. Implementation

Given public policy's focus on the bureaucratic aspects of policymaking, the discipline has shown a long-running interest in the implementation phase of policymaking. While the agenda setting, formulation and adoption stages of the process have also been extensively researched by political scientists, they often neglect the implementation stage. However, implementation can make or break a policy. Well-intentioned as political deciders may be, the policy orientations that they fix upon will never have the intended effect if the bureaucracy refuses to implement them properly. In France, for example, bureaucrats deliberately delayed the implementation of further education reforms as a negotiating tactic in a dispute over salary and working conditions.[11] Similarly, if a policy does not meet the expectations or desires of the public, they will not engage with it and once again it will fail.

Indeed, many researchers concluded from their investigations of the implementation process that bureaucrats – far from being neutral executors – often have a preponderant effect on the practical effects of political decisions. As well as deciding whether and how policies will be implemented, they also control much of the information that is passed upwards concerning the public's responses to the policies and their requests for changes.[12] Yet other researchers argued that policy implementation is both a bottom-up and a top-down process, a perpetual conflict between the various different interest groups in the policy chain.[13] This differs widely between states, however. Some countries give civil servants more leeway than others in implementing policy, and some insist more on civil service neutrality than others.

5. Evaluation

Long neglected, the evaluation phase of the policy process has recently attracted much more attention from researchers.

In mainstream visions of political science and philosophy, at the end of the day evaluation falls to the public, which gets the final say on all political and policy issues. If they feel that a government is not making or ensuring the implementation of the policies they want, they can vote it out or simply begin a mass revolt. However, we argue against this mainstream view. We argue that the people are bad at evaluating policy, and this should be done by experts. Bureaucrats and politicians should conduct periodic review exercises, by either running investigations themselves, soliciting public comments or commissioning an independent enquiry. Once again, however, conflicts of interest can arise. As mentioned earlier, bureaucrats often have an interest in presenting failed policies as successful and perpetuating them, as long as their jobs rely upon their continuation. While some models of the policy process mention a termination stage, in practice it is exceptionally rare for those responsible to be willing to both admit failure and risk redundancy by recognising that they have failed in a core part of their jobs. Instead of being formally terminated, failed policies tend either to be revised, forgotten or overlaid with new policies.

This process is often simplified into an iterative cycle:[14]

However, in practice, the process is often much messier:[15]

This is why the frameworks described in this book are necessary to bring some order to the situation. However, while the circular model may be an idealised version of the truth, it nevertheless provides an essential framework for anyone wishing to understand how policy works and to attempt to influence it. If you wish to influence policy, the first stage is to work out where your pet issue is situated in the policy cycle, and thus which actors are likely to have the most influence on its future trajectory. If an issue is at the agenda-setting stage, then you would be well-advised to stir up public awareness, build a relationship with the media. If it is at the decision stage, then a better approach would be to lobby the politicians involved in passing the relevant measures, in order to reassure them that this decision will earn public support.

In this book, we will provide a history of the various trends in public policy and public management that have emerged across the history of the discipline, and

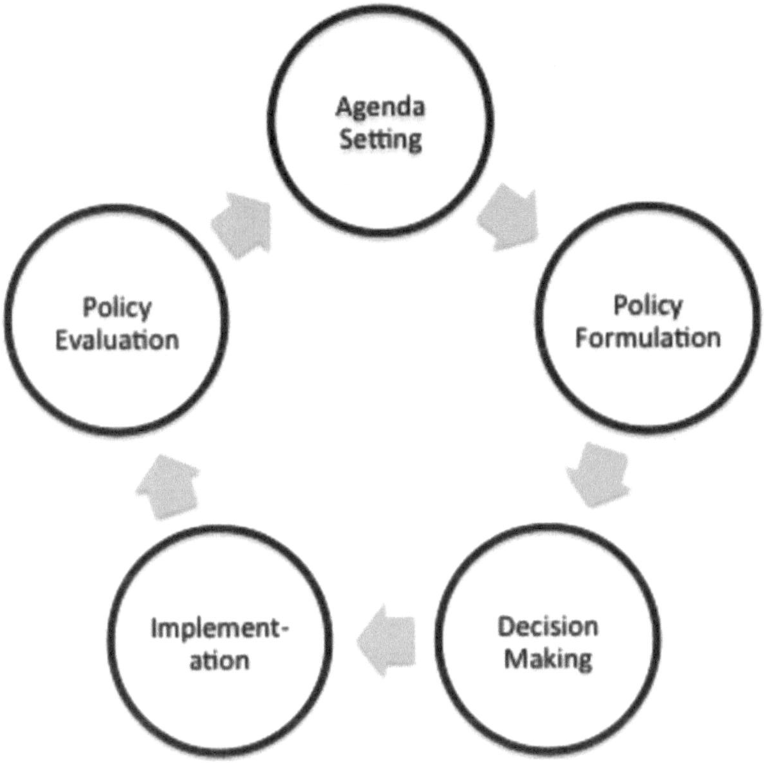

FIGURE 2.3 Policy Cycle (Adapted from Howlett et al., 2009)

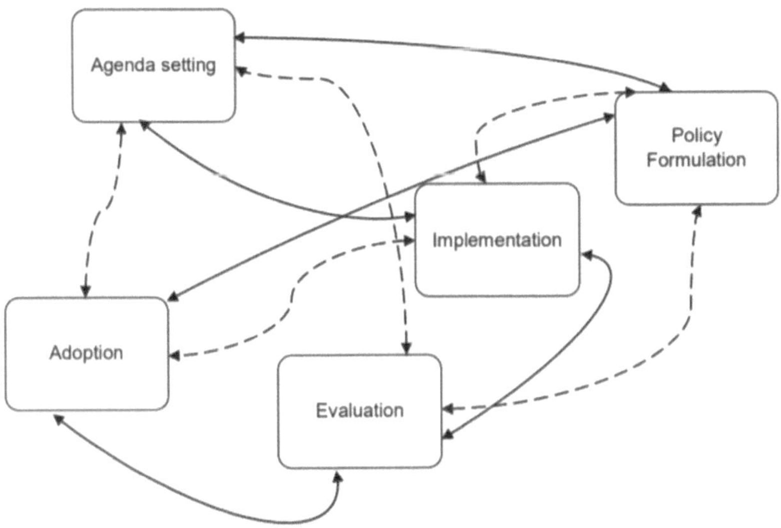

FIGURE 2.4 Messy Policy Process (Adapted from Benoit, 2013)

the various means that people have adopted to influence policy. Then, we will go on to look at the various tools that governments and administrations use to make policy, and which you can also use to influence it. We first look at the methods for evaluating and monitoring the environment and one's own advantages and disadvantages. We then go on to look at problem definition: the moment at which issues are laid out and described in detail. Finally, we look at how it is possible to become a policy innovator, opening up new spaces in which to act and improve your community, your state or the world. In all cases, we provide examples and counterexamples from around the world aimed at inspiring readers to take action in their own communities.

Notes

1 Howlett, Michael, and Ben Cashore. "Conceptualizing public policy." In *Comparative policy studies*, pp. 17–33. London: Palgrave Macmillan, 2014.
2 Hochadel, Amy M. "Case studies: Barking & Dagenham, Hackney and Tower Hamlets." In *Local leadership in a global era*, pp. 125–179. London: Palgrave Macmillan, 2018.
3 Leith, Murray Stewart, and Martin Steven. "Party over policy? Scottish nationalism and the politics of independence." *The Political Quarterly* 81, no. 2 (2010): 263–269.
4 Fischer, Frank, and Gerald J. Miller, eds. *Handbook of public policy analysis: Theory, politics, and methods*. Oxon: Routledge, 2017.
5 Dasgupta, Nabarun, Leo Beletsky, and Daniel Ciccarone. "Opioid crisis: No easy fix to its social and economic determinants." *American Journal of Public Health* 108, no. 2 (2018): 182–186.
6 Fossedal, Gregory. *Direct democracy in Switzerland*. Oxon: Routledge, 2018.
7 Souza, Celina. "Participatory budgeting in Brazilian cities: Limits and possibilities in building democratic institutions." *Environment and Urbanization* 13, no. 1 (2001): 159–184.
8 Balla, Steven J. "Is consultation the 'new normal?': Online policymaking and governance reform in China." *Journal of Chinese Political Science* 22, no. 3 (2017): 375–392.
9 Howlett, Michael, and Ishani Mukherjee, eds. *Routledge handbook of policy design*. Oxon: Routledge, 2018.
10 Isaksen, S.G., K.B. Dorval, and D.J. Treffinger. *Creative approaches to problem solving*. Dubuque, IA: Kendall/Hunt Publishing Company, 2000.
11 Malan, Thierry. "Implementing the Bologna process in France." *European Journal of Education* 39, no. 3 (2004): 289–297.
12 Lipsky, Michael. *Street-level bureaucracy: Dilemmas of the individual in public service*. New York: Russell Sage Foundation, 2010.
13 Fischer, Frank, and Gerald J. Miller, eds., *op cit*, 2017.
14 Howlett, Michael, Michael Ramesh, and Anthony Perl. *Studying public policy: Policy cycles and policy subsystems* (Vol. 3). Oxford: Oxford University Press, 2009.
15 Benoit, François. *Public policy models and their usefulness in public health: The stages model. National Collaborating Centre for Healthy Public Policy*. Quebec: Institut national de santé publique Québec, 2013.

Bibliography

Balla, Steven J. (2017). "Is consultation the 'new normal?': Online policymaking and governance reform in China." *Journal of Chinese Political Science* 22(3): 375–392.

Dasgupta, Nabarun, Leo Beletsky, and Daniel Ciccarone. (2018). "Opioid crisis: No easy fix to its social and economic determinants." *American Journal of Public Health* 108(2): 182–186.

Fischer, F., G.J. Miller, and M.S. Sidney (Eds.). (2007). *Handbook of public policy analysis: Theory, politics and methods*. Boca Raton: CRC Press.

Fossedal, Gregory. (2018). *Direct democracy in Switzerland*. Oxon: Routledge.

Hochadel, Amy M. (2018). "Case studies: Barking & Dagenham, Hackney and Tower Hamlets." In *Local leadership in a global era*, pp. 125–179. London: Palgrave Macmillan.

Howlett, Michael, and Ben Cashore. (2014). "Conceptualizing public policy." In *Comparative policy studies*, pp. 17–33. London: Palgrave Macmillan.

Howlett, Michael, and Ishani Mukherjee (Eds.). (2018). *Routledge handbook of policy design*. Oxon: Routledge.

Howlett, Michael, Michael Ramesh, and Anthony Perl. (2009). *Studying public policy: Policy cycles and policy subsystems* (Vol. 3). Oxford: Oxford University Press.

Isaksen, S.G., K.B. Dorval, and D.J. Treffinger. (2000). *Creative approaches to problem solving*. Dubuque, IA: Kendall/Hunt Publishing Company.

Leith, Murray Stewart, and Martin Steven. (2010). "Party over policy? Scottish nationalism and the politics of independence." *The Political Quarterly* 81(2): 263–269.

Malan, Thierry. (2004). "Implementing the Bologna process in France." *European Journal of Education* 39(3): 289–297.

Souza, Celina. (2001). "Participatory budgeting in Brazilian cities: Limits and possibilities in building democratic institutions." *Environment and Urbanization* 13(1): 159–184.

3

MACRO-SITUATION ANALYSIS

Environment Analysis

"They don't think it be like it is, but it does".

–Oscar Gamble

Environment is the basis of all policy. In an ideal environment, no policy would be needed, because there would be no problems requiring fixing. Every good policy is a direct response to the defects (or perceived defects) that originally produced it: crime happens, and so penal laws are made, diseases occur and so public health policies are introduced. While the concrete details of any given policy may be inspired by experiences of other states or governments elsewhere, their application will only be successful insofar as they are relevant to the situation at hand. Strict water use regulations might solve a great many problems in an arid country but cause conflict and resentment in one where water is naturally abundant, for example. Policies designed to encourage enrolment in tertiary education may be helpful in a country aiming to move from a manufacturing to a service economy, but harmful in one suffering a lack of qualified vocational workers.

Not only are policies a response to their environment but also their success or failure can only be judged based on how efficiently they mitigate the natural defects of this environment, and thus better the lives of those for whom they were designed.

In the business world, many tools have been designed to help leaders evaluate and respond to their environments. These are usually based largely on economic measures: a favourable environment is one in which it is easy to make money and an unfavourable environment is one in which it is not. Similarly, a company with good policies is one that makes large amounts of money from its environment, while a company with bad policies is one that loses money.

DOI: 10.4324/9781003307228-3

Companies can effectively measure the "fit" between their policies and their environment via the concept of competitive advantage – the degree to which they outperform their rivals.

McGee et al. (2010) define competitive advantage thus: "Delivering superior value to customers and in so doing earning an above average return for the company and its shareholders".[1] Companies achieve competitive advantage by adopting strategies that are better adapted to their environment than those of their competitors. These strategies are defined by four key contextual factors:

1. **The supply side**: The cost, quality and ease of obtaining the resources upon which the company depends – cost advantage.
2. **The demand side**: The willingness of consumers to pay for the company's products, as compared to other companies' products – differentiation advantage.
3. **Market rivalry**: The number and characteristics of other firms supplying the same or similar products.
4. **Industry analysis**: The size, configuration and prospects for the industry in which the firm operates.

Obviously, these factors do not translate exactly to the public sector. Governments, like companies, are subject to supply and demand: they have limited resources with which to provide public services and have to allocate the services that they provide in such a way as to satisfy enough citizens to prevent the populace from turning against it. However, most governments are not subject to day-to-day competition from other actors. While it is possible for citizens dissatisfied with their government to vote it out (in a democratic polity), engage in violent revolt or move to a different area, exchanging one government for another remains far harder than – for example – switching between two different brands of toothpaste. The result is that it is much harder for governments to evaluate their own performance than it is for companies. A company that is losing money can observe where the leaks are and conclude that these are where its strategic deficiencies lie, but governments tend to provide public services at a loss by design, meaning that this metric is of no use to them. Instead, they have to use other measures – polling, audits and internal evaluations, for example – to judge their performance and work out where they will need to improve if they wish to maintain their position.

This chapter will look at the ways that public sector leaders – deprived of profit and loss streams to use as performance indicators – can assess their environment accurately, preparatory to situating themselves and their policies within it. While the present chapter focuses on environmental analysis, borrowing heavily from models used in the private sector, the next chapter will look at the ways in which public sector leaders can judge their own performance within this context.

We begin by giving a brief overview of intelligence gathering methods, and then go on to look in greater depth at four methods, in particular: ESTEMPLE, stakeholder management, internal analysis and the Diamond/Five Forces. These should not be understood as alternative approaches to strategy, but as complementary ones. This is why we have broken them down into three steps. The first step involves broad environmental scanning: identifying the trends, issues, people and entities that will affect your organisation's existence in the coming months and years. This not only focuses on the ESTEMPLE and EFAS approaches but also touches upon other methods, and focuses on categorical and structural factors. In the third section, we go from the general conceptual environment to look at the specific actors that have a capacity to influence your day-to-day functioning, their interests and goals, and how you should interact with them: stakeholder management, setting agents within the structures in which they work. Then, we look at ways for situating policies in time, and acknowledging that citizen demand will change, and some areas of public policy will grow obsolete while other new ones develop. Finally, we will focus on the Diamond model/Five Forces Framework; we also cover other ways of looking at the challenge and conduct holistic whole-country environmental analysis and holistic country–country analysis. When undertaking an analysis of your strategic situation, it is not necessary to apply every framework, but it is necessary to apply at least one framework from every section, in order to conduct a full horizon scan. If it is the first analysis exercise that you have conducted, it may be a good idea to use all frameworks, in order to decide which ones work best for you, but if you already know that your team likes and understands the power–interest matrix approach, then it is fine to stick with that for the stakeholder management stage. As often in strategic planning, it is often more important that you have a systematic approach than that you have a particular strategic approach. As long as, you are covering all three parts of the analysis process – environmental scanning, stakeholder management and policy lifecycle – it is up to your organisation to establish the frameworks that you use for doing it.

1. Environmental Scanning: By Categories: ESTEMPLE

In order to evaluate one's environment, it is first necessary to be aware of it. While most of us have a broad idea of the political, economic and social trends that surround us, good decision-making demands that these be listed, organised and interpreted with reference to the business in question and the threats and opportunities that they represent. This relates to the agenda-setting part of the policy cycle.

Most public sector contexts imply dealing with multiple different environments. A ministry will need to deal with other ministries or departments, service users, political actors, commercial suppliers and contractors, and potentially other entities at the local, national or international levels. This means that any given environment scanning or analysis exercise must be repeated at multiple levels, usually local, national and international. In some cases, separate analyses will also be required for the various different sectors in which a ministry intervenes. Thus, for example, a Singapore's Ministry of Manpower has to deal with entirely different local, national and international environments when dealing with migrant labourers and when dealing with SME training programmes.[2]

While governments cannot usually use revenue as a measure of consumer preferences, they do have access to a wealth of other data: from polling, research, national statistics agencies or even clandestine intelligence from satellite observation and spying.

The research should be done in as systematic a way as possible, to avoid omissions and potential confirmation bias. This involves four key stages:

TABLE 3.1 Environment Scanning Stages (Adapted from Hanson et al., 2016)

Scanning	Identifying early signals of environmental changes and trends (this is strongly linked to the scenario-planning technique described later)
Monitoring	Assigning significance to the information obtained during the scanning stage
Forecasting	Making projections based on the information obtained and interpreted in stages one and two
Assessing	Determining the relative importance of likely outcomes and their implications for the organisation

The information collected during this stage of the process can be broken down further to identify opportunities and threats using a selection of different frameworks. One of the most frequently used within the business world is the ESTEMPLE (PESTEL, STEEPLE, etc.) framework.[3]

ESTEMPLE stands for "economic, social, technological, ecological, media, political, legal and ethical" – a way of breaking down the external factors liable to affect an organisation's operations. It is the latest in a long line of similar acronyms, all aimed at performing the same broad functions: PEST ("political, economic, social and technological"), STEEPLE ("social, technological, economic, environmental, political, legal and ethical") and PESTEL ("political, economic, social, technological, environmental and legal").[4] These provide simple, memorable checklists for leaders to fill in as they brainstorm factors that could affect their organisations – often in the context of performing SWOT or TOWS analyses (which will be covered in the next chapter), they were also used by approximately 40% of public and non-profit organisations according to one US-based survey[5] – something that reflects their high degree of transferability between sectors.

- "Economics" refers to a wide variety of factors: GDP growth, exchange rates, taxes, public debt, inequality, wages, etc. While the effects of each factor will be different for commercial and non-commercial organisations, the same factors have an impact on both. Thus, high taxes may be bad for business and good for public services, but they have an equally strong effect on both sectors.

- "Social" factors cover demographic trends, cultures and attitudes. In the private sector, these can affect preferences for different products – for example, the growing willingness to pay extra for environmentally friendly products. In the public sector, they are more likely to be felt via opinion polls reflecting public perceptions of government and public institutions.
- "Technological" factors are often disruptive: new technologies force actors that would have been more comfortable sticking with the status quo to adapt or fail. They can provide new opportunities but also create new threats – the development of IOT (internet of things) technologies may have made police surveillance easier, but the growth of the internet has also opened up new ways to commit crimes anonymously, for example.
- "Ecological" or "Environmental" influences are those that relate to natural risks and resources. Climate change, for example, may improve farm yields in some areas and reduce them in others, affecting food security.
- "Media" refers to the organisation's relations with other stakeholders as mediated by the press, radio and television. Media may help to amplify public relations messages via interviews and press releases, but they can also do significant damage to an organisation's reputation by reporting on scandals and rule breaking. This is strongly linked to social and political factors.
- "Politics" is usually used to refer to the electoral politics of the state or region, and to lobbying relationships when the framework is applied in a private sector context. In a public sector context, "politics" is more likely to refer to the party-political situation in which bureaucrats operate, and the likely effects of electoral changes upon their budget and constraints.
- "Legal" factors refer to the regulatory constraints to which an organisation is subject. This is strongly related to the "politics" item mentioned earlier – a change in government is likely to lead to changes in regulation, and either an increase or a reduction in compliance costs. Conversely, an organisation may use lobbying and media relations techniques to attempt to modify political and regulatory trends in its own favour.
- "Ethical" refers to the deontological and other constraints to which an organisation may be subjected. These are often – though not always – related to the legal factors mentioned earlier. An organisation may act in such a way that it is technically within the law while still generating public opprobrium for acts perceived to be unethical.

These approaches have been used frequently in both the public and the private sectors. The PESTEL approach is well known for having been used by PepsiCo in strategising:

Political	PepsiCo is regulated by the FDA in the United States and conducts lobbying activities to ensure that the regulatory environment remains favourable. It is also affected heavily by subsidies and tariffs affecting its raw ingredients
Economic	As an economic entity, PepsiCo has to keep track of general economic developments, but as a producer of relatively low-priced products it is not necessarily as heavily affected as companies whose demand is more inelastic. The main economic trend affecting its business environment in recent years has been the growing disposable wealth enjoyed by citizens of developing states, which has brought PepsiCo products within the reach of more and more people
Social	This is an important factor for PepsiCo, as sales of its products are significantly affected by trends in consumption. A large component of its revenue comes from snacks and drinks, and these are being affected significantly by the growing popularity of healthier and more environmentally friendly options.
Technological	PepsiCo's production processes are growing increasingly automated as technology improves. The development of social media has also changed the ways in which it advertises its products
Environmental	Environmental factors do not generally affect PepsiCo directly, but they do have a significant effect on the cost of its agricultural raw materials and on the distribution costs (as governments' tax petrol to attempt to slow global warming)
Legal	This is closely related not only to the political aspects described earlier but also to corporate liability. For example, a chemical leak at a PepsiCo plant in India was suspected of having used water from a contaminated source, leading to a massive product recall

As described earlier, it is important to adapt and potentially re-run this analysis at all levels in which an organisation operates – local, national and international – and to repeat it whenever circumstances change. Thus, for example, the German Ministry of Justice is obliged to deal with very different contexts depending on whether it is operating at the regional, national or international levels.[6]

Context	*Environment*
Local	State governments, local police and prison authorities, local suppliers, state regulations, local lobbying and pressure groups
National	Federal government, national suppliers, federal laws, federal regulations, the Constitution, national suppliers, national lobbying and pressure groups
International	The EU, Interpol, international agreements, multinational suppliers

2. Environmental Scanning: By Time: Scenarios

While these points can simply be used as a way to brainstorm potential threats and opportunities, they can also be combined with other frameworks to create matrices. Johnson et al. (2009) suggest looking for megatrends, inflexion points (potential shifts in a particular trend) and weak signals (small precursors of large potential changes).[7] They also suggest feeding the data points and conclusions into scenario-planning exercises. This involves attempting to imagine the ways in which an organisation's environment would change if key trends identified continue or develop. This is usually done in five steps:

- Defining scenario scope: This refers to setting out the temporal and geographic limits of the planning exercise. Are you interested in the local, national or international levels? Do you intend to look 1, 5 or 10 years ahead?
- Identifying the key drivers for change: Which trends will have greatest impact on your organisation?
- Developing scenario stories: Creating and elaborating upon likely narratives as the changes progress and evolve. This is done in much the same way as a novelist or a scriptwriter would plan out his or her work.
- Identifying impacts: Working out the effects that this is likely to have on your organisation. What negative and positive impacts are the changes likely to have? What are the threats and the opportunities inherent within the developments? How can you extract maximum benefit from the opportunities and mitigate the risks as much as possible?
- Establishing early warning systems: In order to benefit from all the effort, put into identifying trends and making predictions, it is important to continue to monitor developments and alert your organisation if the situation changes.

Ideally, this exercise should be carried out as a group, with multiple scenarios being developed. The best way to conduct the exercise is for the entire management team to get together to identify three or more key future scenarios, before splitting up into smaller groups, each of which will elaborate in a particular scenario in greater detail. While analysing more potential scenarios is usually better, this is not practical given the limits on time and resources. This will mean that some possible outcomes will always be neglected. To minimise this problem, it helps to pick three or four general scenarios that can be combined or concatenated in various ways, and which all cover a variety of sub-scenarios. The group then reunites to compare their conclusions and decide upon any actions that should be taken.[8]

Scenario planning is a technique that has been used extensively by the Singapore government, inspired by its use in the Shell Oil Company.[9] During policy formulation, Singapore applies long-term scenario planning and futures thinking. As former PM Lee Kuan Yew put it: "My job is to be a long-range radar, to look ahead and then share with the government and give them my advice".[10] Scenario planning was imported from Shell Petroleum and actively practised in various ministries. Diverse scenario-planning methodologies ("future forward" and "future backward", for example), which are now widely available in open-source literature, were also used. Former Civil Service Head, Peter Ho, was a firm believer in these methods and established the Centre for Strategic Futures. Various Ministries now have dedicated staff responsible for "futures" work. Where futures methodologies attempt to anticipate new complexity and unexpected events, scenario planning takes a linear, goal-oriented approach.[11]

An example of this scenario planning can be found in Singapore's urban planning system. Urban planners use three types of plans: concept plan, master plan and development guide plans. Concept plans are 30–40-year plans, while master plans seek to operationalise and adjust concept plans in shorter time periods of 5–10 years. Singapore is divided into 55 planning areas, and future development plans are prepared by Urban Redevelopment Authority as development guide plans to systematically and transparently communicate to the private sector.[12] For example, the 1971 Concept Plan sets out the development needs of projected population of four million by 1992. Similarly, the 1991 Concept Plan incorporated 55 Development Guide Plans, which in turn fed into the 1998 Master Plan.

This said, it is cautionary to note that earlier versions of scenario planning posit linearity. Hence, it depends on which key drivers are chosen and why they are chosen. The more the key drivers are chosen, the more possible permutations of scenarios there may be. Hence, it is a judgement call to decide on how many drivers: 2, 4 or 20. A middle-way option of 4 to 6 drivers is recommended. After scenarios are developed, there is a false sense of security to assume reality will pan out according to scenarios anticipated. In reality, many drivers interact and complexity breeds emergence (novel phenomenon from such interactions). Besides, there are many combinations of actions that could lead present to future (future forward), or future to present (future backward). As such, policymakers must be cautious to note the anticipated scenarios, have preventive policies that can account for such scenarios including high impact, low probability black swan scenarios, yet not forget the importance of near- and medium-term planning that is grossly needed to bridge the long-term vision/scenario. Hence, scenario planning is a strategy tool but cannot be the only strategy tool. It is worth to note that scenario planning has evolved through the years too, with the latest work by Oxford Scenarios led by Rafael Ramirez and Angela Wilkinson (2016) that has made steps to refine the methodology to account for more complexity assumptions.

Other authors have discussed various different ways of dividing up the factors you identify: Wheelen and Hunger (2017), for example, also suggest breaking each set of factors down into threats and opportunities or ranking potential outcomes by impact or likelihood.[13] Another way to approach the task is via the external factors analysis summary framework, which we shall discuss next.

TABLE 3.2 Risk Management Framework (Adapted from Wheelen and Hunger, 2017)

		Probable impact on corporation		
		High	*Medium*	*Low*
Probability of occurrence	**High**	High priority	High priority	Medium priority
	Medium	High priority	Medium priority	Low priority
	Low	Medium priority	Low priority	Low priority

The External Factors Analysis Summary (EFAS) is another framework heavily related to the SWOT analysis schema, which will be covered in Chapter 5.[14] It involves listing and ranking external factors according to their importance and the organisation's performance in tackling them. In this example, we have used the US Department of Agriculture:

TABLE 3.3 External Factors' Analysis Summary (Adapted from Wheelen et al., 2017)

External factors	*Weight*	*Rating*	*Weighted score*	*Comments*
Opportunities				
Brexit	0.20	4.1	0.82	Opportunity for greater trade links with the United Kingdom
Automation of farming	0.10	5.0	0.50	Reduce costs of managing land
Changing patterns in domestic consumption	0.05	2.0	0.10	Growing preference for high-quality local products, increasing suspicion of agribusiness
Increasing national debt/ small government preference	0.05	2.0	0.10	Risk of reductions to farm subsidies
Reduction in world poverty	0.10	1.80	0.18	Increased meat consumption in developing states
Threats				
Fluctuating oil prices	0.10	4.3	0.43	Well positioned
Climate change	0.10	4.0	0.40	Change in the nature of the crops it is possible to cultivate in the United States, and increased risk of natural disasters
Trade war with China	0.15	3.0	0.45	Reduced exports
Water scarcity	0.05	1.2	0.06	A particular threat in certain areas – California, Colorado, etc.
Massive decline in world fish stocks	0.10	1.6	0.16	Severe threat
Total scores	**1.00**		**3.15**	

To make this table, a standard process was applied:

1. List opportunities and threats in column 1.
2. Weight each factor from 0.0 (not important) to 1.0 (very important) based on their likely impact on the organisation's strategic position. These scores are listed in column 2.
3. Rate the organisation's performance in each area from 1.0 (poor) to 5.0 (excellent) and list these scores in column 3.
4. Explain your justifications in column 4. This may be tempting to omit, but purely quantitative data – particularly when you have assigned the scores yourself – give only a tiny proportion of the information you need. Especially if the team is likely to change between now and the next time you conduct this exercise, it is important to have notes on why you made the choices you did and which concepts and factors seemed important to you a year ago. It also gives team members a chance to argue through the reasoning behind your model.
5. Multiply the numbers in column 2 by the numbers in column 3, and list the results in column 4.
6. Use column 5 to justify the scores given in each case.
7. Add the scores to evaluate the organisation's total performance in the final cell in column 4.

This technique has the significant advantage of providing numerical scores for each domain, which can be added up and compared year-on-year. As before, it is important to conduct this exercise repeatedly, and to adapt it in the event that different parts of the organisation face differing opportunities and threats.

However, it is often important to be able to zoom in on a particular part of the strategic environment, and in particular, on the interests of stakeholders. While ESTEMPLE and EFAS describe the categorical environment, other methods are better-adapted to describing the stakeholder environment – that is, the human environment.

3. Organisational/Sector-Level Stakeholder Management for Competitive Advantage: Five Forces Model

Stakeholder management is a crucial part of the formulation and decision-making stages of the policy cycle. While the ESTEMPLE and EFAS models are useful for brainstorming and even for identifying priorities, it is not particularly useful for showing how the various factors involved interact with one another, and the different directions in which they may pull and push a given organisation. To do this a more structural approach needs to be applied, such as the Five Forces model.

This matrix was developed by Michael Porter in the 1970s as a way for companies to monitor their competition landscape on an ongoing basis.[15] While the model is expressly designed for a business environment, it is equally well adapted to assessing the environment in which a public sector entity operates.[16] It is particularly well suited to dealing with polycentric visions of government, in which managing a country, region or sector is not a purely top-down approach, but a product of overlapping authorities and multiple layers of governance.[17] It is designed to effectively perform an ESTEMPLE analysis from the perspective of every individual or entity capable of affecting or being affected by your actions.

The original framework shows:

- **The bargaining power of suppliers**. When supply is dominated by just a few companies, they have a greater potential for exercising power over buyers (oligopolistic competition), and this is also the case when switching from one supplier to another carries high costs. The supplier power structure is also affected by the use or otherwise of intermediaries: in the airline industry, for example, airline companies have been able to use the rise of online booking to negotiate less favourable contracts with travel agents. In a public sector context, "suppliers" are essentially taxpayers, whether individuals or corporations. They are in a position to reject the authorities above them, both at an individual level (by moving away) and a collective level (by voting out the current authorities or rebelling). However, this is not a daily process and often involves a great deal of effort, weakening taxpayers bargaining power.
- **The threat of substitute products or services**. If buyers can obtain similar or better products from other sellers, any given seller's power is lessened. Related to this is the potential for technological advantages that will render a given supplier's products obsolete. In a public sector context, this can refer to other sources of goods and services: other authorities (whether bureaucratic or political, local, national or international), but also corporations, self-help groups and NGOs.
- **The threat posed by new entrants to the market**. This is often a product of the barriers to entry and economies of scale in a given industry. The costlier it is for new entrants to join a market, the safer existing market players are. Existing companies can work to create or increase barriers to entry by convincing suppliers not to sell to new entrants, for example, or by launching price wars against new entrants. In the public sector, this refers to new iterations of the same organisations as mentioned in the previous point. Thus, if a government agency performs badly a new one may be set up to replace it; if people are tired of all their current political parties, new ones may be created. Similarly, corporations and NGOs may move into states that are performing poorly in order to provide the services that it is unable to cope with. Once again, this ties in with the concept of polycentric governance described earlier.
- **The bargaining power of buyers**. The more oligopsonistic a market is, and the lower the switching costs that buyers face, the less power sellers have. Similarly, if a buyer has the potential to bypass its suppliers and get resources directly from the source, this weakens sellers' power. In the public sector, buyers often have a strong overlap with suppliers. The same people who pay for

services through their taxes also benefit from them. However, not every taxpayer benefits from the same services in the same ways. A person who pays high taxes is unlikely to use public education or health services, for example, as he is likely to prefer to pay for higher quality private services.

Some analysts also include a sixth force: the presence or absence of complimentary products, companies or industries.[18] Thus, for example, movie streaming services compliment television manufacture, and breweries compliment pub chains. In the government sector, complementary services are often provided by international organisations – Interpol makes it easier for national police services to perform their core tasks, for example.

These five (six) forces can be used to create a typology of different markets based on the level and type of competition present: monopolistic industries, oligopolistic industries, hypercompetitive industries and perfectly competitive industries. This, in turn, allows companies to make strategic decisions about the markets that it should enter or leave, and how it should do so. In doing this, it is important to clearly define the term "industry". Many industries have sub-sectors in which the forces that apply differ from one another. Similarly, industries may merge or split over time.

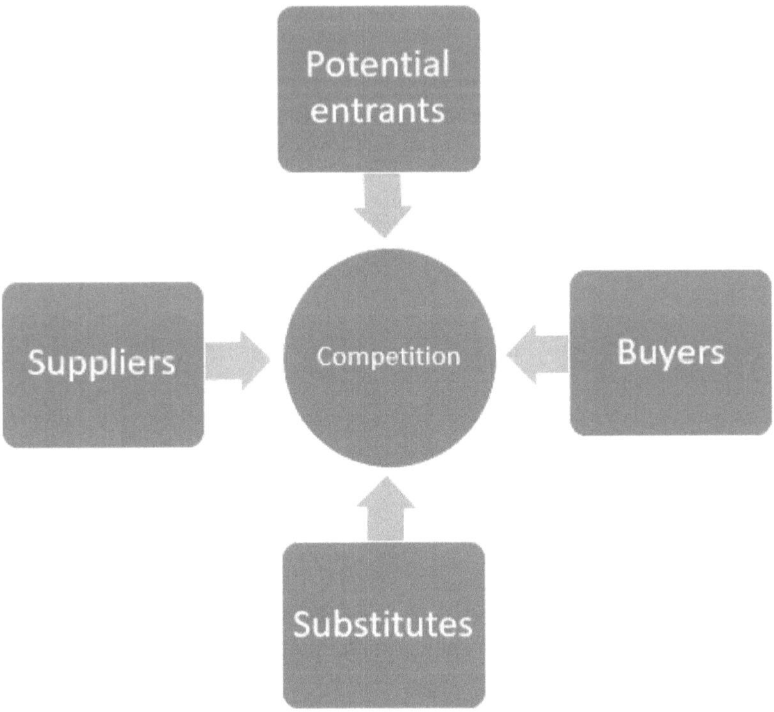

FIGURE 3.1 Five Forces Model (Adapted from Tsiligiris, 2018)

While public sector organisations are not generally subject to the same market forces as companies, they do deal with inputs, outputs and competitors.

For example, the Five Forces model has previously been used to analyse the state of the market for public transport in Spain.[19] This is an interesting case study, given that it is a market upon which public and private companies both collaborate and compete, each with its own advantages and disadvantages. In some cities, bus routes are staffed by public companies owned by the municipality, while in others the job is done by private companies that have a contractual relationship with the local government. The authors note that barriers to mobility, the long duration of contracts and the control of the public sector over the industry produce a series of long-running local monopolies, with users being a relatively captive audience given the lack of alternative options for many of them. However, the users are not only the people who buy tickets but also society as a whole:

> It is our belief that these customers are, on the one hand, public transport users in particular, and on the other, Society in general. Sustainable mobility plans are increasingly more frequent, as is the creation of public transport policies that contribute towards the sustainable development of cities by reducing pollution, traffic jams, noise, etc., thus making cities more habitable, which not only has repercussions on users, but on society as a whole. From the users' point of view, a concentration of customers who acquire or demand the service in large quantities does not exist, and rather the contrary, i.e., there is a huge quantity of customers who make journeys whose maximum consideration is that of buying a monthly, or even yearly, season ticket and who have to make journeys because they have no choice, signifying that their strength or bargaining power would appear to be fairly limited. What is more, although alternative modes of transport exist, the cost of changing from one to another may, in some cases, be steep (for example, deciding not to use the bus for a week and travelling by taxi or car. In the case of the taxi, the cost is obvious, while in the case of the car, the costs of parking must be added to fuel costs). Itis not therefore easy to decide to use an alternative, and as explained previously, those who use public transport do so for reasons that make them, in certain respects, constant users. All in all, users have no bargaining power to allow them to impose conditions, nor do they seek them, and they simply decide to use the service because they usually have no alternative. The service is provided because it is necessary, independently of whether there are more or less users.
>
> *(which could be resolved by increasing or decreasing the frequency of the service)*

Finally, it is important to point out that, although users have no bargaining power, it is important to encourage the use of public transport, not only for reasons of economic and social policies but also to permit a greater coverage of operating costs according to the number of passengers transported.

The factors involved may differ from organisation to organisation, but the main differences emerge when one compares political and civil service organisations. Political parties (under democratic regimes, at least) are subject to "market pressure" insofar as that providing good services at a low cost is likely to increase the number of votes that a party receives, while providing poor services at a high cost is likely to lead to electoral losses. Even in undemocratic systems there exists a threat of violent revolt if the party fails consistently to provide satisfaction – it is noteworthy that the Chinese Communist Party conducts extensive polling exercises, despite not being subject to the same level of inter-party competition as its counterparties in more democratic states.[20]

This example looks at competition from the point of view of a political actor/party, for example:

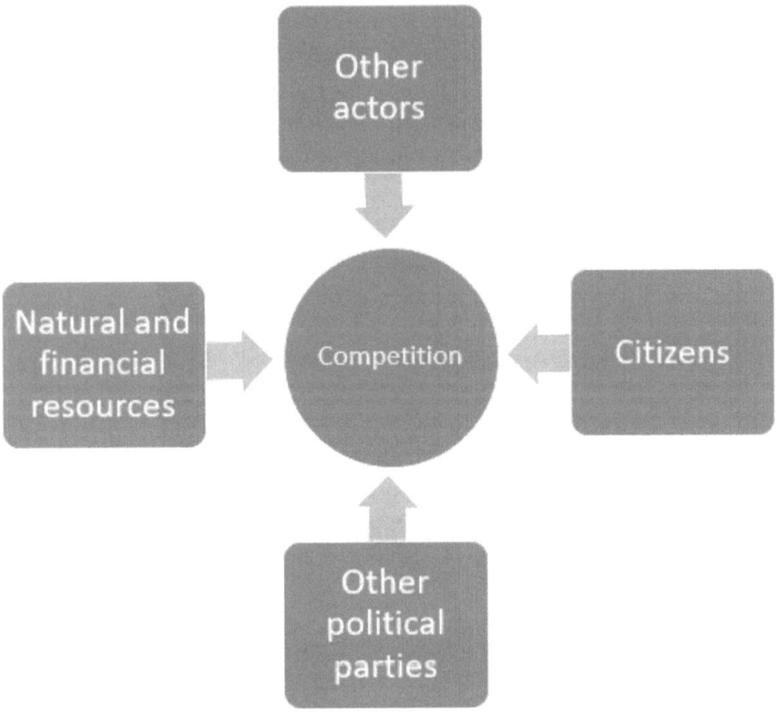

FIGURE 3.2 Adapted Five Forces Model (Adapted from Cummings and Angwin, 2015)

In this scenario, the government is under pressure to use the resources to which it has access (natural resources, tax income, financial reserves) in such a way as to maintain or increase citizen satisfaction with its performance. In doing this, it is subject to external pressure from other political parties, which promise to extract more utility from the resources available and thus procure greater citizen satisfaction. It also has to work out a modus vivendi for dealing with other entities: pressure groups, other states, local authorities, businesses and so on.

Thus, it is possible to analyse a country's political situation and understand how the public services on offer should be modified to increase citizen satisfaction and maintain government stability. Thus, a party ruling a state with abundant natural resources will have a greater a priori capacity to supply public services than one with few. However, a state with few resources may also make strategic decisions to increase them while one with plentiful resources may make poor choices and waste them (the famous resource curse). A party ruling a one-party state will obviously be subject to greater electoral competition than one in a state with a proportional representation system, but competition does not only come from other parties. Other organisations such as NGOs and religious groups offer public services and may succeed in usurping government power as a result of this.[21]

There are abundant examples of this phenomenon occurring in both democratic and undemocratic states. In the United Kingdom, for example, the Labour government faced increasing popular dissatisfaction with the management of the economy throughout the 1970s. The poor financial state of the country forced the government to approach the International Monetary Fund (IMF) for a loan, effectively begging for help from an outside actor in running the country. The IMF demanded budget cuts, which led to protests by trade unions that further weakened the country's economic situation. As a result of this, opposition parties grew stronger, winning multiple by-elections until the Labour Party found itself in charge of a minority government. It finally lost the 1979 general election with the greatest swing to the Conservative Party since the end of World War II.[22]

Alternatively, it is possible to employ the same framework in a purely bureaucratic context. Civil service organisations are less directly subject to popular sanction than political parties, but this does not mean that they are entirely immune. Their budgets and remit are subject to control by political parties via the executive and legislative branches, thus the popular pressure on political parties filters through and has repercussions upon the civil service. If a department consistently performs badly, it puts its political controllers at risk of electoral sanction. In response to this, they may increase the department's budget, but they may also compel it to undergo reorganisation, transfer its responsibilities to other departments, or even outsource them to the private sector – as in the Spanish example described earlier.

This approaches the same framework from the perspective of a departmental director within the civil service (or similar). His or her department is allocated a particular budget for the year, which it must try to deploy in such a way as to maximise the satisfaction of the people who use its services. It can maximise its resources by performing well or persuading government to allocate more cash to its tasks. If it fails to use the money effectively, it is at risk of having its portfolios transferred to other departments or outsourced to private sector contractors, which provides additional pressure to perform well.

In both of these cases, the final judge is the people: the citizen body as a whole in the first instance and a particular department's service users in the second. These are often the same individuals that contribute resources to the state via their taxes. Their interest is to extract as much utility from the government at minimal cost,

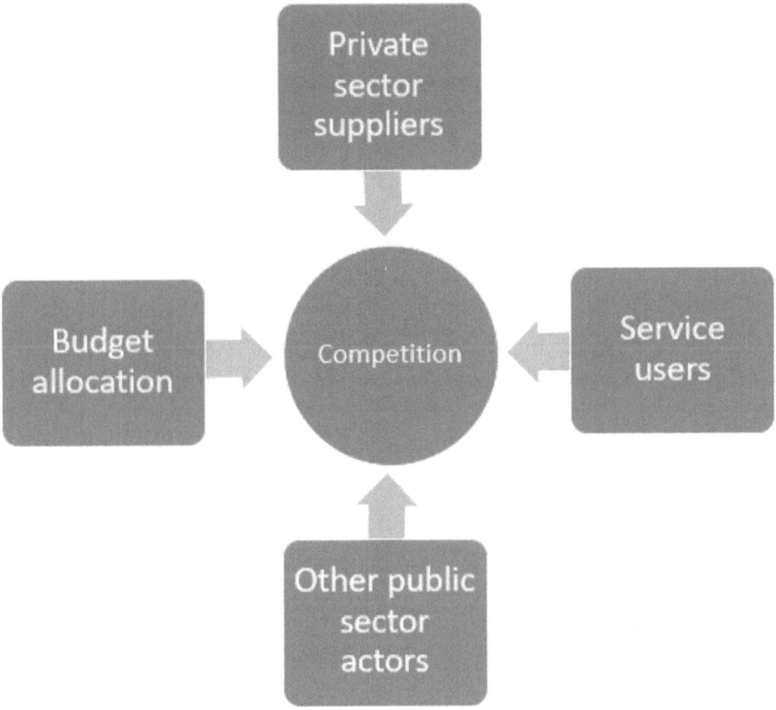

FIGURE 3.3 Adapted Five Forces Models (Adapted from Cummings and Angwin, 2015)

though the nature of the utility gained differs based on whether they consider the issue from the point of view of a taxpayer, a citizen or a service user.

An individual considering an issue from the perspective of a citizen has an interest in increasing the utility of society, as a whole. Thus, a childless citizen may still favour increased investment in education, though he or she will not benefit personally, as they believe it will produce benefits for society, as a whole. An individual considering an issue from the perspective of a service user is interested primarily in the ways in which he or she benefits personally from a service: a citizen who is also a parent is likely to have clear and precise ideas concerning how education should be delivered to maximise the utility gained by themselves and their children. Meanwhile, an individual considering education as a taxpayer is most likely to be concerned about getting value-for-money.

In taking this approach, it is important to be clear who the service users are, and this is not always easy. Prison service staff, for example, spend most of their time interacting with prisoners, but the principal beneficiaries of the service are not the prisoners themselves but the law-abiding citizens who are protected when criminals are withdrawn from society.

Successive French governments have integrated this conception of differing citizen interesting into their official budgetary process. When justifying any new expense in multi-year budgeting plans, civil servants are obliged to assess the impact of the spending from three perspectives: that of the taxpayers, that of the citizens and that of the service users.[23] If a policy cannot be justified from any of the three perspectives, it will not be implemented. The goal of this is to ensure that any policy change is justified according to democratic principles. Thus, for example, if a policy is of benefit only to corporate donors and not to ordinary citizens, it cannot – in theory – be implemented.

This is related to the identification and analysis of key stakeholders, which is the central goal of the next framework we will cover: power–interest matrices.

This idea was created as a brief mention in a conference paper in 1991 but proved to be so useful that academics and businesspeople have been using it extensively ever since.[24] Briefly put, it is a way to sort stakeholders in an organisation based on the extent to which its decisions can affect them and the extent to which their decisions can affect it. For a public sector agency, stakeholders include other government agencies, political actors, corporate actors, non-profit organisations, citizens and international organisations. The goal of the exercise is to work out how best to engage whichever of these stakeholders are relevant to a particular organisation. On this basis, strategies for dealing with each stakeholder can be designed or refined. As with the other frameworks, it is normal to repeat this exercise regularly, as strategies must be changed as stakeholder positions shift. This can be done by applying agile methodologies (which will be covered later in the book).

Once again, this is a framework from the business sector that can easily be transferred to a public context. It has, for example, been used to evaluate the factors that can help or hinder the development of science parks in Brazil.[25]

Stakeholders	*Primary interests*
Universities and Research Centers	To commercialise the results of academic research in order to broaden the sources of financial resources and expand the labour market for researchers and students
Entrepreneurs and academic entrepreneurs	Take advantage of the results of academic research activities in order to enhance the corporate R&D activities Improve financial returns Access qualified human resources
Financial agents and venture capitalists	Investments in promising technology companies with high potential for economic growth and rapid payback
Government and development agencies	Support technological innovation activities Revitalise economically depressed regions Generate jobs

Interestingly, in this case, the authors noted that

> it was revealed that many of these actions were not formally structured but were conducted by members of the project team because they perceived

> the need to motivate stakeholders to keep their engagement or support in specific situations during the life cycle of the project. It was also found that the team maintained a constant monitoring of stakeholder engagement and a proactive approach towards changing strategies when necessary.

Indeed, this is something that all of us do to a greater or lesser degree. The aim of the framework is to make this process more systematic, as described later.

The technique involves situating all stakeholders within a grid based on their interest in any given project or decision and their ability to affect the outcomes. Stakeholders that have a high level of interest and a high level of power should be engaged directly. Stakeholders with a high level of power but a low degree of interest should be kept happy but not involved in day-to-day management decisions. Stakeholders with a high level of interest and a low degree of power should be kept informed of changes, though there is no need to comply with any demands that they may make. Stakeholders without any particular power or interest do not need to be managed or engaged, though they do need to be monitored in case anything changes.

This has been widely applied in both the private and the public sectors. Thus, Cummings and Angwin (2015) uses the example of the Australian Transport Ministry to illustrate the concepts. The Ministry had grown stagnant and unresponsive to its environment. To change this, it decided to revise its perceptions concerning key stakeholders and thus its interactions with them. Originally, the Minister (a political appointee) had been treated as a high-power, high-interest stakeholder. The staff conducting the exercises revised this position and decided that while he

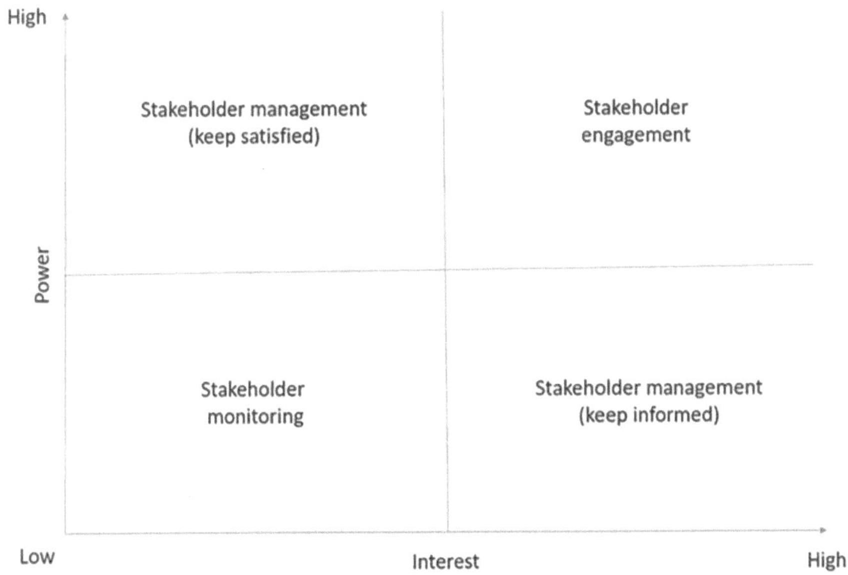

FIGURE 3.4 Stakeholder Matrix (Adapted from Cummings and Angwin, 2015)

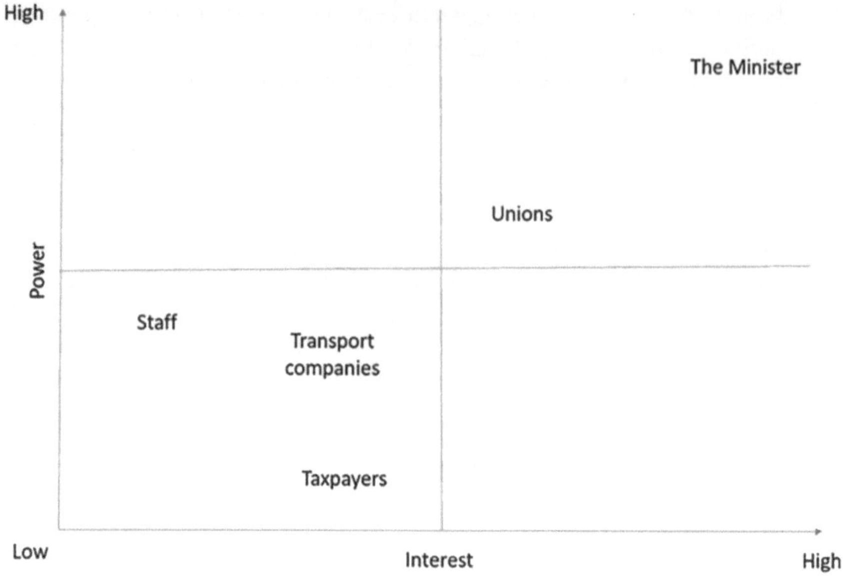

FIGURE 3.5 Power–Interest Matrix for Stakeholders (Adapted from Cummings and Angwin, 2015)

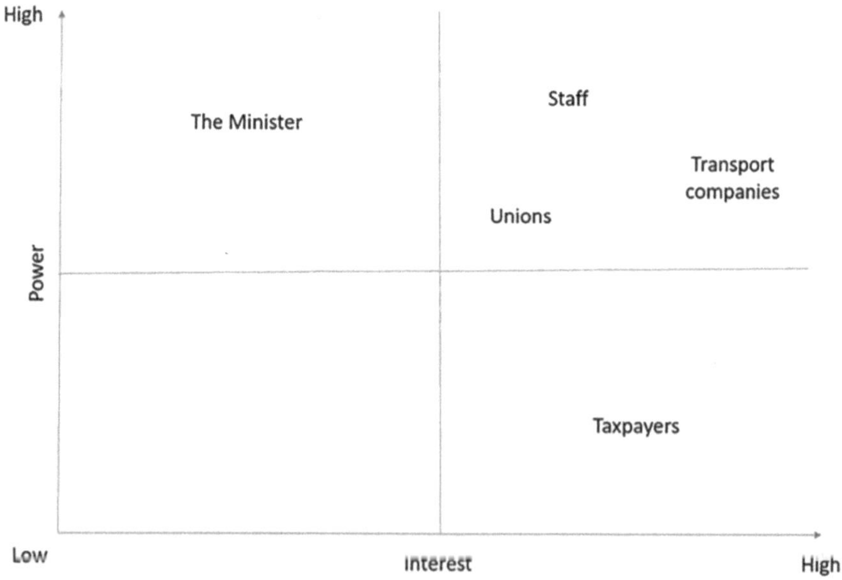

FIGURE 3.6 Power–Interest Matrix for Stakeholders (Adapted from Cummings and Angwin, 2015)

had a high level of power, his other interests meant that he lacked the time or the inclination to involve himself in day-to-day decisions.

As a result, the Minister was shifted to the top left quadrant. He was replaced by the staff within the ministry, the relevant trades unions and the transport companies that the ministry interacted with regularly. All of these groups had a strong interest in Ministry decisions, and the capacity to ensure the failure of any given policy should they wish. Meanwhile, taxpayers were moved to the high-interest, low-power quadrant, their relative lack of ability to take coordinated action making them unlikely to influence policy directly, despite their strong interest in the outcomes.

However, while this approach helps bureaucrats to prioritise tasks at hand, it tends – as the previous example shows – to minimise the role of customers (in a corporate setting) and citizens (in a public sector setting). While this may be necessary on a day-to-day basis, in order to ensure that work gets completed, in the long run the organisation runs the risk of becoming alienated from the very people who decide whether it succeeds or fails.

4. National-Level Competitive Advantage: Diamond Model

The concept of comparative advantage is strongly related to the five forces model that we will discuss in Chapter 4. In fact, both were developed by the same person – Michael Porter.[26] It is also known as Porter's "diamond model".[27]

The main difference is that the five forces model focuses on an organisation's present position as compared with its competitors, while the competitive advantage concept focuses on the ways in which it can create a clear distinction between itself and them. Nevertheless, the principal factors affecting both are the same, and in trying to identify your organisation's competitive advantage it is helpful to also conduct a five forces analysis. This will help you work out who your target users are, and hence who your competitors are. This is particularly important in the public sector because your competitors will not always be obvious. If you work for the Ministry of Defence, then your competitors will be the military forces of other countries. If you work for a political party, then your competitors will be other parties. On the other hand, if you run a waste management department or a public statistics department, then identifying competitors might be more difficult. In the former case, your competitors may be private companies or public entities at other levels of the administration. In the latter, they will probably be large-scale international consulting companies and international organisations.

The diamond model was originally developed to help identify why a country may have advantages over its competitors, but it can also be used for other organisations, whether firms or public sector entities.

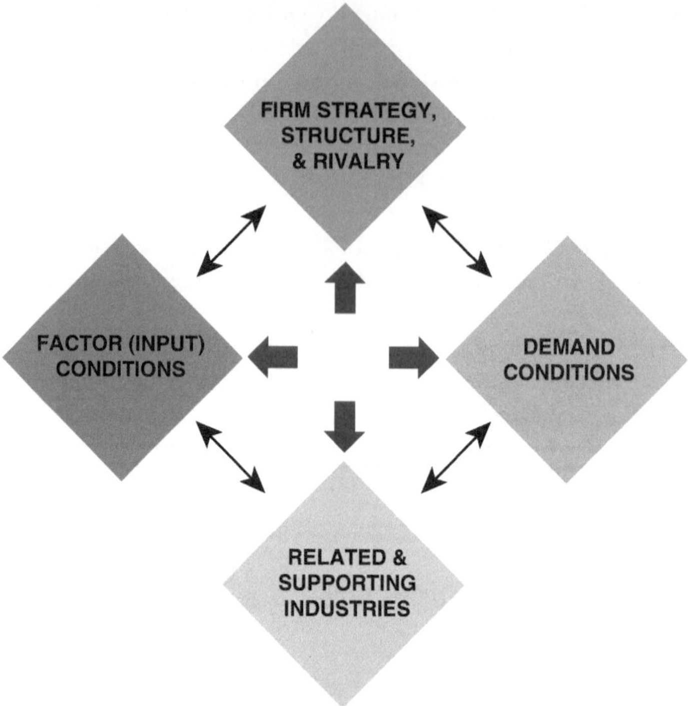

FIGURE 3.7 Adapted Diamond Model (Inspired by Tsiligiris, 2018)

Firm Strategy, Structure and Rivalry refers to the environment in which the organisation operates, and particularly the degree of competition that exists. Strong competition tends to foster innovation. Often government entities have no real competition, leading to a lack of innovation.

Factor Conditions refers to labour, capital and other resources that are required for an organisation in order to function well. If an entity lacks the personnel, the money or the natural resources to function, it is unlikely to be competitive.

Demand Conditions refers to the opinions of the service users. If citizens within a state have low expectations of their public services or no means of recourse against an unpopular government, then there is less pressure to succeed. If they are highly likely to get rid of a poorly performing government, then the pressure is much higher, which is likely to lead to better performance.

Related and Supporting Industries refers to suppliers and partners, whether in the public or the private sector.

Within this context, Porter highlighted two key ways for organisations to distinguish themselves from one another: price and product differentiation. Many public organisations tend to "compete" with the private sector on price. Usually, public hospitals provide far less luxurious treatment than private ones, for example, but they do it at little or no upfront cost. On the other hand, product differentiation is not entirely unheard-of in the public sector. Armed forces, for example, compete purely on effectiveness – providing national defence more cheaply than your neighbours is seldom effective.

Companies can distinguish themselves based on cost and product differentiation, but they can do so at different levels: they can target the entire market or just a segment. Thus, an organisation may attempt to be a cost leader over the entire market that it serves or just a part of that market. An organisation aiming for cost leadership will try to produce its output at a lower price than all of its competitors, for either the same users or a smaller subset of them. For example, ride sharing apps compete principally on price, trying to be as cheap as possible to capture as much of the total transport market as they can. On the other hand, low-cost airlines focus on being the price leaders for just a small part of the total market for airline tickets – the economy segment. Organisations that aim to distinguish themselves through product differentiation, however, focus on design and branding to stand out from their competitors. This is often the case in non-essential sectors such as fashion and entertainment. Most of the people who buy Air Jordans, for instance, are not buying them primarily for practical reasons, but because of the aesthetics and the branding attached to them. Similarly, a ticket to a romantic comedy is not a substitute for a ticket to an action movie. Indeed, a ticket to one romantic movie is not even necessarily a substitute for a ticket to another romantic movie.

		Source of Competitive Advantage	
		Cost	*Differentiation*
Scope	**Broad**	Cost leadership	Differentiation
	Narrow	Cost focus	Differentiation focus

A company that fails to choose one of the four options will tend to find itself in a stuck-in-the-middle position, attempting to compete with companies in all four quadrants without a significant advantage over any. In this case, it is important to factor in the organisation's rivals in setting its agenda.

This can also be applied at the state level. Indeed, various analyses have been conducted using this approach to try to identify ways in which states can become more competitive. Armen Chobanyan, Laurence Leigh, for example, applied the approach to the case of Armenia, concluding that

> The authors conclude that while achieving the required legislative and institutional framework, market liberalization and a stable macroeconomic environment are necessary, they are not sufficient conditions for ensuring continued economic growth and the achievement of sustainable development. In particular, based on the "Diamond Model" framework, they advocate Government policies to attract foreign direct investment with the objective of creating new industrial "clusters".[28]

Richard Hodgett applied the same approach to show why Mexico's leading industrial clusters – petrochemicals and automobiles – give it a comparative advantage in dealing with the United States.[29] Christian Bellak and Andreas Weiss performed a similar exercise in analysing the Austrian economy.[30] The same approach has also been used to analyse relationships between public sector enterprises and their competitors. Mohammad Hosein Rezazadeh Mehrizi and Mohammad Pakneiat used the approach to look at how Iran's telecoms companies – both public and private – have adapted to competition, with foreign firms being attracted by the low levels of technological rivalry from local firms but also intimidated by US sanctions against Iran.[31] Paul Curran used the same approach to analyse the ways in which the United Kingdom's further education system, formerly dominated by public sector organisations, changed with the increasing participation of private sector entities.[32]

In order to be able to position your organisation among other similar organisations and – more importantly, as far as this chapter is concerned – find underserved sectors in which there is room for innovation, it is necessary to understand where the other actors in the area are situated. There is no point in offering state-subsidised health insurance if private providers are already offering cheap and serviceable products, for example – you will simply be duplicating their work. Similarly, if a particular strategy is not within your capabilities, then it is not an option for you. A public hospital may wish to distinguish itself based on quality by providing luxury single rooms for all patients, but this is unlikely to be within the resources of a public entity, particularly one that has a large number of competing priorities. However, it may be able to look into providing other services that are either not supplied or supplied at too high a price for all citizens to access them. If there is a shortage of opticians or dentists in the area, a local hospital can consider providing walk-in services. Alternatively, several public hospitals may possibly band together to distribute the provision of services that are important but not in such high demand that they are necessary in every region, such as child heart surgery or gene therapy. There may also be particular populations that fall through the gaps in existing public services, and their problems end up being ignored. While targeting them may involve extra work, it can also be a way to demonstrate effectiveness and augment the departmental budget. As the example of the UK Higher Education sector shows, just because public sector workers are not generally used to thinking in terms of competition, the increasing interpenetration of the public and private spheres across the globe means that increasing competition is definitely coming.

In order to prepare for this, your organisation must maintain a good awareness of the environment in which it operates, using desk research to monitor the competition and tools such as design thinking and the job-to-be-done approach to keep an eye on the services that your users and potential users need or want.

However, this approach to innovation is only useful in making small, incremental changes, and ones for which there is an existing demand. Moreover, unless it is conducted on a very regular basis, it will tend to miss the emergence of new macro-trends. To do this, it is necessary to take a more global and proactive vision of change. However, as research shows, this is extremely difficult to do. In the following sections, we will look at why this is so, and take in several methods adopted to attempt to deal with this problem.

Conclusion

In this chapter, we ran through a variety of methods for approaching the environmental strategic analysis: environmental scanning by categories and by time, organisational/sector-level stakeholder management and national-level competitive advantage. While it is important to socialise oneself with the different models, it is not necessary to use every framework in a strategic analysis study. The crux is a FIT. Whichever model you choose to use, it must fit the problem you are trying to solve and the policy stage you are at. Using Diamond model for an organisational competitive advantage study may not be useful. Using ESTEMPLE by itself, without corroborating with organisational analysis may end up being a laundry list of ESTEMPLE factors.

While it is important to have a strategic approach to environmental analysis, it is also important not to get hung up on it. Thus, while the frameworks discussed in this chapter are a necessary first step towards building and improving public sector strategies and policies, there is no point in carrying out any of these exercises if they are not relevant to the organisation in question. In order to work out whether or not they apply to any given entity, it is necessary to evaluate not only the environment but also the organisation itself. Once you have a vision of your horizons, the next thing to do is to interact with your organisation within this environment. In the next chapter, we will examine this.

Notes

1 McGee, John, David Wilson, and Howard Thomas. *Strategy: Analysis and practice*. New York: McGraw-Hill Higher Education, 2010.
2 Osman-Gani, Aahad M. "Human capital development in Singapore: An analysis of national policy perspectives." *Advances in Developing Human Resources* 6, no. 3 (2004): 276–287.
3 Babatunde, Bayode O., and Adebola O. Adebisi. "Strategic environmental scanning and organization performance in a competitive business environment." *Economic Insights-Trends & Challenges* 64, no. 1 (2012).
4 Angwin, Duncan. *Business strategy pathfinder: Core concepts and micro-cases*. New York: John Wiley & Sons, 2008.
5 Cummings, Stephen, and Duncan Angwin. *Strategy Builder: How to create and communicate more effective strategies*. New York: John Wiley & Sons, 2015.
6 Bröhmer, Jürgen. "Subsidiarity and the German constitution." In *Global perspectives on subsidiarity*, pp. 129–156. Dordrecht: Springer, 2014.
7 Johnson, Gerry, Kevan Scholes, and Richard Whittington. *Exploring corporate strategy: Text & cases*. London: Pearson Education, 2009.
8 Ramirez, Rafael, and Angela Wilkinson. *Strategic reframing: The Oxford scenario planning approach*. Oxford: Oxford University Press, 2016.

9 Schein, Edgar H. *Strategic pragmatism: The culture of Singapore's economic development board* (Vol. 11). Cambridge, MA: MIT Press, 1996.
10 Song, Ng Kok. *Up close with Lee Kuan Yew: Insights from colleagues and friends*, p. 153. Singapore: Marshall Cavendish, 2015.
11 Lecture by Peter Ho, "Scenario planning and horizon scanning." 5 September 2013.
12 Centre for Liveable Cities. "Urban development: From urban squalor to global city." In *Urban Systems Studies*, pp. 16, 81–82, 86–87. Singapore: Centre for Liveable Cities, 2016.
13 Wheelen, Thomas L., J. David Hunger, Alan N. Hoffman, and Charles E. Bamford. *Strategic management and business policy*. Boston, MA: Pearson, 2017.
14 Dobbins, Craig. "Strategic planning: External environmental scanning." *Center for Food and Agricultural Business* (2003). Accessed from: https://studylib.net/doc/8351559/strategic-planning--external-environmental-scanning. Accessed on 25 October 2020.
15 Grundy, Tony. "Rethinking and reinventing Michael Porter's five forces model." *Strategic Change* 15, no. 5 (2006): 213–229.
16 Vining, Aidan R. "Public agency external analysis using a modified 'five forces' framework." *International Public Management Journal* 14, no. 1 (2011): 63–105.
17 Ostrom, Elinor. "Beyond markets and states: Polycentric governance of complex economic systems." *American Economic Review* 100, no. 3 (2010): 641–672.
18 Wheelen, Thomas L., J. David Hunger, Alan N. Hoffman, and Charles E. Bamford. *Strategic management and business policy*. Boston, MA: Pearson, 2017.
19 Ortega, Alba Gómez, M. Luisa Delgado Jalón, and José Ángel Rivero Menéndez. "A strategic analysis of collective urban transport in Spain using the Five Forces Model." *Investigaciones europeas de dirección y economía de la empresa* 20, no. 1 (2014): 5–15.
20 Zhu, Jian-Hua. "Public opinion polling in China: A descriptive review." *Gazette* (Leiden, Netherlands) 41, no. 2 (1988): 127–138.
21 Flanigan, Shawn Teresa, and Mounah Abdel-Samad. "Hezbollah's social jihad: Nonprofits as resistance organizations." *Middle East Policy* 16, no. 2 (2009): 122–137.
22 Hay, Colin. "The winter of discontent thirty years on." *The Political Quarterly* 80, no. 4 (2009): 545–552.
23 Moretti, Delphine, and Dirk-Jan Kraan. "Budgeting in France." *OECD Journal on Budgeting* 18, no. 2 (2018): 8–72.
24 Mendelow, A. "Stakeholder mapping: The power interest matrix." Proceedings of 2nd International Conference on Information Systems, Cambridge, MA, 1991.
25 Pacagnella Júnior, Antônio Carlos, Geciane Silveira Porto, Ornella Pacífico, and Alexandre Pereira Salgado Júnior. "Project stakeholder management: A case study of a Brazilian science park." *Journal of Technology Management & Innovation* 10, no. 2 (2015): 39–49.
26 Porter, Michael E. "Competitive advantage, agglomeration economies, and regional policy." *International Regional Science Review* 19, no. 1–2 (1996): 85–90.
27 Tsiligiris, Vangelis. "An adapted Porter diamond model for the evaluation of transnational education host countries." *International Journal of Educational Management* 32, no. 2 (2018): 210–226.
28 Chobanyan, Armen, and Laurence Leigh. "The competitive advantages of nations: Applying the 'Diamond' model to Armenia." *International Journal of Emerging Markets* 1, no. 2 (2006): 147–164.
29 Hodgetts, Richard M. "Porter's diamond framework in a Mexican context." *MIR: Management International Review* (1993): 41–54.
30 Bellak, Christian J., and Andreas Weiss. "A note on the Austrian 'diamond'." *MIR: Management International Review* (1993): 109–118.
31 Hosein Rezazadeh Mehrizi, Mohammad, and Mohammad Pakneiat. "Comparative analysis of sectoral innovation system and diamond model (the case of telecom sector of Iran)." *Journal of Technology Management & Innovation* 3, no. 3 (2008): 78–90.
32 Curran, Paul J. "Competition in UK higher education: Competitive advantage in the research assessment exercise and Porter's diamond model." *Higher Education Quarterly* 54, no. 4 (2000): 386–410.

Bibliography

Angwin, Duncan. (2008). *Business strategy pathfinder: Core concepts and micro-cases*. New York: John Wiley & Sons.

Babatunde, Bayode O., and Adebola O. Adebisi. (2012). "Strategic environmental scanning and organization performance in a competitive business environment." *Economic Insights-Trends & Challenges* 64(1).

Cummings, Stephen, and Duncan Angwin. (2015). *Strategy builder: How to create and communicate more effective strategies*. New York: John Wiley & Sons.

Dobbins, Craig. (2003). "Strategic planning: External environmental scanning." *Center for Food and Agricultural Business*. Accessed from: https://studylib.net/doc/8351559/strategic-planning--external-environmental-scanning. Accessed on 25 October 2020.

Dunleavy, Patrick, and Christopher Hood. (1994). "From old public administration to new public management." *Public Money & Management* 14(3): 9–16.

Flanigan, Shawn Teresa, and Mounah Abdel-Samad. (2009). "Hezbollah's social jihad: Nonprofits as resistance organizations." *Middle East Policy* 16(2): 122–137.

Grundy, Tony. (2006). "Rethinking and reinventing Michael Porter's five forces model." *Strategic Change* 15(5): 213–229.

Hanson, Dallas, Michael A. Hitt, R. Duane Ireland, and Robert E. Hoskisson. (2016). *Strategic management: Competitiveness and globalisation*. London: Cengage.

Hay, Colin. (2009). "The winter of discontent thirty years on." *The Political Quarterly* 80(4): 545–552.

Johnson, Gerry, Kevan Scholes, and Richard Whittington. (2009). *Exploring corporate strategy: Text & cases*. New York: Pearson.

Mailland, Julien, and Kevin Driscoll. (2017). *Minitel: Welcome to the internet*. Cambridge, MA: MIT Press.

McGahan, Anita M., Nicholas Argyres, and Joel AC Baum. (2004). "Context, technology and strategy: Forging new perspectives on the industry life cycle." *Advances in Strategic Management* 21: 1–24.

McGee, John, David Wilson, and Howard Thomas. (2010). *Strategy: Analysis and practice*. New York: McGraw-Hill Higher Education.

Mendelow, A. (1991). "Stakeholder mapping: The power interest matrix." Proceedings of 2nd International Conference on Information Systems, Cambridge, MA.

Moretti, Delphine, and Dirk-Jan Kraan. (2018). "Budgeting in France." *OECD Journal on Budgeting* 18(2): 8–72.

Ortega, Alba Gómez, M. Luisa Delgado Jalón, and José Ángel Rivero Menéndez. (2014). "A strategic analysis of collective urban transport in Spain using the Five Forces Model." *Investigaciones europeas de dirección y economía de la empresa* 20(1): 5–15.

Ostrom, Elinor. (2010). "Beyond markets and states: Polycentric governance of complex economic systems." *American Economic Review* 100(3): 641–672.

Pacagnella Júnior, Antônio Carlos, Geciane Silveira Porto, Ornella Pacífico, and Alexandre Pereira Salgado Júnior. (2015). "Project stakeholder management: A case study of a Brazilian science park." *Journal of Technology Management & Innovation* 10(2): 39–49.

Porter, Michael. (1998a). *Competitive strategy: Techniques for analysing industries and competitors*. New York: Free Press.

Porter, Michael. (1998b). *Competitive advantage: Creating and sustaining superior performance*. New York: Free Press.

Ragusa, Jordan Michael. (2010). "The lifecycle of public policy: An event history analysis of repeals to landmark legislative enactments, 1951–2006." *American Politics Research* 38(6): 1015–1051.

Ramirez, Rafael, and Angela Wilkinson. (2016). *Strategic reframing: The Oxford scenario planning approach*. Oxford: Oxford University Press.

Schein, Edgar H. (1996). *Strategic pragmatism: The culture of Singapore's economic development board* (Vol. 11). Cambridge, MA: MIT Press.

Tsiligiris, Vangelis. (2018). "An adapted Porter diamond model for the evaluation of transnational education host countries." *International Journal of Educational Management* 32(2): 210–226.

Vining, Aidan R. (2011). "Public agency external analysis using a modified "five forces" framework." *International Public Management Journal* 14(1): 63–105.

Wheelen, Thomas L., J. David Hunger, Alan N. Hoffman, and Charles E. Bamford. (2017). *Strategic management and business policy*. New York: Pearson.

Zhu, Jian-Hua. (1988). "Public opinion polling in China: A descriptive review." *Gazette (Leiden, Netherlands)* 41(2): 127–138.

4

MACRO-SITUATION ANALYSIS

Organisational Strategies

> *"If you know the enemy and know yourself, you need not fear the result of a hundred battles".*
>
> – *Sun Zi*

It is necessary for organisations to have a clear understanding of their environment if they wish to craft a well-adapted strategy for dealing with it, as we saw in the previous chapter. However, this strategy has to be realistic in the light of their specific capacities. Recognising that AI is a growing industry and deciding to join it may be a reasonable decision from the perspective of a software development firm, but it is far less practical for a fried chicken franchise. The market is the same, but the existing capacities of the firms are not – what is feasible for one organisation may not be for another. Similarly, while Singapore may look enviously at Indonesia's oil wealth, the government does not currently consider invading Indonesia to take possession of its resources to be a feasible plan.

An organisation's capacities are not defined in isolation. Indeed, they cannot be defined in isolation. Any capacity is the capacity to do *something*, which implies interaction with the outside world. A capacity to retain staff depends partially not upon an entity's human resources policy but also upon the local, national and international job markets, for example.

In this chapter, we will look at various frameworks used by public sector entities to assess their own capacities and thereby to settle upon a strategy that will allow them to reconcile these capacities with the environment in which they find themselves, playing to their strengths to provide the best possible service to their users and to maximise the value provided to taxpayers. Once again, we will run through them in the order in which they should – ideally – be undertaken. In the first stage,

DOI: 10.4324/9781003307228-4

it is important to conduct an internal analysis in a similar way to the environmental analyses described in the previous chapter. In the next stage, internal and external analyses are brought together, and the places in which they either complement or contradict one another are identified. Finally, the internal and external forces at work are analysed in detail, in order to create a strategy. However, it is not enough to go through the motions. These projects need to be conducted as a good-faith effort to change, rather than merely a box-ticking exercise. In the final part of this chapter, we go into more detail on how to ensure participant buy-in.

We will run through several well-known and less well-known frameworks, taken mainly from the business world, describing the ways in which they are applied and how they can be transferred to the public sector. While the New Public Management (NPM) movement of the 1980s led to the transfer of models from business to the public sector, one of the results of this was an increased awareness of the fact that – though these frameworks do transfer across – they also require significant modification. In this chapter, in particular, we show how these approaches have changed as they were moved from the private to the public sectors. We will first run through the key concepts involved in internal analysis. We then go on to look at resource-based strategies, and, in particular, the VRIO approach, as well as the value chain analysis approaches and 7-S. Finally, we look at the best-known framework for comparing capacities and environment: SWOT analysis. In the years since its development, the SWOT framework has been expanded into a more precise comparison matrix: TOWS, which we will go on to look at in detail. SWOT and TOWS help to uncover the strategic levers of an organisation, and these can then be embedded into a VRIO analysis and understand which levers are most important within that organisation's value chain. Then, when using these levers, a balanced scorecard approach can be used to get alternative perspectives on the same issues.

1. Organisational Analysis: 7S

Every organisation exists for a purpose, and any attempt to analyse the organisation's strengths and weaknesses must constantly return to this purpose. If one department within the organisation performs with outstanding efficiency but is working counter to the overall aims of the organisation, then it is contributing nothing to the overall goal, and may even be harming the organisation as a whole. It essentially depends upon the ability to take a meta-perspective in considering the formulation and decision-making stages of the policy cycle.

To evaluate each component of the organisation, it is necessary to identify the extent to which they contribute to the realisation of its global goals. As Hanson et al. (2016) put it, "The strategic decisions managers make about the internal organisation are nonroutine, have ethical implications, and significantly influence the firm's ability to earn above-average returns. These decisions involve choices about the resources the firm needs to collect and how best to leverage them".[1]

In the past, when social progress was slower and technology had less influence on government, public sector entities' efforts to improve their performance were largely geared towards providing a static service to a stable and familiar user base. This stability could often lead organisations to neglect or underestimate the role of their own resources and competencies, in both maximising efficiency under current circumstances and anticipating new challenges.

As we saw in the previous chapter when discussing the policy lifecycle, focusing principally on past experience tends to lead organisations to get stuck in a rut, simply repeating familiar procedures, rather than to work with their unique advantages to transform their environment. There are various ways to change this mindset, but they all begin with a thorough awareness of an organisation's core competences and resources, as well as the ways in which they fit into their environment.

Resources can be broken down into tangible and intangible resources. Tangible resources are things that can be observed and measured: equipment, contracts with suppliers, staff, etc. Intangible resources are harder to analyse but are not necessarily less important: things like user goodwill, experience in a given field, reputation or relationships with other governments. While these things are not always easy to quantify, they are nevertheless given a monetary value in the commercial world: often their value is factored in when a business is sold and assigned a monetary value. In a public sector context, however, this is harder to do. While polls or election results can measure citizen engagement and treaties and trade agreements can be seen as a reflection of goodwill abroad, the relative effects of these things upon the functioning of a state or a given department within a state are almost impossible to measure. Instead, approximations such as social cost–benefit analysis must be used.[2]

TABLE 4.1 Tangible and Intangible Resources (Adapted from Hanson et al., 2016)

Tangible resources	
Financial resources	Tax revenues
	Sovereign wealth
	Capacity to borrow
Organisational resources	Formal structures
	Administrative organisations
Physical resources	Land
	Plant, equipment and real estate
	Stock
Legal resources	Legislative and regulatory capacity
	Contracts, agreements and property rights
Executive resources	The right and the capacity to use force in legal relations (police, army, etc.)
Intangible resources	
Human resources	Knowledge
	Trust
	Skills
	Abilities to collaborate
Innovation resources	Ideas
	Scientific capabilities
Reputational resources	Soft power
	Positive perceptions

The two often help to complement each other. For example, ideas cannot be transformed into innovations without support from administrative structures, while an organisation's capacity to borrow depends to a great degree on its reputation (states are accorded credit ratings by financial institutions based partially on concrete financial data and partially upon analysts' perceptions of their prospects and risks).

This combination of tangible and intangible resources is what defines an organisation's capabilities. These capabilities tend to be concentrated in particular functional areas: human resources, information systems, distribution and logistics, public relations and image management, organisation and strategy, research and development. The distribution of these capacities and their focus are what define an organisation's core competencies. Thus, Apple's capacities are centred on design, innovation and public relations, defining its core competencies in high-end technology. Meanwhile, Walmart's principal capacities lie in logistics and organisation, skills that are necessary for its core competency: the large-scale distribution of consumer goods. This framework is hard to apply to states – which are expected to demonstrate transversal competence rather than focusing on a particular area – but it can easily be transferred to the analysis of a given department within a state. Thus, for example, a Ministry of Education and a Ministry of Defence will have different tangible and intangible resources, capacities and core competencies. While it is good to aim for excellence in all fields, in reality, some departments will always be better at certain things and worse at others. A telecommunication regulator is likely to be more comfortable with innovation than a park management board, for example, while the armed services will be better at handling logistics issues than a telecommunications regulator. It is important to recognise this in order to recognise where improvements should be made, and to prioritise specific changes.[3]

However, the tangible and intangible resources' vision of organisations tends to focus on highly concrete aspects of an organisation. This can lead those who apply it to omit aspects of an organisation that can be the key to its functioning: things such as its strategy and its values. These can keep an organisation going when both tangible and intangible resources fail, or their absence can provoke the collapse of an organisation that is otherwise well-resourced. The McKinsey 7-S framework is an attempt to pin down and analyse these more nebulous concepts. The 7-S framework was developed by consultants at McKinsey in the late 1970s and singles out seven key factors that need to be aligned in order for an organisation to be successful.[4]

The framework includes three hard factors:

- Strategy – The organisation's plans for maintaining or improving its position. A good strategy should be clearly articulated, cover both short- and long-term eventualities, aid the organisation in becoming more effective than its counterparts elsewhere, and be reinforced by a strong mission, vision and values.
- Structure – How your entity is organised. This refers to the organisation of the various business divisions and units, and the chain of accountability. In larger

organisations, this will be highly formalised, while in smaller ones it may be more informal with people taking on multiple roles.

- Systems – Your daily activities and procedures. These are the standard processes by which decisions are made and implemented throughout the company. Who has the final say in which circumstances? How do you interact with customers or users? How does information circulate throughout the organisation?

And four soft factors:

- Shared values – Why you do what you do? These are the core of the 7-S model. These may not always be obvious to people outside or even inside the organisation, and often they do not entirely align with the PR-boosting mission and vision statements published by almost every medium or large organisation these days. Values may include cynicism, hostility to outsiders and hypocrisy, just as well as quality, integrity and environmentalism, for example.
- Skills – Your practical competencies. This refers to your employees' capabilities, and their various levels of competence in each area. Remember that a low-level skill remains a skill, and should be borne in mind if it is to be improved upon.
- Style – Your approach to leadership. This is the management approach taken by the senior leaders in the company.
- Staff – The employees. This is highly related to the "skills" item, though it also includes the number, location and motivation of staff.

It is important that every factor within the framework be given equal weight, in order to achieve optimal outcomes. The links between these different elements are then inspected to look for gaps or inefficiencies. This is done by the following four steps:

1. Are your shared values consistent with the other values? If not, what do you need to change?
2. Do the hard elements support or detract from one another?
3. Do the soft elements support or detract from the hard elements?
4. Iterate. Changing one element will affect all of the others. In planning strategies, it is necessary to look at each possible change successively, evaluating its likely impact on all the other elements.

Through this iterative process, it should be possible to work out what your organisation would look like in ideal circumstances. Once this map has been made, it can be compared with the map as it is currently, in order to identify the changes that need to be made in order to maximise the organisation's potential.

One place where this has actually been implemented in a public sector context is in Kenya, where the Revenue Authority has used the 7-S framework to carry out internal reforms.[5] The approach was used to create consensus around the organisation's vision and chart the way towards successfully implementing the strategies that they developed. A study on the process concluded that:

> The element of shared values has also been crucial in enabling employees regardless of their job or grade to piece together how their individual roles fit into the whole organization and therefore provided purpose for their day-to-day work. This has made the strategy implementation process an inclusive affair within the organization, therefore creating ownership and responsibility. The application of the McKinsey 7S model in strategy implementation has been acclaimed as the major factor that has contributed to the emergence of KRA as one of the leading public bodies in terms of achieving its core objective of collection of revenue on behalf of the government of Kenya. The model has enabled the authority to exploit its internal resources so as to respond to the dynamic environment within the country.

It is important to note that this should not be seen as a one-time exercise. It must be repeated on a regular basis in order to prevent slippage and remain up to date. However, it should also not be conducted in isolation.

2. Organisational Analysis: Threshold Versus Core Resources and Capabilities

Cummings and Angwin (2015) offered a simple matrix for evaluating resources, capabilities and core competencies of any given organisation.[6] This approach emphasises the evaluation stage of the policy cycle, as the data collected during the evaluation stage are necessary for any organisation to gain a reliable perspective on its strengths and weaknesses.

Threshold resources tend to be static and similar throughout a given field, while unique resources are what makes a given organisation special. In a public sector

TABLE 4.2 Threshold vs. Core/Resources vs. Capabilities (Adapted from Cummings and Angwin, 2015)

	Similar to other organisations or easy to imitate	*Better than other organisations and difficult to imitate*
Resources	**Threshold resources** Examples: administrative structures, office management software	**Unique resources** Examples: specially designed equipment, legal privileges
Capabilities	**Threshold capabilities** Examples: recruiting procedures, management techniques	**Core capabilities** Examples: military and police capacities, international relations

context, this is not only what distinguishes one department from another but also what distinguishes it from private entities. Threshold capabilities, on the other hand, are those capabilities that are necessary to meet customers' or service users' minimum requirements, while core competencies are what gives the organisation its key advantages over other similar organisations.

Thus, for example, while a government-operated health service has different resources from a government school or a government prison, it also has different resources from a private hospital, and both comparisons need to be made in order to get a full, 360-degree view of the situation. The comparison can also be made at an international level: US military force projection capabilities are unique and hard to challenge, making them a core competency. Similarly, its military resources are more extensive and – largely – more advanced than those of any other state. On the other hand, the US Drugs and Alcohol Administration uses resources and approaches that are commonplace elsewhere and does not have any significant head start when compared to its Canadian counterpart, for example.

3. Organisational Analysis: VRIO

This is not the only way to approach this task, however. The VRIO framework was designed by Jay Barney and Bill Hesterly to help organisations look in more depth at their core competencies. VRIO stands for "value, rarity, inimitability and organization".[7] In other words:

- **Value**: Does the organisation have the capacity to produce a good or service that is valued by those who use/consume it?
- **Rarity**: How many other organisations exist with these capacities?
- **Inimitability**: How easy would it be for competitors to acquire these capacities?
- **Organisation**: Do the managerial and structural capacities exist to exploit the opportunities available?

Clearly, there is a significant overlap between this and the previous framework. In a commercial context, **value** is easily measured via willingness to pay for goods or services. In a public service context it is far harder to assess. The usual way to do so is via polls, elections and other forms, since many services are provided either free at the point of use or at a heavily subsidised price, while others are compulsory (police and justice, military service, etc.). We will look in more detail at this point in the next section (value chain analysis).[8]

Rarity is also measured in different ways in commercial and public sector contexts. In the private sector, the means used by companies to restrict supply of their products and thus maintain price levels and minimise competition include intellectual property, trade secrets, economies of scale and market power. In the public sector, the degree of competition and potential competition differs greatly between various departments. The police and the military, for example, are not – in theory – subject to any competition on their own state's territory. In practice, however, this is not always the case. Many countries rely on alliances for defence, for example, meaning that they lack monopolistic control over their military affairs. Similarly, while national or local police forces may be the only organisations enabled to enforce the law within a given territory, in practice they may face competition from private security firms, organised crime gangs and militias. In other areas, competition from private entities is even more widespread: private schools and hospitals, for example, are frequently seen as being preferable to their state equivalents.

Rarity is strongly linked to **inimitability**. While rarity measures the existence of similar resources or capabilities among competitors at the present point in time, inimitability is used to evaluate the potential acquisition or emergence of similar resources and capabilities in the future.

Organisation is the factor that best crosses the boundaries between the public and the private sectors, and assesses the ability of a given company or department to deliver the good or service that customers/service users require. A great product or idea is worth nothing if its owner has no way of getting it to the people who want it. This includes not only human resources and logistics chains but also particular production techniques and company culture.

In a commercial context, a company aims to maximise all four factors: the goal is to create a unique and high-quality product or service, to deliver it consistently and effectively, and to prevent other companies from attempting to copy it. This is not necessarily the case in a public context. Governments may want to deliver (organisation) a quality health service (value) that fills the gaps left by private providers (rarity); if private providers find a way to provide for-profit services that are as good or better as those provided by the government, this is generally seen as a positive rather than a negative outcome. Indeed, in recent years, it has become a popular trend in public administration, with many governments striving for polycentricity and public–private partnerships.[9] It is thus important to be clear that while the goal of these frameworks in a commercial context is to improve services in order to outcompete other services, the goal in a public sector context is to improve services in order to improve citizen satisfaction. Comparison with other services is useful insofar as it helps with benchmarking and understanding what is expected of the organisation, but it is not usually a driver of competition with these other services.

This can be of particular use when public agencies' remits overlap or lead to inefficient allocation of resources, and a way needs to be found to draw clear and reasonable lines between their various areas of responsibility. In the United States, for example, frozen cheese pizza is regulated by the Food and Drug Administration (FDA), while frozen pepperoni pizza is regulated by the Department of Agriculture (USDA). The nutrition information labels on both are produced by the FDA, but they feature the USDA logo because the USDA carries out most inspections.[10] The result is that the companies that are obliged to comply with the relevant regulations are obliged to jump through multiple hoops and interact with two separate industries when it would be far more efficient to have a single point of contact. In practice, this has been used in the real world to analyse the situations faced by various organisations that sit on the border of the public and the private.[11] For example, the approach was used to analyse competition between "Academic Health Sciences Centres" in the United Kingdom, which are public entities but which also compete among themselves to recruit the best researchers, produce results and thereby ensure the renewal of their public accreditation. A similar approach was also used in Denmark to improve the effectiveness of hospital services.

As described earlier, however, the absence of direct commercial competition can make it difficult to assess public organisations' performance. While a company that is outperforming its competitors can tell this is the case from its profit and loss statements, this method cannot be applied to compare – for example – the performance of two public hospitals. If both hospitals are receiving equal amounts of funding and one is achieving better outcomes than another, this can be a sign that one is performing better than another – though this is not always the case, since one may deal with trickier cases.[12] Indeed, in the public service there can often be a pressure for departments to spend as much as possible to ensure that their budget will not be cut in the following year. If this is the case, it is important to identify where the deficiencies are occurring.

4. Organisational Analysis: Value Chain Analysis

Once again, an approach often used in business – value chain analysis – can be applied to public sector cases.

The goal of value chain analysis is to identify where money is leaking from a given organisation, and hence where efficiency can be improved.[13] This fits in with the SWOT and TOWS analyses conducted (see later) insofar as that value leakages tend to be evidence of the places where your organisation is weakest. Every organisation has its own specific value chain, but a generic example can be seen here.

The table should be read in the direction of the arrow. The bottom row includes all activities directly relating to the good or service delivered. Taking the example of a public health department, citizen demand may include phone calls to the emergency services as well as walk-ins and elective patients. Operations refer to the organisational processes via which this demand is fulfilled. Service delivery involves

TABLE 4.3 Value Chain Analysis (Adapted from McGee et al., 2010)

	→				
Support activities	Infrastructure Human resource management Technology development Procurement				Service
Primary activities	Citizen demand	Operations	Service delivery	Marketing and sales	

actually carrying out medical treatments. Marketing and sales would include publicising the services on offer (though not necessarily as aggressively as is the case for private businesses), letting people know what they can access and how, as well as publicising public health campaigns. However, these functions cannot be delivered without the support activities described in the top row: it is impossible to treat patients adequately without hospitals, doctors and nurses, equipment and drugs. Together with the primary activities described earlier, these come together to make up the service as it is received by the end users.

This breakdown of an organisation's activities is often used in cost analysis. This is done in six distinct steps:[14]

1. Define the key elements of the chain for the organisation in question. These may be the same as in the previous example diagram, or they may be different. It is important that the activities be distinct and clearly defined; if they overlap it becomes impossible to identify where exactly inefficiencies originate.
2. Establish the relative importance of the various activities in the total cost of providing the service. This can be done through management's accounts or other forms of internal audit. It is best to have this done by a trained accountant, who will be able to distinguish clearly between different types of costs and factor in capital depreciation, etc.[15]
3. Compare these costs against benchmarks from similar organisations. In the hospital example, these may be other public hospitals (whether at home or abroad) or private hospitals (ditto).
4. Identify cost drivers. In the case of a highly distributed customer base, logistics may be a major driver of costs. If the organisation is a labour-intensive one, then wage rates will be a major driver of costs.
5. Identify linkages between activities. Often leakages of cash come from gaps or inefficiencies in the coordination between different activities. Thus, for example, inefficient management may mean that more frontline staff have to be hired, which pushes up costs. The cost is in the wages of the frontline workers, but the root of the problem lies in organisational structures.
6. Identify opportunities for reducing costs. These will often coincide with the inefficiencies identified in question 5. It is important to note that these will be different for every organisation. For some organisations, it may make sense to subcontract out parts of the production process, for others it may be less risky to bring them in-house. This will be determined by the cost and risk profiles of each organisation.

Taking the example given above of the overlap between the FDA and the USDA, it is common for both organisations to be obliged to inspect the same companies as part of their statutory duties, rather than sending two inspectors from two departments to inspect a single frozen pizza company. This means that the inspection process is far more expensive than it would be if one department ran all inspections on its own. A value chain analysis of the inspections process would quickly identify this duplication of activities and allow the analysts to work out which of the two departments would be better equipped to handle all inspections. While the inefficiency of the present situation may seem obvious to an outsider, the inherently conservative nature of the bureaucracy has maintained this *status quo* for decades. The approach has been used in the past, particularly at the intersection of public and private sector activities. In Indonesia, for example, it was applied to the cocoa bean industry in the context of a joint public–private effort to fight cocoa pod borer infestations.[16] However, its utility is not limited to business-adjacent sectors. In Canada, a value chain approach has been applied to analyse the reasons between the decline in public trust in government institutions, concluding:

> the "public sector service value chain" helps us to understand that public managers should give greater attention to measurement and accountability for both internal and external performance. Implementing systems of accountability for measurable improvement in employee engagement (satisfaction/commitment) results and in service satisfaction (and other results valued by citizens) can contribute, in measurable ways, to the larger goal of improving citizen trust and confidence in public institutions.[17]

Conclusion

In this chapter, as in the last one, we ran through the key steps required to analyse your organisation's strengths and weaknesses. First, 7S looks at categories within an organisational health. Second, threshold and core lenses can be applied to assess resources and capabilities/competencies. Third, adopting VRIO allows one to accentuate the unique value proposition of one's organisation. Fourth, value chain analysis adopts a "value chain" process lens to determine critical leverage points. Now that we have evaluated both our environment and organisation, the next thing to do is to interact with your organisation within this environment. In the next chapter, we will examine this.

Notes

1 Hanson, Dallas, Michael A. Hitt, R. Duane Ireland, and Robert E. Hoskisson. *Strategic management: Competitiveness and globalisation*. London: Cengage AU, 2016.
2 Cinca, Carlos Serrano, Cecilio Mar Molinero, and Alexandre Bossi Queiroz. "The measurement of intangible assets in public sector using scaling techniques." *Journal of Intellectual Capital* 4, no. 2 (2003): 249–275.
3 Zigan, Krystin, Fraser Macfarlane, and Terry Desombre. "Intangible resources as performance drivers in European hospitals." *International Journal of Productivity and Performance Management* 57, no. 1 (2008): 57–71.
4 Ravanfar, Mohammad Mehdi. "Analyzing organizational structure based on 7s model of McKinsey." *Global Journal of Management and Business Research* 15, no. 10 (2015). Accessed from: https://globaljournals.org/GJMBR_Volume15/2-Analyzing-Organizational-Structure.pdf. Accessed on 25 October 2020.
5 Maru, Beatrice W. "Application of the McKinsey 7S model in strategy implementation at the Kenya revenue authority." PhD diss., University of Nairobi, 2015.

6 Cummings, Stephen, and Duncan Angwin. *Strategy Builder: How to create and communicate more effective strategies*. New York: John Wiley & Sons, 2015.
7 Scholes, Kevan, Gerry Johnson, and Richard Whittington. *Exploring corporate strategy*. New York: Financial Times Prentice Hall, 2002.
8 Olsen, Jan Abel, and Cam Donaldson. "Helicopters, hearts and hips: Using willingness to pay to set priorities for public sector health care programmes." *Social Science & Medicine* 46, no. 1 (1998): 1–12.
9 Ostrom, Elinor. "Polycentric systems as one approach for solving collective-action problems." *Indiana University, Bloomington: School of Public & Environmental Affairs Research Paper 2008–11* (2008): 2.
10 Sugarman, Carole. "Who's minding the store?" *Washington Post*, 11 May 1988. Accessed from: www.washingtonpost.com/archive/lifestyle/food/1988/05/11/whos-minding-the-store/2af04559-d212-4a64-bc6e-b3b7adb7f49f/. Accessed on 25 October 2020.
11 Rosenberg Hansen, Jesper, and Ewan Ferlie. "Applying strategic management theories in public sector organizations: Developing a typology." *Public Management Review* 18, no. 1 (2016): 1–19.
12 McKee, Martin, Anne-Marie Rafferty, and Linda Aiken. "Measuring hospital performance: Are we asking the right questions?" *Journal of the Royal Society of Medicine* 90, no. 4 (1997): 187–191.
13 Ensign, Prescott C. "Value chain analysis and competitive advantage." *Journal of General Management* 27, no. 1 (2001): 18–42.
14 McGee, John, David Wilson, and Howard Thomas. *Strategy: Analysis and practice*. New York: McGraw-Hill Higher Education, 2010.
15 Hergert, Michael, and Deigan Morris. "Accounting data for value chain analysis." *Strategic Management Journal* 10, no. 2 (1989): 175–188.
16 Panlibuton, Henry, and Frank Lusby. "Indonesia cocoa bean value chain case study." *USAID Microreport* 65 (2006).
17 Heintzman, Ralph, and Brian Marson. "People, service and trust: Is there a public sector service value chain?" *International Review of Administrative Sciences* 71, no. 4 (2005): 549–575.

Bibliography

Cinca, Carlos Serrano, Cecilio Mar Molinero, and Alexandre Bossi Queiroz. (2003). "The measurement of intangible assets in public sector using scaling techniques." *Journal of Intellectual Capital* 4(2): 249–275.

Cummings, Stephen, and Duncan Angwin. (2015). *Strategy Builder: How to create and communicate more effective strategies*. New York: John Wiley & Sons.

Dess, Gregory, Alan Eisner, G.T. Lumpkin, and Gerry McNamara. (2011). *Strategic management: Creating competitive advantages*. New York: McGraw-Hill Higher Education.

Ensign, Prescott C. (1982). "Value chain analysis and competitive advantage." *Journal of General Management* 27(1): 18–42.

Eriksson, Päivi, and Anne Kovalainen. (2015). *Qualitative methods in business research: A practical guide to social research*. London: Sage.

Hanson, Dallas, Michael A. Hitt, R. Duane Ireland, and Robert E. Hoskisson. (2016). *Strategic management: Competitiveness and globalisation*. London: Cengage.

Heintzman, Ralph, and Brian Marson. (2005). "People, service and trust: Is there a public sector service value chain?" *International Review of Administrative Sciences* 71(4): 549–575.

Maru, Beatrice W. (2015). "Application of the McKinsey 7-S model in strategy implementation at the Kenya revenue authority." PhD diss., University of Nairobi.

McGee, John, David Wilson, and Howard Thomas. (2010). *Strategy: Analysis and practice*. New York: McGraw-Hill Higher Education.

McKee, Martin, Anne-Marie Rafferty, and Linda Aiken. (1997). "Measuring hospital performance: Are we asking the right questions?" *Journal of the Royal Society of Medicine* 90(4): 187–191.

Olsen, Jan Abel, and Cam Donaldson. (1998). "Helicopters, hearts and hips: Using willingness to pay to set priorities for public sector health care programmes." *Social Science & Medicine* 46(1): 1–12.

Ostrom, Elinor. (2008). "Polycentric systems as one approach for solving collective-action problems." Indiana University, Bloomington: School of Public & Environmental Affairs Research Paper 2008–11: 02.

Panlibuton, Henry, and Frank Lusby. (2006). "Indonesia cocoa bean value chain case study." *USAID Microreport* 65.

Ravanfar, Mohammad Mehdi. (2015). "Analyzing organizational structure based on 7s model of McKinsey." *Global Journal of Management and Business Research* 15(10). Accessed from: https://globaljournals.org/GJMBR_Volume15/2-Analyzing-Organizational-Structure.pdf. Accessed on 25 October 2020.

Rosenberg Hansen, Jesper, and Ewan Ferlie. (2016). "Applying strategic management theories in public sector organizations: Developing a typology." *Public Management Review* 18(1): 1–19.

Scholes, Kevan, Gerry Johnson, and Richard Whittington. (2002). *Exploring corporate strategy*. London: Prentice Hall.

Zigan, Krystin, Fraser Macfarlane, and Terry Desombre. (2008). "Intangible resources as performance drivers in European hospitals." *International Journal of Productivity and Performance Management* 57(1): 57–71.

5

MESO-ANALYSIS FOR POLICY STRATEGY

Interaction Strategies

It is important to bring your newfound awareness of the characteristics of your organisation together with the information about your environment that you collected to form a coherent strategy from interactional analysis. This is the meso-enabler for policy strategy. There are several options.

1. Interacting Your Organisation in Its Environment for Competitive Advantage: SWOT

SWOT is by far the most frequently used analytic framework, in both the public and private sectors. It is favoured by many organisations as a quick and easy way of judging an organisation's position within its environments. SWOT stands for "strengths, weakness, opportunities and threats".[1] These are usually listed as part of a matrix, which can be used in the context of a particular decision or of the business as a whole:

- Strengths: The areas in which the organisation outperforms the competition;
- Weaknesses: The areas in which the organisation is not performing as well as it could do;
- Opportunities: External factors that present a potential for the organisation to improve its performance;
- Threats: External factors that are liable to have a negative effect on the company's performance.

Once again, issues are broken down into internal and external factors. Strengths and weaknesses are internal factors, with opportunities and threats being external factors. Each individual factor is then assessed to work out whether it presents a strength or a weakness for the company in the present context.[2]

DOI: 10.4324/9781003307228-5

Internal factors:

- Financial resources (borrowing, revenue, subsidies, etc.)
- Physical resources (real estate, equipment)
- Human resources (employees and customers)
- Legal rights (patents, copyrights, trademarks, access to natural resources)
- Processes (staff training, hierarchies, software, organisational culture, etc.)

External factors can similarly be classified on the basis of whether they present an opportunity of a threat to the company.

External factors:

- Market trends (new technologies, trends and fashions, evolving preferences, etc.)
- Economic trends (market growth, exchange rates, interest rates, tax rates, etc.)
- Demographics (size and make-up of customer base)
- Relationships with suppliers and other partners
- Relationships with political and administrative actors

This is usually presented in the form of a two-by-two grid:

Strengths	*Opportunities*
Weaknesses	**Threats**

This approach is one of the most common strategic tools used by public and private organisations. It has, for example, been used throughout Scandinavia to orient many regional programmes in areas as diverse as education, technology, agriculture and business promotion.[3] An analysis of these exercises concluded:

> As a general conclusion of the project it can be argued that SWOT analysis can result in a certain value added for strategic planning. Yet this potential often remains untapped, as the actual strategic relevance of SWOT is not acknowledged and the learning potential underlying the utilisation of this instrument is only secondary to the formal standards of planning process. SWOT, as well as the strategy formation process in its entirety should be more directed towards emphasising the learning aspects, allowing for regional specialisation and therefore potential comparative advantage . . . The fact that the utilisation of SWOT analysis as a strategic instrument is more or less explicitly expected of most regional development programming documents is indicative of a semi-institutionalised planning practice that is taken for granted, but often not sufficiently elaborated on or consciously worked through for all of its potential value added to be realised.

TABLE 5.1 External Factors' Analysis Summary (Adapted from Wheelen et al., 2017)

Internal factors	*Weight*	*Rating*	*Weighted score*	*Comments*
Strengths				
Strong trade bargaining power	0.15	5.0	0.75	Driven by size of the US market
Strong research capacities	0.05	4.2	0.21	Can innovate way out of trouble
Stock of equipment	0.10	3.9	0.39	As a result of economic prosperity
Highly trained personnel	0.15	2.8	0.42	As a result of economic prosperity
Weaknesses				
Reduced political lobbying capacity	0.05	2.2	0.11	The Trump administration is less susceptible to influence and pork-barrel politics
Sclerotic bureaucracy	0.05	2.0	0.10	Little pressure to improve
Low adaptability	0.05	4.0	0.20	Little pressure to improve
Total scores	**1.00**		**3.05**	
External factors	**Weight**	**Rating**	**Weighted score**	**Comments**
Opportunities				
Brexit	0.20	4.1	0.82	Opportunity for greater trade links with the United Kingdom
Automation of farming	0.10	5.0	0.50	Reduce costs of managing land
Changing patterns in domestic consumption	0.05	2.0	0.10	Growing preference for high-quality local products, increasing suspicion of agribusiness
Increasing national debt/small government preference	0.05	2.0	0.10	Risk of reductions to farm subsidies
Reduction in world poverty	0.10	1.80	0.18	Increased meat consumption in developing states
Threats				
Fluctuating oil prices	0.10	4.3	0.43	Well positioned
Climate change	0.10	4.0	0.40	Change in the nature of the crops is possible to cultivate in the United States, and increased risk of natural disasters
Trade war with China	0.15	3.0	0.45	Reduced exports
Water scarcity	0.05	1.2	0.06	A particular threat in certain areas – California, Colorado, etc.
Massive decline in world fish stocks	0.10	1.6	0.16	Severe threat
Total scores	**1.00**		**3.15**	

To be truly worthwhile, SWOT analysis needs to be combined with other methods. If you have completed the environment scanning exercise described in the previous chapter, you should already have a good idea of the opportunities and threats you are facing, so you should be able to fill in these items first. After you have done this, you can then go on to look at your own strengths and weaknesses.

This can be resolved by modifying the framework. This can be done by adapting the EFAS framework from Chapter 3.

As described earlier, this approach to quantifying threats and opportunities makes it far easier for managers to rank and track factors affecting its position. The ranking system can assist management in identifying the low-hanging fruit: places where an extra dollar spent will have the greatest effect on customer/user satisfaction. Once again, it is worth noting that the final column is not an optional extra – it is essential for understanding why particular scores have been given, particularly if the exercise is repeated year-on-year by different teams.[4]

2. Interacting Your Organisation in Its Environment for Competitive Advantage: TOWS

Another more advanced way to leverage the information collected during a SWOT analysis into an operational tracking and planning tool is via a similar related framework: TOWS. TOWS analysis, developed in 1982 by Heinz Weihrich, uses the same basic information as is used in a SWOT analysis, but combines and compares them with one another in order to produce a list of feasible options for dealing with each factor. While this is possible to do via a SWOT matrix, the TOWS approach allows users to take a more systematic approach and helps them to spot linkages that they may otherwise miss. The goal of this framework is to help organisations make the most of their strengths, circumvent their weaknesses, capitalise upon opportunities and manage threats.[5]

If well conducted, the TOWS approach can help your organisation transform threats into opportunities via innovation. TOWS addresses the earlier weakness of

TABLE 5.2 TOWS (Adapted from Johnson et al., 2009)

	Strengths	*Weaknesses*
Opportunities	SO Strategic Options (maxi–maxi strategies) Ways to use strengths to take advantage of opportunities	WO Strategic Options (maxi–mini strategies) Ways to overcome weaknesses to take advantage of opportunities
Threats	ST Strategic Options (mini–maxi strategies) Ways to use strengths to avoid threats	WT Strategic Options (mini–mini strategies) Ways to minimise weaknesses in order to avoid threats

SWOT which may end up a static framework of S, W, O, T points, whereas TOWS forcefully interacts S with O, S with T, etc.

If we apply this to the situation faced by the USDA as covered in the previous chapter, it produces a result that looks like the following.

	Strengths *Strong trade bargaining power* *Strong research capacities* *Stock of equipment* *Highly trained personnel*	*Weaknesses* *Reduced political lobbying capacity* *Sclerotic bureaucracy* *Low adaptability*
Opportunities Brexit Automation of farming Changing patterns in consumption Increasing national debt/small government preference Reduction in world poverty	**SO Strategic Options** Use bargaining power to negotiate favourable bilateral agreements to provide high-demand goods to newly wealthy developing nations	**WO Strategic Options** Use increasing outside pressure to force existing organisation to modernise and become more efficient
Threats Fluctuating oil prices Climate change Trade war with China Water scarcity Massive decline in world fish stocks	**ST Strategic Options** Use technology to mitigate the effects of environmental change and diplomatic strengths to mitigate effects of trade war	**WT Strategic Options** Improve the organisation's innovative capacities to better address current threats

Elsewhere, the TOWS framework has notably been used in Oman to assess the impact of e-government initiatives.[6]

They first listed their strengths and weaknesses: a growing IT sector but one which is weak when it comes to innovation. They then listed their opportunities and threats: a well-trained population and good ease of doing business combined with recent fluctuations in the economy. They then combined these into a TOWS matrix.

	Strengths	*Weaknesses*
Opportunities	Network strategy: Expanding available broadband capacity through the enhancement of investments in infrastructure and networks	**Broad band speed strategy:** Conducting external innovations especially in ICT would enhance the strategy and increase local education and experience

	Strengths	*Weaknesses*
Threats	Human capital strategy: The government should focus on the empowerment of skilled human capital in order to enhance training and education within local citizens	Funding strategy: Government must approach different kinds of funds in order to minimise weakness especially in ICT development in infrastructure and network

While SWOT and TOWS give organisations a helpful way to align themselves with the challenges and opportunities that they face, it does not necessarily tell them how to apply their competencies to best effect. To do this, other frameworks can be helpful, whether in mobilising your advantages (VRIO) or in minimising your disadvantages (Value Chain Analysis, Balanced Scorecard). These will be covered in the following section.

3. Interacting Your Organisation in Its Environment for Internal Buy-In and Monitoring: Balanced Scorecard

These steps may seem simple on the surface, but it is often difficult to judge where a business is performing less well than it could do. One of these is the balanced scorecard approach.

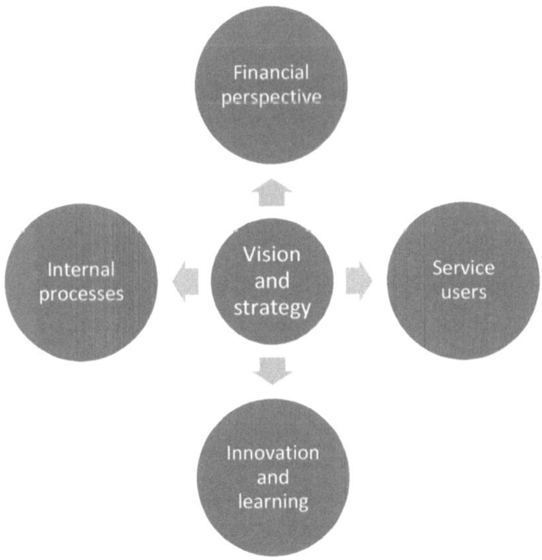

FIGURE 5.1 Balanced Scorecard (Adapted from Kaplan and Norton, 2005)

This method was developed by Kaplan and Norton, to give managers a fast and comprehensive view of a given organisation.[7] The balanced scorecard approach (BSC) asks managers to look at their organisation from four key perspectives: the customer/user perspective, the internal perspective, the innovation and learning perspective and the financial perspective.

Service user/customer perspective: As described in the previous chapter, a public organisation has three types of "customers" – service users, citizens and taxpayers. While the three groups often overlap, and indeed the same person may belong to all three, the perspectives differ. A service user simply wants the best service possible. A citizen wishes for the service to be provided in such a way as to promote overall social welfare. A taxpayer wishes the service to be provided at minimal cost. Various methods can be used to assess these groups' satisfaction: polling, focus groups and feedback forms.

Internal process perspective: When customer indicators have been fixed upon, they must be translated into internal indicators. It is important to work out which internal processes must be changed to create the greatest possible improvements to the customer/user experience. Thus, for example, if users are complaining that the service is slow, it becomes necessary to identify the internal processes that are slowing down the service and work out how to improve them. In one organisation, this may be due to equipment breakdowns and require more money to be put into maintenance. In another, it may be due to management bottlenecks, in which case an administrative reorganisation is indicated.

Innovation and learning perspective: Efficiency in current processes is not enough to ensure long-term success. Even if customer/user evaluations are good and little room for improvement can be found in internal processes, this still does not necessarily future-proof the organisation. At any moment a social or technological change could arise that obliges it to completely revise its operating model. Conversely, an organisation that is not operating at maximum efficiency may be doing so deliberately in order to better prepare itself for future changes – by shifting to a new IT system, for example, or by switching to green methods of production.

Financial perspective: This is not considered in raw terms, but in terms of margins. This means that it is as applicable in a public as in a private context. The aim is to work out how much energy (and hence money) needs to be spent in any given area to procure an extra unit of customer/user satisfaction. Once this has been worked out, efforts can be targeted at the areas where they will produce the greatest results.[8]

Each of these perspectives is then related to the organisation's vision and strategy:[9]

In a BSC exercise, all relevant entities within the organisation use the framework diagram to list the resources that they already have in each area, as well as the goals that they aim to attain in each. These are then compared, and strategy is adjusted to try to make existing resources align as closely as possible with goals. In order to be effective, the goals should be as concrete as possible – for example, it is better to set "serve 10% more users per day" as a goal than "provide more efficient service to users".

The BSC approach is useful for aggregating ideas and suggestions for improvement in a bottom-up manner, discussing them among senior management and then experimenting with and iterating new policies on this basis. It is also extremely useful for letting the different components of the organisation know what their goals should be and why these particular goals have been selected. Thus, it can be a valuable negotiation tool when trying to establish useful and reasonable goals for the various branches of a given organisation.

The BSC approach is used widely among private sector organisations, but it is also used within the public sector in certain circumstances. The Singapore Armed Forces (SAF), for example, have used it to gather and aggregate feedback from ordinary armed forces personnel. It has also been used extensively in local government in Australia as well as in the public sector in New Zealand.[10] In the Australian context, many local authorities had trouble adapting the framework to public sector circumstances, with managers saying that,

> the complexity of the LGA (local government authority) coupled with a top down approach to implementation also led to communication problems and difficulties in measurement. It was also acknowledged by most managers that it was difficult to link rewards and incentives with performance in a large LGA where performance was often difficult to measure in the first place.

It was also criticised for being an overly hierarchical and top-down approach.[11] However, over time, organisations gradually began to adapt it to fit their specific needs. Thus, while the financial component was not necessarily seen as highly relevant to the SAF in a national security context, the other items in the framework have been found to provide a useful way to pass information concerning organisational changes up and down through the organisation, effectively establishing a conversation that incorporates all layers. In such a context, the financial component is replaced by other feedback mechanisms, such as interviews, surveys and focus groups, directed at both armed service members and the citizens who benefit from the services that they provide.

It should be noticed that many organisations misuse the BSC concept to simply present a graphical description of the vision, direction and strategies of an organisation from a top-down perspective. In fact, it was originally intended to be a planning tool, by means of which individuals at both the top and bottom of an organisation can share information and set out a collaborative vision for the future. The goal is to allow everyone to lay out their aspirations, resources, working objectives and the broad direction in which they wish the organisation to travel, creating a strategy dialogue even within large organisations. It should not be used as a means for senior management to transmit their KPIs to those lower in the hierarchy.

However, the BSC approach is not the only one. The Singapore government, for example, looked at the BSC approach but found that the explicitly financial method for assessing performance was not necessarily well adapted to all departments. It may be well adapted to hospital's procurement unit but not to a mental health community programme. For this reason, the Singapore government went with the Baldridge National Quality Award criteria.[12] However, the Baldridge criteria involve dozens of questions split into various different rubrics and require a large amount of training, reading and literature to apply, which can be difficult for organisations that are small or pressed for time (and which is also why we are not covering them in detail here – they require entire books to explain).

Whichever option you choose, it can often be helpful to have each sub-department conduct its own exercise – whether using the BSC or Baldridge or some other systems – and then pass them upwards to give the management a perspective on how each part of the organisation sees its situation and its prospects. It is normal that each unit will try to frame their situation in a way that is as favourable as possible to them, so their answers should not necessarily be taken as the final truth but serve as a basis for discussion and negotiation concerning next year's budget and planning, as well as to elaborate a coherent strategy in which all units of the organisation work together as a coherent whole.

4. Interacting Your Organisation in Its Environment for Ops Monitoring: OKR

Often the implementation phase of the policy process is under-regarded, but it is important to remember that it is not enough that these exercises be carried out. They must also be carried out in an effective manner – indeed, if done so they in themselves constitute an important component of a company's strengths. If a TOWS or a S-7s analysis is conducted by only a small group of executives, or one highly subject to groupthink, or one that is lacking in information regarding key factors affecting the organisation, it will effectively be useless. The problem with this is that often senior management is convinced that no one knows its organisation better than it does itself, and therefore is unwilling to listen to other opinions. The result is that the output is skewed and tends to minimise or ignore weaknesses and threats. Even when organisations begin the process with the best will in the world, there can be a tendency for the exercises to come to be seen as a mere formality. Identifying serious flaws in an organisation will compel internal change, which is liable to threaten the interests of those in power within the hierarchy or – at the very least – cause a large amount of extra work for everyone involved. It is for this reason that stakeholder engagement, as described in this and the previous chapter, is so important, and also part of the reason that policy co-creation has grown in popularity over recent years.

One helpful way to do this is to have everyone in the organisation take responsibility for a set of written goals in which how success will be measured is included within the goal itself. This is the OKR (Objectives and Key Results) approach used by Google, where employees and teams regularly create lists of goals in this way within their hierarchy. At Google they use the format "I will ____________ as measured by ____________".[13]

Another approach involves setting up a system of internal checks and balances that will ensure that the various departments within the organisation work to keep each other up-to-speed and oblige them to deal with their problems before they begin to pose a serious problem for the organisation, as a whole.

While each organisation will want to do this in its own way, useful examples can be found in political systems around the world. One helpful example comes from the United States political system, which is organised to channel conflict in such a way as to ensure that actors keep tabs on one another while still being able to compromise. While electoral politics forces candidates to differentiate their politics, in order to attract attention from the grassroots, government then forces them to soften their positions and compromise in order to get their policies through the legislative system.

While it is hard to replicate the competing branches of power within the US government in smaller organisations, other checks and balances systems can be designed, potentially based on the exercises described in the previous two chapters. (It is also important to note that the aim of the US Constitutional system is to ensure that in the event of irreconcilable differences the system will come to a halt rather than descending into tyranny or anarchy. In a small government department, this is not necessarily ideal, and someone may need to step in from time to time, in order to break up deadlocks.)

If it becomes clear that two or more departments are working at odds with one another, this can be a source of friction and conflict within the organisation, but it can also be a way to make sure that each corrects the others' faults and both work with senior management to improve their performance. Nevertheless, this needs to be conducted carefully and diplomatically. A constructive process can quickly descend into paranoia and backstabbing if not handled carefully.

Conclusion

In this chapter, we looked at interactional analysis. First, SWOT articulates the environmental factors of opportunities and threats and organisational factors of strengths and weakness. Second, TOWS, in a more structured manner, force the interaction between environment and organisational factors to elicit the dynamic interactions, for example, using strength to mitigate threats, using strength to maximise opportunities, using opportunities to cover weakness, using threats to initiate actions to improve weaknesses. Third, balanced scorecard is an interaction between environment and organisational factors in a structured manner of finance, user/customer, internal process and innovation and offers a democratic way to elicit ground ideas and garner ground support for seed ideas, and transform into a layered governance and monitoring for change management. Fourth, Objectives–Key Results (OKR) is a targeted manner for ops and progress monitoring.

This macro (environment + organisation + interaction)-situational analysis serves as the policy context for policy strategy and innovation. All potential policy innovations will need to be embedded and aligned to its policy context, before it can aspire to shape the policy context and situation through implementation of successful strategic policy innovation. The next chapter will kick-start the policy innovation process.

Notes

1 Helms, Marilyn M., and Judy Nixon. "Exploring SWOT analysis – where are we now?" *Journal of Strategy and Management* 3 (2010): 215–251.
2 Korableva, Olga N., and Olga V. Kalimullina. "Strategic approach to the optimization of organization based on BSC-SWOT matrix." 2016 IEEE International Conference on Knowledge Engineering and Applications (ICKEA), pp. 212–215, IEEE, 2016.
3 Karppi, Ilari, Merja Kokkonen, and Kaisa Lähteenmäki-Smith. *SWOT-analysis as a basis for regional strategies*. Nordregio, Vol. 4, 2001. Accessed from: https://archive.nordregio.org/en/Publications/Publications-2001/SWOT-analysis-as-a-basis-for-regional-strategies/index.html. Accessed on 22 October 2020.
4 Eriksson, Päivi, and Anne Kovalainen. *Qualitative methods in business research: A practical guide to social research*. London: Sage, 2015.
5 Weihrich, Heinz. "The TOWS matrix – A tool for situational analysis." *Long Range Planning* 15, no. 2 (1982): 54–66.
6 Al Salmi, Muatasim Anwar Ahmed, and Norlena Bt Hasnan. "SWOT and TOWS matrix e-government analysis review on Sultanate of Oman." *International Journal of Learning and Development* 4 (2015).
7 Kaplan, R.S., and D.P. Norton. "The balanced scorecard: Measures that drive performance." *Harvard Business Review* 83, no. 7 (2005): 172.
8 Dess, Gregory, Alan Eisner, G.T. Lumpkin, and Gerry McNamara. *Strategic management: Creating competitive advantages*. New York: McGraw-Hill Higher Education, 2011.
9 Kaplan, R.S., and D.P. Norton. "The balanced scorecard: Measures that drive performance." *Harvard Business Review* 83, no. 7 (2005): 172.
10 Griffiths, John. "Balanced scorecard use in New Zealand government departments and crown entities." *Australian Journal of Public Administration* 62, no. 4 (2003): 70–79.
11 Hoque, Zahirul, and Carol Adams. "The rise and use of balanced scorecard measures in Australian government departments." *Financial Accountability & Management* 27, no. 3 (2011): 308–334.
12 Lee, S.M., B-H. Rho, and S-G. Lee. "Impact of Malcolm Baldrige national quality award criteria on organizational quality performance." *International Journal of Production Research* 41, no. 9 (2003): 2003–2020.
13 Steiber, Annika, and Sverker Alänge. "A corporate system for continuous innovation: The case of Google Inc." *European Journal of Innovation Management* 16, no. 2 (2013). Accessed from: https://www.researchgate.net/publication/263251371_A_corporate_system_for_continuous_innovation_The_case_of_Google_Inc. Accessed on 22 October 2020.

Bibliography

Al Salmi, Muatasim Anwar Ahmed, and Norlena Bt Hasnan. (2015). "SWOT and TOWS matrix e-government analysis review on Sultanate of Oman." *International Journal of Learning and Development* 4.

Cinca, Carlos Serrano, Cecilio Mar Molinero, and Alexandre Bossi Queiroz. (2003). "The measurement of intangible assets in public sector using scaling techniques." *Journal of Intellectual Capital* 4(2): 249–275.

Cummings, Stephen, and Duncan Angwin. (2015). *Strategy Builder: How to create and communicate more effective strategies*. New York: John Wiley & Sons.

Dess, Gregory, Alan Eisner, G.T. Lumpkin, and Gerry McNamara. (2011). *Strategic management: Creating competitive advantages*. New York: McGraw-Hill Higher Education.

Eriksson, Päivi, and Anne Kovalainen. (2015). *Qualitative methods in business research: A practical guide to social research*. London: Sage.

Griffiths, John. (2003). "Balanced scorecard use in New Zealand government departments and crown entities." *Australian Journal of Public Administration* 62(4): 70–79.

Hanson, Dallas, Michael A. Hitt, R. Duane Ireland, and Robert E. Hoskisson. (2016). *Strategic management: Competitiveness and globalisation*. London: Cengage.

Heintzman, Ralph, and Brian Marson. (2005). "People, service and trust: Is there a public sector service value chain?" *International Review of Administrative Sciences* 71(4): 549–575.

Helms, Marilyn M., and Judy Nixon. (2010). "Exploring SWOT analysis – where are we now?" *Journal of Strategy and Management* 3: 215–251.

Hoque, Zahirul, and Carol Adams. (2011). "The rise and use of balanced scorecard measures in Australian government departments." *Financial Accountability & Management* 27(3): 308–334.

Johnson, Gerry, Kevan Scholes, and Richard Whittington. (2009). *Exploring corporate strategy: Text & cases*. New York: Pearson.

Kaplan, R.S., and D.P. Norton. (2005). "The balanced scorecard: Measures that drive performance." *Harvard Business Review* 83(7): 172.

Kaplan, R.S., and D.P. Norton. (2006). *Alignment: Using the balanced scorecard to create corporate synergies*. Cambridge, MA: HBS Press.

Karppi, Ilari, Merja Kokkonen, and Kaisa Lähteenmäki-Smith. (2001). *SWOT-analysis as a basis for regional strategies*. Nordregio, Vol. 4. Accessed from: https://archive.nordregio.org/en/Publications/Publications-2001/SWOT-analysis-as-a-basis-for-regional-strategies/index.html. Accessed on 22 October 2020.

Korableva, Olga N., and Olga V. Kalimullina. (2016). "Strategic approach to the optimization of organization based on BSC-SWOT matrix." 2016 IEEE International Conference on Knowledge Engineering and Applications (ICKEA), pp. 212–215, IEEE.

McGee, John, David Wilson, and Howard Thomas. (2010). *Strategy: Analysis and practice*. New York: McGraw-Hill Higher Education.

McKee, Martin, Anne-Marie Rafferty, and Linda Aiken. (1997). "Measuring hospital performance: Are we asking the right questions?" *Journal of the Royal Society of Medicine* 9(4): 187–191.

Olsen, Jan Abel, and Cam Donaldson. (1998). "Helicopters, hearts and hips: Using willingness to pay to set priorities for public sector health care programmes." *Social Science & Medicine* 46(1): 1–12.

Ostrom, Elinor. (2008). "Polycentric systems as one approach for solving collective-action problems." Indiana University, Bloomington: School of Public & Environmental Affairs Research Paper 2008-11: 02.

Rosenberg Hansen, Jesper, and Ewan Ferlie. (2016). "Applying strategic management theories in public sector organizations: Developing a typology." *Public Management Review* 18(1): 1–19.

Scholes, Kevan, Gerry Johnson, and Richard Whittington. (2002). *Exploring corporate strategy*. London: Financial Times Prentice Hall.

Steiber, Annika, and Sverker Alänge. (2013). "A corporate system for continuous innovation: The case of Google Inc." *European Journal of Innovation Management* 16(2). Accessed from: https://www.researchgate.net/publication/263251371_A_corporate_system_for_continuous_innovation_The_case_of_Google_Inc. Accessed on 22 October 2020.

Weihrich, Heinz. (1982). "The TOWS matrix – A tool for situational analysis." *Long Range Planning* 15(2): 54–66.

Zigan, Krystin, Fraser Macfarlane, and Terry Desombre. (2008). "Intangible resources as performance drivers in European hospitals." *International Journal of Productivity and Performance Management* 57(1): 57–71.

6

AGENDA SETTING, DATA COLLECTION AND ANALYSIS TOOLS

What's Your Problem?

Hopefully, if you have read the previous chapters, you will already have a good idea of what issues your organisation is facing. However, this does not necessarily tell you what the major problems are that you need to deal with.

Take, for example, the problem of piracy off the coast of Somalia. In the late 2000s pirate attacks on ships in the Gulf of Aden increased dramatically. Local pirate groups became increasingly organised and well-equipped. Diaspora investors and local underwriting clubs began funding pirate voyages, paying for weapons and boats, and spreading the risk of the venture. Multiple large container ships, fishing boats and oil tankers were targeted, with crews being killed and ships and cargoes held to ransom. Insurance premia went up and shipping companies were obliged to hire mercenaries to protect their boats travelling through this key strategic chokepoint.

The problem here may seem obvious: pirates are attacking ships. The solution may well seem equally obvious: send in military patrols to ensure the security of boats travelling in the region. However, the locals only took to piracy because their fish stocks had been exhausted by huge foreign trawler fleets fishing illegally in Somali waters. From this perspective, the problem takes on an entirely different complexion, and the solution changes likewise. From this point of view, sending in the military to protect foreign boats is actively making the situation worse, since these foreign boats include the illegal trawlers that were the root cause of the problem in the first place. From this perspective, a better solution would be to regulate the waters in such a way as to prevent illegal fishing.[1]

In design thinking, this is referred to as the "iceberg model". This is based on the idea of trying to start from visible factors (events) to deduce trends (patterns) and the influences that drive these trends (underlying structures), as well as the assumptions that create these trends (mental models).[2] However, this is just one way

DOI: 10.4324/9781003307228-6

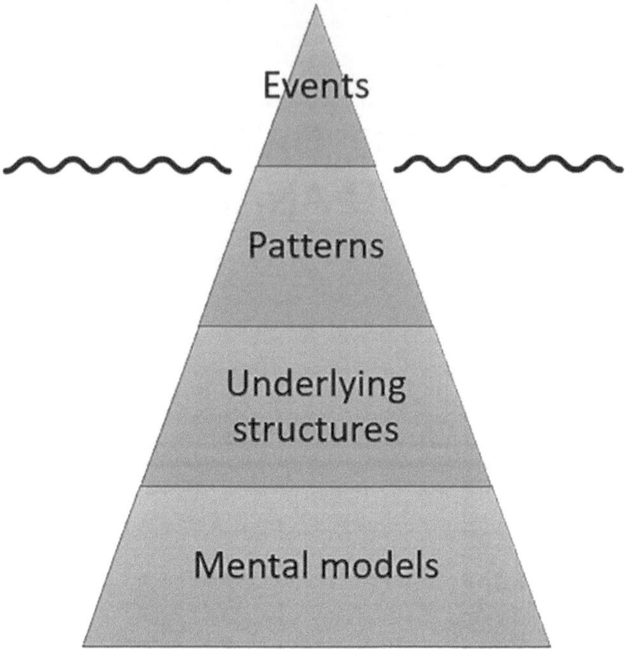

FIGURE 6.1 Iceberg Model (Inspired by Booth and Meadows, 2010)

to separate a problem into multiple levels. As we have described elsewhere, other approaches do this in different ways – the scenarios planning approach focuses on time horizons, for example.

Whatever method is used, however, a clear understanding of the problem is vital if you wish to avoid doing more harm than good, and to do this we need to cycle back to the policy lifecycle concept, in order to understand where exactly a given policy is in its lifecycle. At the same time, it is possible to adopt a systems thinking approach in order to situate the problem within the larger ecosystem of problems. Finally, it is helpful to get into the nitty gritty of problem definition, in order to set out the precise parameters of the problem that needs to be solved.

In the 1980s and 1990s, US legislators took a zero-tolerance approach to drugs, substantially increasing penalties for selling all drugs, including relatively innocuous substances such as marijuana. The result was that more people were incarcerated for selling soft drugs and found it difficult to find alternative employment upon release due to their criminal records. Many of these subsequently took to dealing with other harder drugs, having realised that the risk was now the same and they had no other way to make money.[3] In this case, the illegal drugs' trade was identified as a problem, but not the poverty and joblessness that led people to feel that selling drugs was the best possible career for them.

In this chapter, we will look at ways to process the information that you gathered during the previous chapters, to correctly identify the right problem to solve and potential problems contained within the data, and brainstorm solutions in such a way as to avoid or minimise perverse incentives and unwanted effects. To do this, problem-finding is crucial. For example, while Amazon and Alibaba may look similar, they were in fact created to solve different problems. In the case of Amazon, the problem to be solved was the time and effort involved in buying books from real-world shops, while for Alibaba the key problem was that small businesses found it hard to reach potential customers. Thus, while the two sites do broadly the same thing, they approach it in very different ways. Thus, problem-centric thinking acts as a spur to innovation.

We will begin by looking at ways to describe the policy lifecycle and pin down the problem using mind mapping and issue redefinition. We will then go on to look at ways for analysing how your policy will affect and be affected by the actions of others, using stakeholder analysis and design thinking. Once this has been done, it's time to make plans, using a scenario-planning approach.

1. Where Are We Now? The Policy Lifecycle

This particular framework was inspired by the Industry Lifecycle Framework, which was designed to help leaders identify whether a particular industry is new, growing, stable or declining, and from this to evaluate the competition that they are likely to face if they join that industry, as well as the likely returns.[4] It involves consciously situating each part of the policy lifecycle in its context.

The utility of this framework may not be readily apparent in a public sector context. Many public services address perennial problems: crime, sickness, poverty, etc. The "crime industry" has always existed and always will exist – in most countries there is no prospect of a terminal decline in crime numbers and a corresponding need to shut down prisons and find other areas in which to spend public money. In other words, it situates a policy in an historical context, seeing how outside factors increase or reduce its relevancy and/or appropriateness over time. Often this can be the most important part of any analysis process and also the hardest to do. It can be extremely difficult for people whose job lies in providing a particular service to acknowledge that this service is either no longer required or no longer adapted to users' needs.[5]

However, throughout the 19th and 20th centuries, technological development has regularly left governments faced with the need to decide whether, or not a new technology is likely to present a field that it will need to regulate or even enter itself: motor transport, aviation, radio, television, space travel, the internet, etc. At the same time, other industries have suffered sudden declines, leading to mass unemployment and requirement for retraining – examples include agriculture, fishing and mining.

As such, this framework can be helpful to public servants in identifying industries whose growth they are likely to have to deal with in the near future, as well as those whose decline they may need to cushion to prevent widespread social consequences.

The standard model identifies five stages in any industry's lifecycle:

- **Development**. This is the disruption stage, with low rivalry and high product differentiation. Innovation is the key to success.
- **Growth**. At this stage, rivalry is still relatively low, but low barriers to entry attract new participants. The ability to scale quickly is the key to success.
- **Shake-out**. As a result of the crowding-in during the previous stage, rivalry is beginning to increase. Growth slows down, and some companies leave the market. Consolidation is the key to success.
- **Maturity**. In this stage barriers to entry increase as the market comes to be dominated by a small number of firms that managed to consolidate their positions in the previous stage. Buyer power increases, and market share becomes the key to success.
- **Decline**. In this stage rivalry intensifies, and companies begin to leave the industry. Price competition is the key to success.

While government decisions about which industries to join or support should not be based purely on profit motives, it is necessary for them to be aware of the ways in which these motives will drive behaviour of other stakeholders in the system, which in turn will determine their own conduct. Thus, for example, different governments have taken differing approaches to the idea of the internet as a public service. While it began as a minority interest supplied mainly through commercial channels, it soon became so essential to everyday life that ensuring fast and consistent internet access came to be seen as a state responsibility in most countries. As the market matured, governments were increasingly obliged to step in to prevent abuse of market power by large corporations at the expense of the poorest in society.

This approach can be particularly useful in deciding when a public service needs to be shut down. Given the tendency of public entities to arrive at a state in which they exist principally to perpetuate their own existence, it can be useful to supervisory authorities to carry out regular checks on whether their various sub-departments are still providing a relevant public service, whether their activities could more efficiently be handled by the private sector, or whether they should cease altogether. This is particularly true when facing pressure from above to cut expenses.

The French Minitel system was an early version of the internet run by the national telephone service and accessed via dedicated household terminals and highly popular during the 1980s. As the world wide web grew and came to dominate the market for such services during the 1990s and 2000s, Minitel became less competitive, being a largely francophone network not accessible from ordinary PCs or mobile phones. Moreover, the need to dedicate resources to Minitel diminished France Telecom's research budget for other internet technologies. However, the service did retain a certain popularity among the older generation, with over ten million connections in 2009 (the last year it was in operation), something that its managers used to justify its continued existence as a public service. While it had begun as a revolutionary technology, the service provision model lacked the flexibility of the internet, and by the 2000s it became clear that it was obsolete. As a result, the service was shut down, but only long after many citizens had forgotten that it existed.[6] It is important to be pragmatic when judging whether a policy is obsolete – particularly given that large numbers of colleagues are likely to have an interest in keeping it going. It is necessary to periodically question assumptions and adopt an innovative approach to policy.

2. Redefining the Problem: Issue Redefinition

As we described earlier, it is often the case when problems are poorly answered that they were badly defined in the initial stage of tackling them. Often, when problems are badly defined, it is because those defining the problem started from their own in-group preconceptions or pre-conceived solutions (without a clear problem in mind), and did not take time to question these. This means that their proposed solution ends up as the practical equivalent of a strawman argument – they are trying to solve a problem that exists only in their own heads, and thus are unlikely to come up with solutions that produce net benefits to the everyday lives of those they are intended to serve.

To minimise the risks of this happening, it is helpful to define problems as part of a group, and this group should ideally be as heterogenous as possible. It is useful to have participants representing all relevant stakeholders and a variety of different opinions in the committee tasked with the project. It is also worthwhile to take steps to make sure that any discussion that certain participants do not dominate the debate and drown out others. As we have seen in recent years with – for example – the election of Donald Trump in the United States and the Brexit vote in the United Kingdom, the temptation for those in power to live in a self-reinforcing media bubble can be compelling but is not sustainable in the long term. While a dominant group can shout over others in most fora, the one place they cannot do so is in the voting booth. This stage is the key to reconciling the policy formulation stage of the cycle with the demands and constraints brought up during the agenda-setting stage.

A more structured way to approach this stage of problem redefinition is via an issue redefinition exercise. This technique involves experimenting with different ways of redefining a problem as a structured divergence process, avoiding confusion, and wasted time while also forcing all participants to consider perspectives other than their own. The process takes place in several stages:

1. **Rephrase**. Try rephrasing the issue without losing or expanding the remit. If the issue you need to deal with is Somali piracy, for example, instead of asking "How can we crack down on piracy in the Gulf of Aden?" you can try asking "How can we disincentivise piracy in the Gulf of Aden?" The first question implies piracy is the problem that needs to be stopped. The second question implies piracy is a situation that can be alleviated. The direction of causality is

different. It will not always be the case that one phrasing is right and the others wrong. Possibly every option will have some merit or (if you are particularly unlucky), none will. The goal is not to come up with a final draft, but merely to consider different perspectives on the matter.

2. **Ask why**. If you know how the problem emerged, you will have a better chance of solving it. Try the Five Whys method:

   1st Q: "Why do Somali fishermen turn to piracy?"
   A: Somali fisherman are not able to have a proper economic livelihood.
   2nd Q: "Why are Somali fisherman unable to have a proper economic livelihood?"
   A: The Somali capitalists deprive them of proper profits from fishing.
   3rd Q: "Why did Somali fisherman deprive them of proper profits from fishing?"
   A: Somali capitalists are able to unfairly set the rules for the economy.
   4th Q: "Why are Somali capitalists able to unfairly set the rules for the economy?"
   A: Somali capitalists are in close contact with the Somali government.
   5th Q: "Why is the Somali government in close contact with Somali capitalists?"
   A: Somali government needs money to run their bureaucracy and Somali capitalists funds that.
   Rephrased Question: How can we help Somali fisherman adopt an honest and sustainable living?

3. **Broaden the focus**. Instead of just looking at the problem itself, there are at least two ways to broaden the focus: macro and micro. For macro-broaden, consider the other factors that surround it. Somali fishermen began to turn to piracy because their fish stocks were being depleted by foreign trawlers. These foreign trawlers were able to operate because the official Somali government was for many years non-functional and unable to enforce its control over its territorial waters, and the government of the stable breakaway state of Somaliland in the North is unrecognised by most other states. The Somali government has long been destabilised by the foreign-funded Islamist group Al Shabaab, which offers an alternative source of protection and income to ordinary citizens. If Somalis cannot make money from fishing or piracy, they may turn to Al Shabaab. For micro-broaden, focus on asking one level up for each key word. For example, for "How can we stop Somali piracy?", there are several key words: (1) how, (2) Somali, (3) stop and (4) piracy. Try asking: "How can we stop global/Gulf of Aden (Somali) piracy?" "How can we stop Somali organised crime (from piracy)?"
4. **Narrow the focus**. Take apart the original problem into its component parts, instead of asking "How can we stop Somali piracy?" There are several key words: (1) how, (2) Somali and (3) piracy. Try asking one level down for each word. For example, "How can we stop Somali pirates (from piracy)?" or

"How (from piracy to pirate to supplies) can we stop Somali pirates' supplies of weapons (from piracy)?" Somali refers to race; how about sub-components of Somali: national government, municipal government, corporate and civil society. Try "How can we stop Somali government's support for piracy".

5. **Redirect the focus**. In this stage, we look for alternative causal factors and potential solutions. Ask yourself, what else? What is the "none of the above" option? Why is the Somali government unable to protect its territorial waters? Why does the international community refuse to recognise the Somalis and government? What alternatives are there to fishing and piracy for jobless Somalis?
6. **Turn 180 degrees**. Whatever question you asked initially, identify the key words and try reversing each word, one at a time and in different combinations. Remember, it is divergence for diversity of ideas. Do not self-censor your creativity process at this stage. If you asked "How can we stop Somali piracy?" There are at least two ways: micro and macro. For micro-180, there are several key words identified, reverse them: (1) how (why, so what), (2) Somali (global), (3) stop (continue) and (4) piracy (security). Try asking: "Why (from how) is Somali (or global) piracy still continuing?" "How is global security supporting piracy?" For macro-180, you ask the reverse of the sentence: from "How can we fight Somali pirates?" now ask "What will Somali pirates fight our attacks on them?"[7] Note there are gross overlaps between 180 and redirect, do not be alarmed.

Once again, it needs to be borne in mind that the goal is not necessarily to come to a final conclusion, but merely to look at the issue from different viewpoints in a structured manner. Since this is necessarily a collaborative process, it is good to write down every suggestion as it is made. This can be done via a Wiki or a Google doc, or just on a whiteboard. One interesting approach to the exercise involves having people contribute and organise their suggestions via a shared Google Slide without any audio communication between them. While the approach may appear chaotic to start with, a spontaneous order soon emerges from the chaos, and it becomes easy to see where participants agree and disagree, thus creating a shared map of everyone's ideas and perspectives.[8]

If done correctly, this method should help you avoid some of the key pitfalls of issue definition: solution-driven thinking ("How can we convince people that war in Iraq is a good idea?"), assumption-driven ("How can we protect the US by toppling the Iraqi government?"), too broad/ambiguous ("What's going on in Iraq?") or too narrow/wrongly directed ("Where are Iraq's WMDs?"). It can also be used to provide physical evidence of your reasoning processes, which allows you to seek feedback on the logic and assumptions of others. It can be combined with the mind mapping and concept mapping approaches described earlier, being useful for interrogating the a priori upon which the former are based. Is A a product of B or is B a product of A? Or is there no causation at all, and merely a correlation (or even no correlation at all)?

3. User Data Collection With Empathy: Design Thinking

Before a problem can be solved, it must be understood in depth. This is a general principle, but it is also a crucial component of the design thinking approach, which we will be covering later in this chapter. Obviously, whole textbooks have been written on this topic, and in one short subsection it is impossible to give a full overview. Nevertheless, we will run through the principal approaches here as a reminder.

Before begin collecting data, there are a few steps to complete. These may seem like mere formalities, but data protection laws are growing ever stricter across the globe, meaning that ignoring issues such as participant consent can have significant consequences. It is thus vital to get permission and consent from all parties involved. Depending on the kind of research you want conduct, you might have to obtain written permission and fill out informed consent forms from all subjects as well as written permission from any organisations and stakeholders involved. It is also important to inform stakeholders of any changes in the study, and possibly to ask them to renew their consent – check the legislation that applies in order to make sure that you are always in full conformity.

Once you have done your preliminary due diligence, then you can begin the research. There are various approaches that are used regularly – surveys, focus groups, interviews and observational research are the main techniques. However, they are often not used in isolation. You may do interviews and focus groups to get an idea of the problem, surveys to evaluate possible solutions and observational research to see how people interact with the solution you propose.

Surveys are among the easiest and most cost-effective ways to collect data. It is possible to conduct them yourself using online platforms, by phone or by email, or you can hire a market research company. Surveys have various advantages: they are anonymous, it is possible to gather qualitative and quantitative data, they provide statistically robust results, and you can cover a large variety of topics. Moreover, modern statistics programmes let you quickly analyse the results. However, they are also subject to self-reporting bias and often lack depth and context. If you cannot afford a survey of your own, it may be possible to get access to previous survey results on similar topics to get a general idea of the state of people's thinking on a given issue.

Individual interviews, on the other hand, are a purely qualitative form of research and tend to be used when market researchers have found the ideal person(s) to provide individual feedback on a specific issue. Often this person is chosen as being representative of a particular demographic or user persona. Often the interviews are structured or semi-structured, using a standard question list for all interviewees, with potentially the option to let them digress and provide additional clarifications if it seems that they may add to the overall dataset. More rarely, entirely unstructured interviews are conducted, when a comprehensive vision of an individual persona is required. Interviews have the advantage of allowing in-depth question exploration, providing rich details and thick description. Moreover, face-to-face contact with respondents is often more productive than surveys, providing deeper and richer insights. Moreover, if there is any confusion regarding the questions or their implications, the interviewer is physically present to clarify. However, they also have significant downsides: they are more time-consuming and more expensive than surveys, and are best conducted by professionally trained interviewers. Moreover, analysis is slow, complicated and generally does not produce generalisable statistical results.

Focus groups are also used for producing qualitative research, but instead of interviewing one person, they involve collecting information from a group of participants. Normally, focus group participants are selected to be representatives of a given target population or profile. During a focus group, interviewers ask a series of questions to generate discussion between participants concerning their subjective experiences and attitudes; ideally, they will include lots of direct interaction and open group participation from everyone.

Focus groups tend to provide a more comprehensive representation of opinions than individual interviews, while also allowing for more detailed questions and greater follow-up than surveys. However, they can also be unpredictable: certain participants may do all the talking, while others do not participate, and thus results may be skewed by peer pressure or if participants do not feel comfortable sharing their real opinions. Similarly, it is important to note that it can be more expensive to conduct a focus group than it is to distribute a survey. Nevertheless, they are useful if you are pretesting ideas, trying to identify their strengths and weaknesses and finding useful recommendations.

Observation research refers to studies in which market researchers observe participants in a natural setting, usually interacting with a specific service. This helps researchers gather clear data on service users' behaviour and the way that they undertake specific processes. They are also less subject to self-reporting bias than other approaches. Often observation requires researchers to go to an off-site location to observe someone in a natural setting, however, and experiment can also be set up to run in a controlled setting where researchers control the variables. However, as with interviews and focus groups, observation is time-consuming and expensive, and it usually takes a long time to code and analyse observational data, and extract the key insights. Moreover, the analysis and experiment design processes require inputs from professionally trained researchers. Also, if participants are aware that they are being watched, their behaviour may change.

Once you have collected the data, it can then be used to get a more accurate vision of your users' requirements and how they interact with your services. It can be analysed according to themes that emerge from the content or via clustering and linkages. It can also be analysed according to the stakeholders involved, per the section on stakeholder integration described earlier. Data can also be analysed over time, comparing previous results with current ones and attempting to identify trends. Once this has been done, other approaches can be tried, such as cost–benefit analysis.[9]

Data analysis will yield a variety of different insights into the state of the situation, and not necessarily just the ones that you were originally searching for.

However, carrying out data analysis is an art, and there is no standards approach. The goal is to identify and solve the major issue that is the key to the problem. For example, when considering the problem of food wastage and public health, the two necessarily involve a trade-off. In order to err on the side of safety, we place a best-before date on products; however, doing this implies that we will be obliged to throw away a certain amount of food before it is necessarily dangerous, thus wasting it. Once this has been recognised, we can look into ways of maximising both.

Remember the crux of user data collection is not the method per se but the approach and thinking behind the method. A survey is a survey. A survey of questions impersonally written and with an agenda to "verify" pre-conceived thoughts about an issue will not be able to suss out critical and real perspectives from users. Hence, this is the empathy with users as seen in the design of questions, regardless of survey, interviews or focus group discussions, that matters. This is where design thinking is useful as a way/system of thinking about data collection.

It is important to realise that everyone involved in the agenda-setting stage of the policy cycle is a stakeholder whose opinions are important to the future of the organisation. In recent years, design thinking has become immensely fashionable in both business and public administrations as a way of trying to put key stakeholders at the centre of their processes. Design thinking is based on the idea of empathy. It posits that the best way to provide a good product or service for your end users is to empathise with their position. This is based on a careful observation and understanding of the ways in which users interact with your service. Are they using it as intended? Have they come up with ideas for it that never occurred to you? Often the originators of an idea are bad at working through its implications, so it is important to seek other perspectives. Incredible as it may seem, bubble wrap was originally developed to be used as wallpaper, while Listerine was intended as a cure for gonorrhoea.[10]

This can be particularly difficult in the public sector, since in theory everyone in your country is a stakeholder in your organisation in some capacity or another. Moreover, the lack of a direct financial feedback system and the ability to compel behavioural changes by law can make it hard for public sector actors to realise that citizens are not interacting with your systems as was originally intended. In colonial India, for example, a famous (and possibly apocryphal) story told of a campaign by the Raj to wipe out pests, offering a reward to anyone who brought in a dead cobra to the state's offices. Unsurprisingly, this did not reduce the total number of cobras in the country but increased it as farmers started deliberately breeding cobras for the reward. This cautionary tale of perverse incentives came to be so well known that the phenomenon became known as the "cobra effect" as a result.[11] The idea behind empathising with other stakeholders is to avoid these outcomes practitioners are asked to continually put themselves in the shoes of those on the receiving end of their policies and imagine how they would react if their roles would be reversed. Bureaucrats often have difficulty doing this, adopting instead a condescending and paternal approach to service users.

The design thinking process involves five stages:

1. **Empathise**. Talk to the people experiencing the problem that you are trying to solve. If possible, experience it yourself. If you are looking to improve public transport services, it will be hard to do if you personally drive to the office every day. If empathy is the first stage of the process and defines everything that is to come, it is with the aim of creating a human-centred design process, in order to make sure that your output is designed around its users rather than produced grudgingly to suit your own convenience (a common problem in bureaucracies). As well as talking to users and trying to experience the problem yourself, you can also conduct surveys and focus groups, and study social media discussions. While this is the first formal stage, it is also the core of the process and should continue through and underlie all of the other stages.
2. **Define the problem**. In this stage, you will need to bring together all the observations you made in the previous stage, analyse and synthesise them to come up with a concise and accurate depiction of the problem being experienced by the population you are hoping to target. You can use the mind mapping and concept mapping approaches to do this, as well as the issue redefinition approaches described earlier. Once again, this should be based on what the user needs rather than your own priorities. So rather than saying "we need to get more people using public transport", it would be better phrased as "people need a reliable and affordable way to get to the places to which they regularly travel". This lets you identify the key features that your offering must possess: in this case, public transport needs to be reliable and affordable and serve popular routes.
3. **Ideate**. This is the point at which you start to begin generating ideas. Having laid out the terms of your problem and the goal to be attained, you are free to think outside the box. It is important to continue to engage stakeholders – for example, by showing them your projects and asking for feedback.
4. **Prototype**. Produce a number of inexpensive, scaled-down versions of the final product. In the context of an attempt to improve public transport services, this may involve increasing the frequency of buses on particular lines, while offering subsidised taxi fares for the elderly in others, for example. This can be difficult to do in a government context – in France, for example, constitutional rules concerning equality and the unity of the state long prevented local governments from rolling out experimental policies in one area that would not be available in another. It may be necessary – as it was in France – to modify regulations, in order to make this possible. This experimental approach can also be difficult to do in a public sector context as bureaucrats are often tempted to minimise, or conceal failed initiatives, rather than recognising their failure and iterating. To prevent this, it is important to foster a "fail fast" culture, difficult though this may be. Once again, engaging stakeholders remains important – feedback on prototypes can prevent useless testing.

5. **Test**. The use and effects of the prototypes must then be tested and evaluated with the same rigour, as the original solution in part one. Once again, it is necessary to approach the task through an empathetic lens. How are users responding to the new solutions? Do they see them as an improvement or not? What suggestions do they have to make? Based on this information, the project begins again.

More so even than in the case of the previous methods, it is important to emphasise the iterative nature of the process. It is central to the design thinking philosophy that the process is never finished: every good or service can always be improved, and to remain a human-centred organisation it is vital to remain in constant contact with your end users in order to be up to date with their perspectives, and continue to empathise effectively with their perspectives. Design thinking is often employed in public sector innovation labs, "islands of innovation" aimed at experimenting with novel solutions to public problems.

Over 60 of these exist in Europe alone, and they can be broken down into several types:

1. **Design-led labs**. Emphasise the application of design thinking to policy and prioritise "user-centred" methods such as ethnography, visualisation techniques and collaboration with citizens and other stakeholders to clarify problem definitions and co-create solutions (see Bailey and Lloyd, 2016; Mintrom and Luetjens, 2016).
2. **Open government/data labs**. Employ innovative approaches in data analytics such as applying new digital and web-based tools to open up and interrogate public data. While they may share an emphasis with design-led labs on participatory methods, "open government" labs can be distinguished by their focus on increasing the accessibility of government data and drawing on expertise from diverse participants to run and apply data analytics, for example, through the organisation of hackathons.
3. **Evidence-based labs**. Are those that focus on the application of rigorous evaluation techniques, principally randomised controlled trials (RCTs) and an adherence to the idea of evidence-based policy.
4. **Mixed Methods**. The label mixed methods were used for labs that showed no preference for one particular set of approaches.[12]

While the design-led labs obviously have the greatest focus on design thinking, all types tend to use the approach to some degree.

However, in a public sector organisation there are often multiple key stakeholders that are not users of the goods or services produced, and yet can have a determining effect upon the way that the organisation provides these goods and services. To deal with these stakeholders, it is necessary to take a different approach: stakeholder diagnostics.

Hopefully, you already conducted the stakeholder analysis processes mentioned in the last two chapters, because it will come in extremely helpful here. In

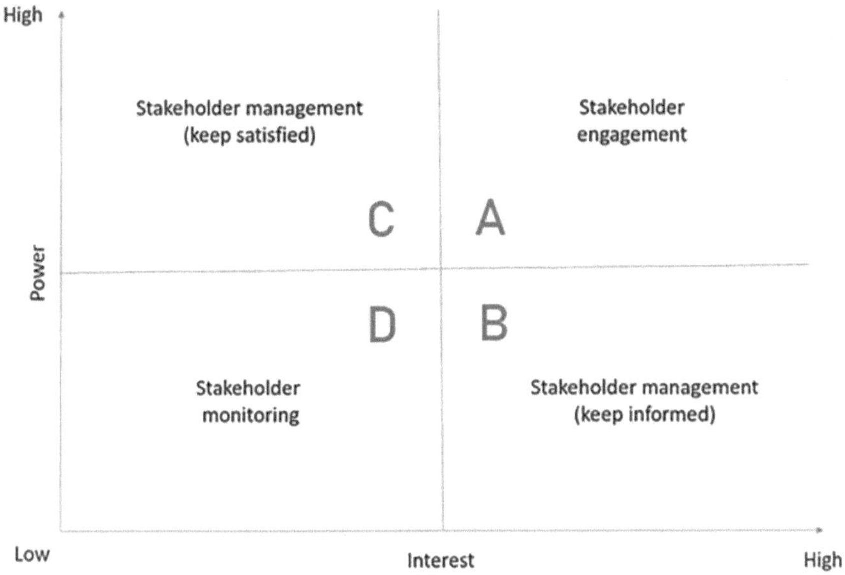

FIGURE 6.2 Power–Interest Matrix for Stakeholders (Adapted from Cummings and Angwin, 2015)

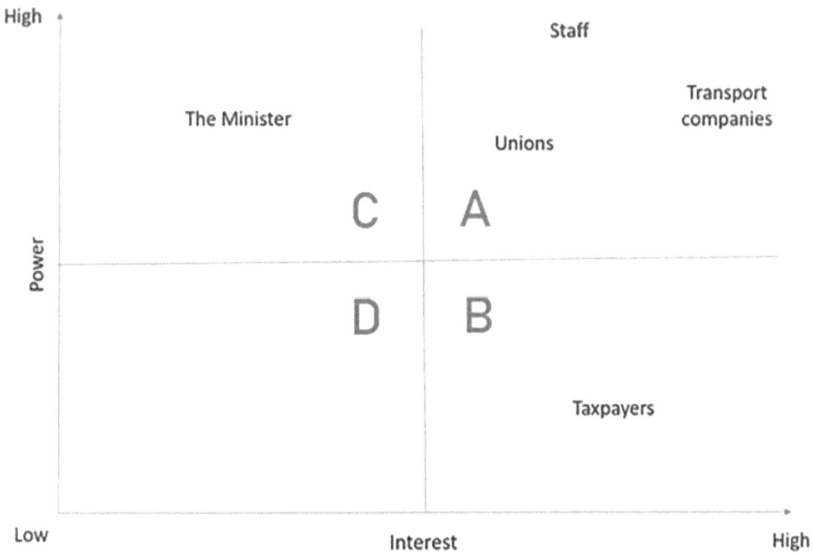

FIGURE 6.3 Power–Interest Matrix for Stakeholders (Adapted from Cummings and Angwin, 2015)

particular, the power–interest matrix framework used in the previous chapter will come in handy.[13] This time around, however, you will need to label each quadrant of the grid with a letter.

We will reuse the example of the Australian transport ministry that we looked at in the previous chapter, so feel free to go back and look over the details there.

In this round, we will not only situate stakeholders based on their capacity to influence our organisation's actions and processes but also evaluate their positions, with regard to a particular decision: the choice to outsource the construction of new trains to China. To do this, it is necessary to put together a stakeholder diagnostic table. This involves identifying not only power and interest levels but also the stakeholders' current levels of support for the proposed decision. As always, do not forget to explain your reasoning for future reference in the final column. First of all, it is necessary to identify stakeholders' levels of support.

Stakeholder	*Impact of project on stakeholder*	*Power category*	*Strongly anti*	*Anti*	*Neutral*	*Pro*	*Strongly pro*	*Reasons*
Minister	M	C		X				Is worried that he will lose votes for moving jobs abroad
Staff	L	A				X		Spending less on new trains will free up budget for other items (including their pay)
Transport companies	H	A	X					Will lose business to Chinese companies
Unions	M	A	X					Concerned about jobs moving abroad
Taxpayers	M	B					X	Savings can be passed on in the form of lower taxes

From this matrix, we can tell how the various stakeholders are likely to interact with one another in order to influence the outcome of the decision. For example, the Minister has the power to make the final decision and is broadly opposed to outsourcing the train contract, but he also has many other claims on his time and may be open to persuasion by actors with more time and energy to commit to the issue. If the unions wish to ensure that he decides not to outsource the contract, they will need to convince him that he and his party will lose significant numbers of votes as a result of this decision. To do this, they may decide to publicise the risk of job losses via media campaigns and protests. On the other hand, if the Ministry staff wish to save money, they will need to persuade the minister that the impact of the decision on his political career will not be significant. To do this they can offer strategies for getting the contract outsourced while attracting as little controversy as possible. In doing this, they could suggest strategies to minimise the effects – proposing that the news concerning the signing of the contract be released on the day of the football cup final, for example. Alternatively, they could strike up an alliance with other stakeholders, coming together with taxpayer groups to mount a counter-campaign against the unions and in favour of the cheapest contract. To help in this process you can construct a leverage matrix, showing how much influence every stakeholder can exercise over the others.

	Who they influence				
	Minister	*Unions*	*Taxpayers*	*Transport companies*	*Staff*
Minister	0	L	M	M	H
Unions	M	0	L	H	M
Taxpayers	H	L	0	L	M
Transport companies	M	H	L	0	M
Staff	M	L	L	M	0

The intent of the exercise is not simply to observe the environment, however. The goal is to identify the stakeholders that need to be engaged, and to work out how best to engage them. Once again, empathy is the key to this, since it is impossible to engage stakeholders effectively without empathising with them. An ideal outcome will satisfy all stakeholders – a so-called win-win outcome. However, if this is not possible, it is logical to either aim to satisfy those stakeholders who have the greatest influence first or aim to reduce their influence.

As with previous exercises, it is very important to remember that this is not a one-time exercise. With every different decision that is made or comes up to be made, these matrices will change, so it is important to keep them up to date if you want to maintain an accurate perspective on your environment.[14]

4. Data Collation and Analysis: Mind Maps and Concept Maps

Once the data are collected, there might be tonnes of data that seems overwhelming to the human mind. One needs to organise the data. The simple way is by timeline (across time), matrix (in excel spreadsheet) and chunking/clustering by themes.

One way to effectively do data collation and analysis in order to tease out interrelationships is via a technique that most people should already be familiar with: mind mapping.[15] While this technique is often done alone, it is also effective group exercise, letting everyone involved get a clear idea of others' perspectives. The idea behind mind mapping is to get as much (potentially) relevant information as possible down on paper, before gradually narrowing it down to the most important points. Indeed, at base it is merely a formalisation of the process that most people go through when trying to solve a problem, letting their minds' wander over a variety of related information and potential solutions before beginning to zero-in on a choice.[16]

When done as a group, however, the process has an added benefit of integrating multiple points of view. Often this is a more chaotic process than individual mind mapping, so it may be helpful to appoint a facilitator to help structure the discussion. Or possibly not. As we will see later, group discussion can often produce a spontaneous order of its own.

While mind mapping is often a free association process, there are specific steps that can be followed to make it more systematic:

1. List all the concepts you can think of that relate in some way to the focal question. If that is "How can we stop piracy in Somali waters?" these might include "maritime law", "naval operations" or "protecting strategic chokepoints".
2. Group them together into related concepts. Try to use your space as efficiently as possible. If you are doing the exercise on paper, it can be helpful to cut up the paper upon which you wrote the initial concepts and physically rearrange them, just like pieces of a jigsaw.
3. Start to make links between the concepts that you feel are related. So, in the previous case, "naval operations" would probably be related to "protecting

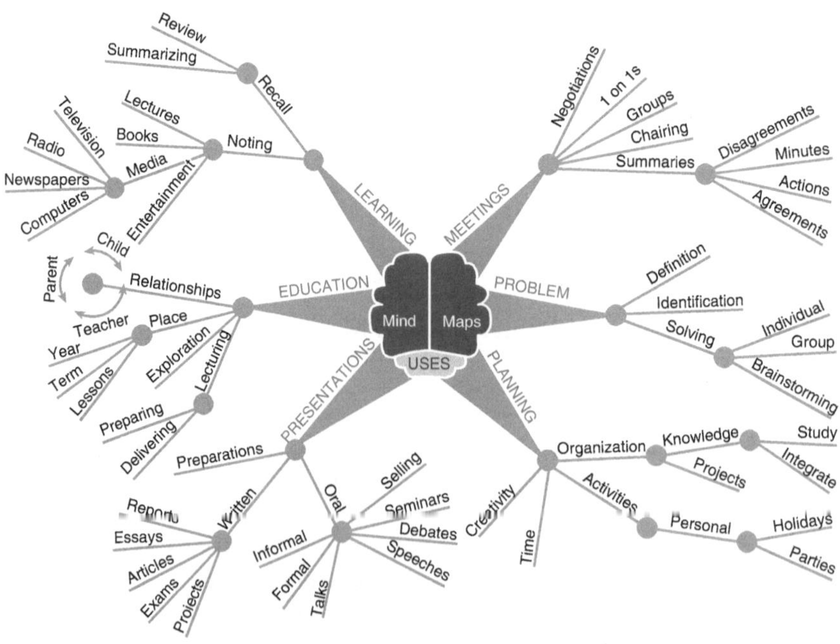

FIGURE 6.4 Mindmap (Inspired by Moon et al., 2011)

strategic chokepoints". Add arrows to show the direction of the relationship. Arrows may go in one or both directions.

4. Next add descriptions of the relationships involved. These can be things such as "causes", "influences" or "necessary for". So, for example, "naval operations work towards protecting strategic chokepoints".
5. Next look for relationships between the concepts, concept clusters and the central question posed at the beginning. As you do this, you may well realise that the question you thought was the key to solving the problem is not as relevant as you thought. You may realise that you need to find another question to account for all of the answers that you have. (Though it is possible to take this too far as well – beware of mission creep.)

Once the mind mapping stage has been completed, a more structured version of the mind map can be produced by transforming the ideas that came out into a concept map. While a mind map focuses on one central idea, concept mapping can have multiple hubs and clusters: you can organise it, however, seems to facilitate the clarification of the problem you aim to solve. It can be shown as a network, a hierarchy, a process or in any other formal that seems appropriate to the participants.

Concept maps were originally developed as teaching aids, and it can be a good thought exercise to continue to treat them as such, even if you do not intend to use yours in a formal teaching setting. It is a good test of your own understanding of an idea that you can explain it clearly and comprehensively to someone else. Creating a concept map is an excellent way to help you to arrive at this point – essentially you are laying out the sum total of your knowledge of the topic in as economical and as easily graspable way as possible.[17]

It can also be useful to include "known unknowns" in the diagram, and even to add an "unknown unknowns" box, in order to avoid operating under the unlikely assumption that you have perfect knowledge of your situation. It can also be useful to note down other perspectives and stakeholder positions, if these are likely to affect the final decision, or even to use the diagram to try to identify the kind of feedback loops mentioned earlier.

However, this organisational stage is not always necessary. Often the principal value of this exercise when conducted as a group is to understand other perspectives rather than to come up with a neat final graphic. It provides a forum to bring disagreements to the surface and allow for debate between different points of view that may be bypassed or sidelined if this stage of the process is skipped. It also allows the group to elaborate a set of shared a priori, preventing confusion and discord later on, as well as to work out what the known unknowns and unknown unknowns are that the group will need to research in greater depth before coming to any formal conclusions. These approaches are so commonly used in public sector strategy exercises that they are often deployed almost unconsciously. However, studies have also been carried out to evaluate their effectiveness. One example involves their use in the UK prison system, where it was implemented via the

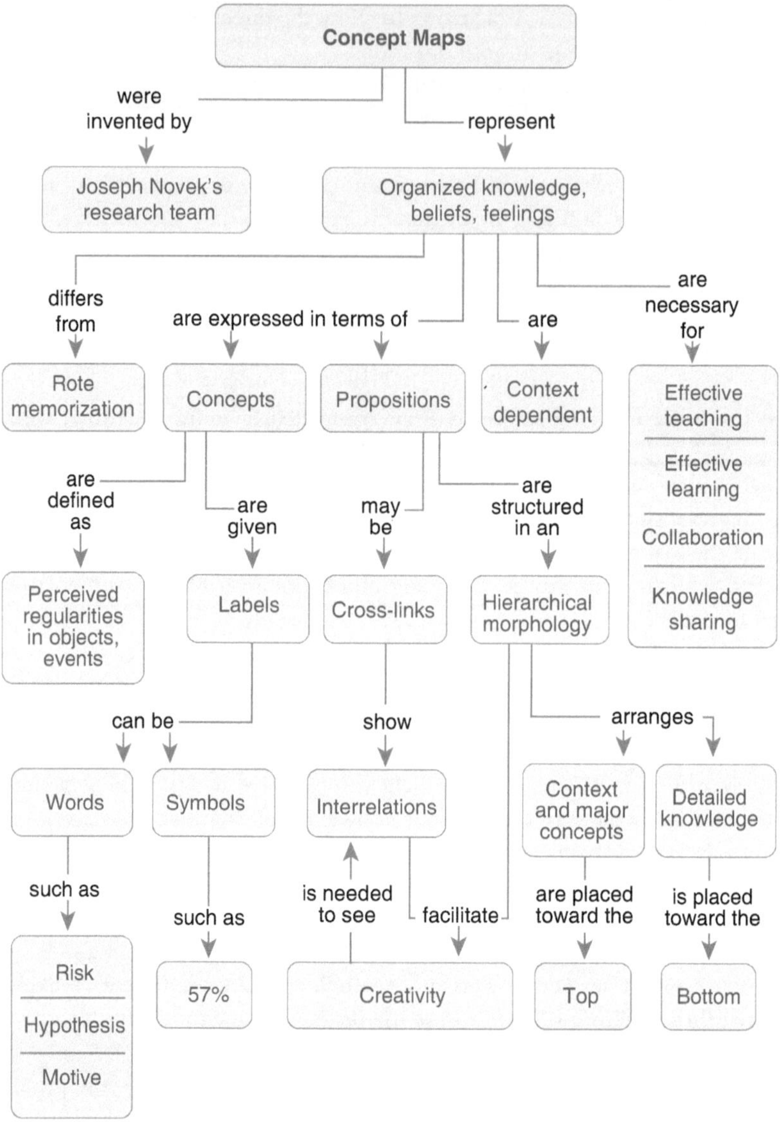

FIGURE 6.5 Concept Map (Inspired by Moon et al., 2011)

Decision Explorer software package. The Director General observed that "The project has been both challenging and stimulating. Each time we reviewed the computer model, its potential capacity to throw up new ideas and its ability to challenge basic assumptions were apparent". Nevertheless, participants observed that the maps tended to quickly grow confusing, particularly when large numbers of participants were involved.[18]

5. Data Analysis by Categories/Entities/Stakeholders: Methodological Note on Systems Thinking

Note that the bubbles (concepts/categories/entities/stakeholders) and arrows (inter-relationships) in the mind maps and concept maps can be taken even further, using a systems thinking approach to identify positive and negative feedback loops (relationships between relationships), which can be reinforced or broken in order to achieve better outcomes. Note that MIT is famous for the engineering version of systems thinking called systems dynamics (Jay Forrester, 1961 and later John Sterman, 2000) and the business version of systems thinking called Learning Organisation: Fifth Discipline where the archetypes are business manifestations of systems dynamics (Peter Senge, 1994).

This said, Open University runs a full master's degree on Systems Thinking which the author was involved, and MIT Systems Dynamics is one of the many systems thinking approaches taught (Reynolds and Holwell, 2020a). While this section will not teach the archetypes, it will present a short note to analyse the types of systems thinking approaches and comment on its utility for what type of problems.

This paper applies systems dynamics (SD) by Jay Forrester (1961) and later John Sterman (2000) from MIT to the situation of interest. Of the five system approaches, Systems dynamics is selected over (VSM), (SODA), (SSM) and (CSH) for the following reasons:

1. If policy need is to map out the macro-forces of interplay between stakeholders and issues underlying the situation of interest (problem) in order to identify inter-relationships particularly reinforcing and balancing feedback loops in the causal loop diagramming (CLD) so as to design systemic interventions (solutions) at strategic leverage point (Morecroft, 2020, pp. 26–31), please use Systems Dynamics (SD).
2. Viable Systems model (VSM) is useful when the government is clear on the vision and strategies for problem, then VSM can map out the complexity drivers in the environment and recommend operations–coordination–delivery/monitoring–development–policy sub-systems to operationalise the strategies (Hoverstadt, 2020, p. 91).
3. Strategic Options Development and Analysis (SODA) is useful as a cognitive mapping tool where there is heavy stakeholder engagement and a need to co-create solutions by capturing wisdom from crowd through facilitation (Ackerman and Eden, 2020, pp. 142–148, 151).
4. Soft Systems Methodology (SSM) is useful as a tool to deepen understanding of stakeholders' perception of the situation in order to co-create solutions because it accentuates different worldviews to find out, build models, discuss and define action (Checkland and Poulter, 2020, pp. 216–218).
5. Critical Systems Heuristics (CSH) is strong in "handling systems boundaries critically" through understanding assumptions, and the picture from

motivation, control, knowledge and legitimacy perspectives, and unfolding multiple perspectives to promote mutual understanding (Ulrich and Reynolds, 2020, pp. 256–258).

6. In conclusion, SD is the preferred systems approach when the situation of interest is at its infancy stage that requires conceptual framing of CLD with policy skill and literature review in order to map out the vision and strategies for the problem. Thereafter, VSM is useful in operationalisation phase. Where there is availability and ability to collect primary data through focus group discussion, then SODA is useful; co-creation sessions with non-government stakeholders and/or internal SINGOV agencies, then SSM and CSH are useful.
7. Data Analysis by Time: Scenarios.

However well you understand your organisation's situation and characteristics, the future remains uncertain. While you may have used design thinking to optimise your output, and applied environment scanning and stakeholder management techniques to anticipate potential problems, the future has a habit of throwing up unexpected new challenges. It is never possible to entirely future-proof your organisation, but you can try to anticipate coming changes before they occur.

One useful way to do this is via scenario planning from current base of knowledge of the situation. This was mentioned in Chapter 3, but we will now go into the methodology in greater detail, describing how it can be used to assess the prospects for any organisational changes that you wish to make.[19]

In this way, you can take the information you learned in previous stage of the process and work out how the data are likely to change based on potential future occurrences. Where mind mapping and concept mapping divide up the world based on practitioner-defined categories, scenario planning does the same thing but using a chronological framework. While various versions of the concept apply it in different ways, we recommend a six-stage process based on that used at Shell Oil:

1. **Identify your basic assumptions and the drivers of change**. Once again, this can be done via brainstorming. For example, if you are planning national police and justice policy, you may decide that crime rates are your key driver of change and assume that since these will never fall to zero, so some sort of criminal justice system will always be necessary. While it is useful to list all possible assumptions and drivers, in moving on to the next round of the process it is necessary to single out those that are *important* and *uncertain*. These will form the basis for your scenario-planning exercises. The process begins with identifying what exactly the scenarios will focus on. Scenarios for the future of the galaxy will not be useful to a department trying to decide whether it should build a new hospital in a particular area. Sometimes the key issue being focused on is specific: Should we invest in high-speed internet? Sometimes it is more open-ended: Are there any potential disruptive events that could

interrupt our current internet connectivity strategy? It may even be geopolitical: What will the technological future of our country look like as compared to our competitors?

2. **Bring the important and uncertain drivers together to form a framework**. For example, if the economy crashes, crime is likely to go up and resources for dealing with it will decline. This part of the process involves bringing together factors that are likely to cluster in real life. While it is possible that a recession will coincide with falling crime rates, this outcome is relatively unlikely and so it may not necessarily be worth planning for this outcome. There will usually be multiple factors entering into play – not merely crime rates and economic growth but also types of crime committed, changes in the law, court capacity and legal aid budgets.
3. **Produce initial mini-scenarios**. Once again, brainstorming comes into play here. Any number of unlikely outcomes can be considered at this stage, as they will be narrowed down at the next stage. It is good to have at least seven mini-scenarios before moving on to the next stage. There are multiple ways to do this: deduction (how are current circumstances likely to evolve?), induction (how are new circumstances likely to affect your environment?), abduction (both of the previous), the normative method (the future you hope for), the incremental method (the default assumptions of the senior management), the alternative futures method (growth, collapse, conservation and transformation), the critical scenarios method (aiming to transform power imbalances that exist currently) and the perspectives-based approach (scenarios based on different worldviews).
4. **Reduce your total number of scenarios to four**. To maximise use of time, your set of scenarios should contain between two and five narratives. More than five scenarios and the results will tend to be confusing and show a strong overlap. Providing three scenarios means that there is a risk that deciders will just try to pick the most moderate or most apparently plausible and forget about the other two. Each scenario that you give should include enough detail to allow deciders to make an informed decision. Ideally, two of the scenarios should be complementary – this prevents those participating in the exercise from merely theorising a "best possible outcome" and a "worst possible outcome". In the criminal justice example, the three scenarios may be "crime outpaces prison capacity and government demands capacity be expanded", "crime outpaces prison capacity and government moves to favour non-penal sanctions" and "crime falls and budgets are cut as a result". Each scenario must pass the participants' respective sniff tests, in order to be validated. Does it make sense according to their knowledge of the organisation and the world? One way to isolate four key scenarios is to fix on just two critical uncertainties to serve as the axes of a 2-by-2 matrix. Four scenario logics are then generated from the labels on the ends of the two axes. Adam Gordon (2020) gave the example of the opening-up of arctic trade routes as a result of climate change.[20]

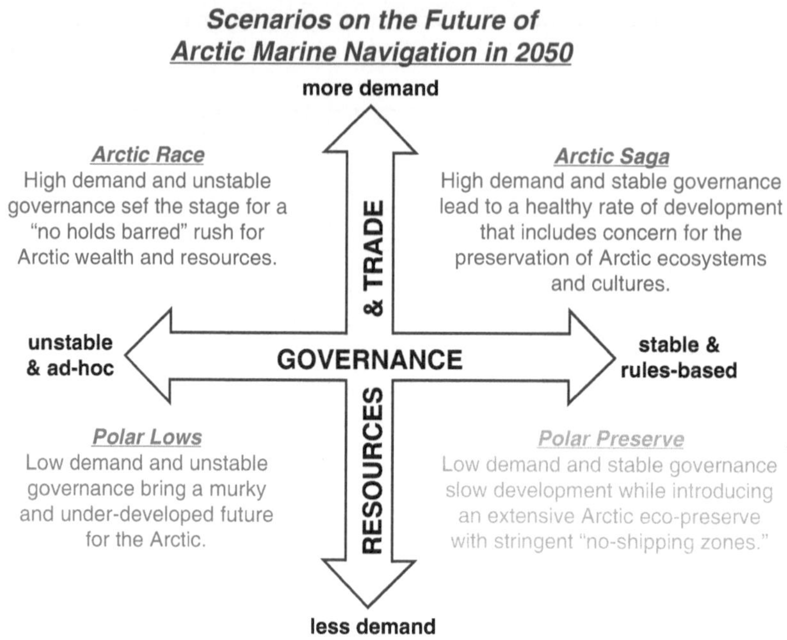

FIGURE 6.6 Scenario Map Sample (Image adapted from A.V. Gordon, 2020)

This can be done in two ways: future forward and future backward. The future-forward approach "projects sets of plausible futures based on analysis of present forces and their likely evolution". In contrast, the future backward method is to "select several significant futures and try to discover the paths that lead to them".[21]

5. **Write the scenarios**. Having a written document to refer to will be immensely helpful in thinking through the implications, particularly if your planning exercises involve a large number of people or the participants are dispersed geographically. The scenarios must be customised to your context. The scenarios that Shell used in anticipating 1986 oil crash were very different from those used by Xerox used to anticipate the convergence of the copier and printer. Each organisation needs to consider its own challenges and environment in writing scenarios. These scenarios can be seen as low-cost insurance policies. While they will not prevent adverse developments in your environment, they will help you to recognise that they are possible outcomes, and hence to begin preparing for them. Scenarios can also help to identify blue ocean opportunities waiting for a first mover to occupy them.
6. **Identify the issues that are likely to arise as a result of each scenario**. How should the organisation change, in order to be robust to these outcomes?

This can be combined with previous methods to work out how your environment and stakeholder relations will likely evolve in the coming months and

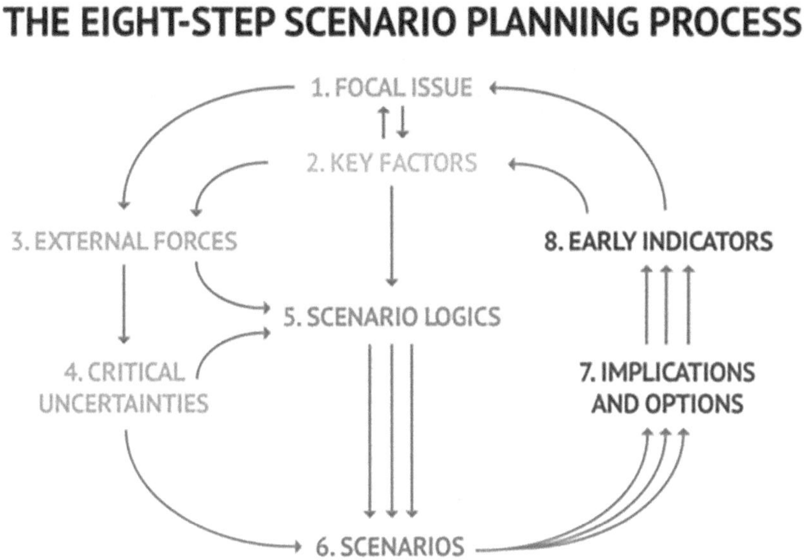

FIGURE 6.7 Scenario-Planning Process (Image from Stratfor.com, 2015)

years, and to help you work out how you will need to modify your organisation and the goods and/or services that you provide, in order to anticipate these changes.

A complete scenario-planning project should take 3 or 4 months, starting with interviews and a kick-off workshop. This is followed by research and writing, which should take around a month. It is helpful to conduct a second workshop to work on the implications of the scenarios produced, the results of which are then summarised and disseminated. Given any given set of scenarios, there are several ways to move from scenarios to strategy. Rather than picking a single scenario and betting the company that this would play out, it is better to find a strategy that will work across the full range of scenarios. It is recommended to then stand back and look at the lists of strategic options that would potentially be appropriate to each scenario. Those that show up on all or most lists are "easy wins". These are the strategic options that work with any and all of the scenarios and can be implemented immediately. If your organisation has enough capacity, this can become a continuous iterative process.

Scenario planning is more often used when considering long-term futures. Though it can be used to look at short-term issues, the time and effort involved in conducting a proper scenario-planning exercise mean that it is often too intensive a process to be used in making day-to-day decisions and can slow down processes that should be conducted quickly. Nevertheless, it provides a useful background against which other short-term decisions can be made and can serve as a useful adjunct to other approaches, such as blue ocean strategy, which will be covered in the next chapter.

Conclusion

In this chapter, we moved on from assessing your organisation's environment and its capacities, to looking at how you can take proactive measures to improve both. We began by looking at ways to identify particular problems faced by your organisation, ways to work out how your choices will affect and be affected by others, and ways to make plans for the future. However, these approaches all involve a relatively passive approach on the part of your organisation, responding to outside factors with the aim of keeping up with changes that are likely to affect you adversely.

In the following chapters, however, we will look at ways in which organisations may recreate themselves and their environments through innovation.

Notes

1 Schbley, Ghassan, and William Rosenau. *Piracy, illegal fishing, and maritime insecurity in Somalia*. Kenya, and Tanzania and Alexandria: CNA, 2013.

2 Sackmann, Sonja A. "Uncovering culture in organizations." *The Journal of Applied Behavioral Science* 27, no. 3 (1991): 295–317.

3 Baum, Dan. *Smoke and mirrors: The war on drugs and the politics of failure*. Boston: Little, Brown, 1996.

4 McGahan, Anita M., Nicholas Argyres, and Joel A.C. Baum. "Context, technology and strategy: Forging new perspectives on the industry life cycle." *Advances in Strategic Management* 21 (2004): 1–24.

5 Ragusa, Jordan Michael. "The lifecycle of public policy: An event history analysis of repeals to landmark legislative enactments, 1951–2006." *American Politics Research* 38, no. 6 (2010): 1015–1051.

6 Mailland, Julien, and Kevin Driscoll. *Minitel: Welcome to the internet*. Cambridge, MA: MIT Press, 2017.

7 Jones, Morgan D. *The thinker's toolkit: Fourteen powerful techniques for problem solving*. London: Currency, 1998.

8 Dennis, A., and M. Williams. "Electronic brainstorming." *Group Creativity: Innovation Through Collaboration* (2003): 160–178.

9 Clemons, Randy S., and Mark K. McBeth. *Public policy praxis: A case approach for understanding policy and analysis*. Oxon: Routledge, 2020.

10 Sweetland Edwards, Haley. "11 successful products originally invented for something else." *Mental Floss*, 8 October 2015. Accessed from: www.mentalfloss.com/article/57861/11-successful-products-originally-invented-something-else. Accessed on 15 November 2020.

11 Warczak Jr, Patrick. "The cobra effect: Kisor, roberts, and the law of unintended consequences." *Akron Law Review* 54, no. 1 (2020). Accessed from: https://papers.ssrn.com/sol3/Delivery.cfm/SSRN_ID3820890_code3917066.pdf?abstractid=3529598&mirid=1. Accessed on 20 November 2020.

12 McGann, Michael, Emma Blomkamp, and Jenny M. Lewis. "The rise of public sector innovation labs: Experiments in design thinking for policy." *Policy Sciences* 51, no. 3 (2018): 249–267.

13 Cummings, Stephen, and Duncan Angwin. *Strategy Builder: How to create and communicate more effective strategies*. New York: John Wiley & Sons, 2015.

14 Silverstein, David, Philip Samuel, and Neil DeCarlo. *The innovator's toolkit: 50+ techniques for predictable and sustainable organic growth*. New York: John Wiley & Sons, 2013.

15 Buzan, Tony. *Mind mapping*. New York: Pearson Education, 2006.

16 Moon, Brian, Robert R. Hoffman, Joseph Novak, and Alberto Canas, eds. *Applied concept mapping: Capturing, analyzing, and organizing knowledge*. Oxon: CRC Press, 2011.

17 Buzan, Tony, *op cit*, 2006.
18 Eden, Colin, and Fran Ackermann. "Cognitive mapping expert views for policy analysis in the public sector." *European Journal of Operational Research* 152, no. 3 (2004): 615–630.
19 Ramirez, Rafael, and Angela Wilkinson. *Strategic reframing: The Oxford scenario planning approach*. Oxford: Oxford University Press, 2016.
20 Gordon, Adam Vigdor. "Matrix purpose in scenario planning: Implications of congruence with scenario project purpose." *Futures* 115 (2020): 102479.
21 Randall, Robert M., and Liam Fahey. *Learning from the Future: Competitive foresight scenarios*. New York: John Wiley & Sons, Inc., 1998.

Bibliography

Ackerman, F., and C. Eden. (2020). "Strategic options development and analysis." In M. Reynolds and S. Holwell (Eds.), *Systems approaches to making change: A practical guide*. Milton Keynes: Springer.

Bailey, J., and P. Lloyd. (2016). "The introduction of design to policymaking: Policy Lab and the UK government." In P. Lloyd and E. Bohemia (Eds.), Future Focused Thinking – DRS International Conference 2016, 27–30 June, Brighton, United Kingdom. Accessed from: https://dl.designresearchsociety.org/drs-conference-papers/drs2016/researchpapers/135/. Accessed on 20 November 2020.

Baum, Dan. (1996). *Smoke and mirrors: The war on drugs and the politics of failure*. Boston, MA: Little & Brown.

Birsel, Ayse. (2017). "To come up with a good idea, start by imagining the worst idea possible." *Harvard Business Review*. Accessed from: https://hbr.org/2017/08/to-come-up-with-a-good-idea-start-by-imagining-the-worst-idea-possible. Accessed on 20 November 2020.

Booth, Sweeney L., and D. Meadows. (2010). *The systems thinking playbook*. London: Chelsea Green Publishing.

Buzan, Tony. (2006). *Mind mapping*. New York: Pearson.

Checkland, P., and J. Poulter. (2020). "Soft systems methodology." In M. Reynolds and S. Holwell (Eds.), *Systems approaches to making change: A practical guide*. Milton Keynes: Springer.

Clemons, Randy S., and Mark K. McBeth. (2020). *Public policy praxis: A case approach for understanding policy and analysis*. Oxon: Routledge.

Cummings, Stephen, and Duncan Angwin. (2015). *Strategy builder: How to create and communicate more effective strategies*. New York: John Wiley & Sons.

Dennis, A., and M. Williams. (2003). *"Electronic brainstorming."* In Paul B. Paulus and Bernard A. Nijstad (Eds.), *Group creativity: Innovation through collaboration*, pp. 160–178. New York: Oxford University Press.

Eden, Colin, and Fran Ackermann. (2004). "Cognitive mapping expert views for policy analysis in the public sector." *European Journal of Operational Research* 152(3): 615–630.

Forrester, J.W. (1961). *Industrial dynamics*. Cambridge, MA: Wright-Allen Press.

Gordon, Adam Vigdor. (2020). "Matrix purpose in scenario planning: Implications of congruence with scenario project purpose." *Futures* 115: 102479.

Hoverstadt, P. (2020). "The viable system model." In M. Reynolds and S. Holwell (Eds.), *Systems approaches to making change: A practical guide*. Milton Keynes: Springer.

Ison, R. (2017). *Systems practice: How to act*. Milton Keynes: Springer.

Jones, Morgan D. (1998). *The thinker's toolkit: Fourteen powerful techniques for problem solving*. London: Currency.

McGann, Michael, Emma Blomkamp, and Jenny M. Lewis. (2018). "The rise of public sector innovation labs: Experiments in design thinking for policy." *Policy Sciences* 51(3): 249–267.

Meadows, D.H. (1972). *The limits of growth: A report for the club of Rome's project on the predicament of mankind*. London: Earthscan.

Meadows, D.H. (1992). *Beyond the limits of growth*. Chelsea Green: Post Mills.

Mintrom, Michael, and Joannah Luetjens. (2016). "Design thinking in policymaking processes: Opportunities and challenges." *Australian Journal of Public Administration* 75. Accessed from: https://www.researchgate.net/publication/305622603_Design_Thinking_in_Policymaking_Processes_Opportunities_and_Challenges_Mintrom_and_Luetjens. Accessed on 20 November 2020.

Moon, Brian, Robert R. Hoffman, Joseph Novak, and Alberto Canas (Eds.). (2011). *Applied concept mapping: Capturing, analyzing, and organizing knowledge*. Oxon: CRC Press.

Morecroft, J. (2020). "Systems dynamics." In M. Reynolds and S. Holwell (Eds.), *Systems approaches to making change: A practical guide*. Milton Keynes: Springer.

Moreno, Diana P., and Maria C. Yang. (2014). "Creativity in transactional design problems: Non-intuitive findings of an expert study using scamper." In *DS 77: Proceedings of the DESIGN 2014 13th International Design Conference*, pp. 569–578.

Ramirez, Rafael, and Angela Wilkinson. (2016). *Strategic reframing: The Oxford scenario planning approach*. Oxford: Oxford University Press.

Randall, Robert M., and Liam Fahey. (1998). *Learning from the future: Competitive foresight scenarios*. New York: John Wiley & Sons.

Reynolds, M., and S. Holwell. (2020a). "Epilogue: Systems approaches and systems practices." In M. Reynolds and S. Holwell (Eds.), *Systems approaches to making change: A practical guide*. Milton Keynes: Springer.

Reynolds, M., and S. Holwell. (2020b). "Introducing systems approaches." In M. Reynolds and S. Holwell (Eds.), *Systems approaches to making change: A practical guide*. Milton Keynes: Springer.

Sackmann, Sonja A. (1991). "Uncovering culture in organizations." *The Journal of Applied Behavioral Science* 27(3): 295–317.

Senge, Peter. (1994). *Fifth discipline field book: Strategies and tools for building a learning organisation*. New York: Currency.

Silverstein, David, Philip Samuel, and Neil DeCarlo. (2013). *The innovator's toolkit: 50+ techniques for predictable and sustainable organic growth*. New York: John Wiley & Sons.

Sterman, J. (2000). *Business dynamics: Systems thinking and modelling for a complex world*. Cambridge, MA: Irwin McGraw Hill.

Ulrich, W., and M. Reynolds. (2020). "Critical systems heuristics: The idea and practice of boundary critique." In M. Reynolds and S. Holwell (Eds.), *Systems approaches to making change: A practical guide*. Milton Keynes: Springer.

Warczak Jr, Patrick. (2020). "The cobra effect: Kisor, Roberts, and the law of unintended consequences." *Akron Law Review* 54(1). Accessed from: https://papers.ssrn.com/sol3/Delivery.cfm/SSRN_ID3820890_code3917066.pdf?abstractid=3529598&mirid=1. Accessed on 20 November 2020.

Wheelen, Thomas L., J. David Hunger, Alan N. Hoffman, and Charles E. Bamford. (2017). *Strategic management and business policy*. Boston, MA: Pearson.

7
IDEA GENERATION

We have already covered the idea of the lifecycle in Chapter 6. However, we previously approached it from the perspective of a public department trying to evaluate which emerging technologies may affect its operation in years to come. The underlying assumption was that public entities will always be responding to innovation, rather than driving it. However, this is not necessarily the case, as NASA – among many others – will tell you. However, innovation is not just limited to military, space and other scientific agencies.

The goal of every public agency should be to provide as much value as possible to stakeholders, and we are all stakeholders. This being so, public workers should have an incentive to make continuous improvements to and expansions of the services that they offer.

In practice, however, many public organisations are sclerotic and unresponsive to environmental change, a frequent result of organisational homeostasis. A larger organisation means more silos, and a mature organisation means more policy layering and path dependency. While a corporate environment offers financial incentives to innovation, in the public sector innovating often carries greater risks than rewards. Thus, organisations limit themselves to providing only the services that their political masters oblige them to offer, and sometimes not even that. Often this is blamed on the fact that these organisations do not experience the same level of competitive pressure as private businesses, but this may not necessarily be the case. Evidence from the business world shows that many large companies experience the same issues, despite the competition to which they are subject to.

Schumpeter's theory of creative destruction is well known.[1] It suggests that innovation generally involves the dismantling of the old order by the representatives of the new one. Thus, for example, the development of online streaming services not only created entertainment behemoths such as Netflix but also led directly

DOI: 10.4324/9781003307228-7

to the bankruptcy of businesses whose services were based on the distribution of physical media such as Blockbuster Video.[2]

This is the central idea behind the concept of disruptive innovation: just as the development of online streaming disrupted the media industry, the invention of the motorcar disrupted the horse buggy industry and the invention of electric lighting disrupted the candle industry. While these developments may seem like bolts from the blue destined to wipe out all businesses that are dependent upon the old technology, this is not always the case. Some companies manage to spot the change coming and adapt. HBO began its existence by supplying infrastructure for cable TV services before moving into providing ad-free pay-per-view movies and sports events. Despite its background in conventional cable services, it took to online streaming like a duck to water, becoming one of the giants of the new industry.

This shows that while large organisations find innovation difficult, it is certainly not impossible. With the right attitude and the right tools, they can not only keep up with changes in their environment but even help to drive them. Nevertheless, it is more difficult in public sector organisations – where there is less competition to spur innovation – than in commercial companies. In public organisations, innovation often carries more risks than rewards, meaning that there is a natural status quo bias. Moreover, large and long-established organisations tend to be particularly subject to the ossification of processes and mindsets. This is not helped by the fact that public organisations often shrink from intrusive evaluations of their performance. Unless compelled by political actors, they naturally tend to be reluctant to engage in any exercise that may reveal them to have performed badly.[3] While issue redefinition (mentioned in earlier chapters) is one way to encourage staff to rethink their assumptions, it is not the only method.

In this chapter, we will look in detail at four mutually reinforcing theories of innovation and change: first, we look at two reasons why otherwise well-managed organisations may find innovation difficult – the concepts of "cultural lock-in" and "the innovator's dilemma". Then, we go on to look at another method for dealing with these problems: the Blue Ocean theory of innovation.

1. Cultural Lock-In

While it may seem easy to conduct periodic strategic analysis exercises to anticipate coming threats and search for new opportunities, it is often even easier to grow reassured by success and fall into a rut, assuming that the strategies that have brought you this far will doubtless carry you onwards without any need to change or re-evaluate them. Sometimes, both phenomena occur simultaneously: a company conducts regular strategic exercises, but the participants are so blinkered by their familiarity with and approbation for the present strategies that they do not genuinely consider alternative approaches.

This tendency was described in detail by Richard Foster and Sarah Kaplan in their best-selling book *Creative Destruction: Why Companies That Are Built to Last Underperform the Market*.[4] The central thesis of the book is that the market will always outperform any given company, simply because many entities always outperform one over the long term. The authors researched the performance of more than 1,000 corporations in 15 countries over 36 years, and none consistently performed better than the market in general. While companies are prone to emotional decision-making and strategic mistakes, the least efficient among them are eliminated by market mechanisms, meaning that market performance remains generally good, despite the errors of the various actors within it. In the public sector, this species-level evolutionary fitness model does not exist. A department that is underperforming is more likely to be given more funds than to be eliminated. The result is that it continues to underperform, but on a larger scale. It can be hard to find alternatives: if your Ministry of Health is not performing well, shutting it down is not an option. Instead, it is necessary to try to find a way to reform it, which is hard to do without seeming to be condoning current incompetence. However, while it is hard to import corporate incentive structures, it is relatively easy to adopt corporate ideas and methods, adapting them to understand and change public sector institutions.

Humans are designed to see patterns, and to learn from rewards and punishments. If adopting a particular approach has brought success in the past, you will be unlikely to take the risk of abandoning it for an untried alternative method. While this is rational to a degree, over time habits based on experience become habits based on hearsay, and finally based purely upon precedent – an organisational culture develops.

Managers, of course, are not idiots, and many of them realise that they must avoid this at all costs if they wish to maintain the relevancy of their organisation, let alone improve. However, as the research described earlier showed, there are very few organisations that have ever achieved this feat, making it extremely difficult to follow existing examples. While a company may manage the feat once or even twice – like HBO switching from cable to pay-per-view to streaming – it is impossible to be lucky every time. This tends to be even harder in the public sector, where adapting to survive simply does not have the same urgency as in the private sector. Consider the Minitel example given previously: everyone involved in the project knew that it was being rendered obsolete by the development of the internet, but too many people had too much interest in seeing it survive, so they came up with excuses to continue pouring money into the network, even as user numbers crashed. Nevertheless, these phenomena are not limited to the public sector, and it can be instructive to consider private sector parallels.

Sterling Drug constitutes one such example. This US company was for many years the principal maker of Aspirin in the United States. While it sold other non-Aspirin painkillers in other markets, in the United States it deliberately refrained from distributing them for fear of cannibalising its own Aspirin market. It stuck doggedly to this strategy, even after Johnson & Johnson released Tylenol on the US market. Signals that change was necessary were omnipresent, but the Sterling Drug leadership did not look for these signs or consider that their strategy may be outdated or require updating. As a result, the company collapsed and was bought out by Kodak Eastman – a company that would itself meet the same fate later as it failed to anticipate the rise of digital cameras.[5]

As Forester and Kaplan put it,

> Cultural lock-in results from the gradual stiffening of the invisible architecture of the corporation and the ossification of its decision-making abilities, control systems, and mental models. It dampens a company's ability to innovate or to shed operations with a less exciting future. Moreover, it signals the corporation's inexorable decline into inferior performance.[6]

These tendencies are reinforced by the natural homophily of all organisations: the founders of a company will tend to share a similar mindset. While this facilitates cooperation in the initial growth stages, it also creates a set of standard procedures that are often based more on personal preferences than rational decision-making. These founders are more likely to recruit people like themselves, and among those recruited, it is the individuals who best fit the company ethos that are most likely to remain. The result is often that camaraderie descends into mere groupthink. Once again, this tends to be an even greater problem in the public sector than in the private sector, where it is harder to isolate poorly performing individuals and teams using financial data, and there is often little inventive to conduct rigorous evaluations. Often, esprit de corps tends to predominate over efficiency.

A big part of the reason that cultural lock-in is so difficult to prevent is because those suffering from it tend to lose their ability to recognise the fact. While there is likely to be a certain level of cultural lock-in in any organisation that has been in existence for a time, there are nevertheless certain signals that it may be growing into a danger for the organisation. A key one of these is the fear of cannibalising one's existing markets, as described earlier. In a public sector context, without financial pressures, this tendency can be even greater than in the private sector. Other common signs of cultural lock-in are increased fears of channel conflict with customers and of earnings dilution. What all of these signs have in common is the fact that they show that the organisation is more worried about losing its existing position rather than concerned about expanding. In the corporate world, this is an untenable position: every company loses customers at a certain rate, and the important thing is not to prevent them from leaving, but to replace them with new ones. If this is not done, collapse is guaranteed. In the public sector, however, a reduction in demand is often hailed as a success: fewer people claiming benefits, going to prison or needing healthcare is seen as something to rejoice over. This makes it difficult to develop reliable indicators of success and failure.

As described earlier, it is difficult or impossible to consistently beat the market, but it is possible to reduce the risks of cultural lock-in. One way to do this is by regarding your organisation as a portfolio rather than identifying with one or two of your key functions. This mindset, long adopted by investors aiming to mitigate risks by diversifying their holdings, can help an organisation abandon the parts of its activity that are no longer in demand, while searching constantly for new opportunities. They do not regard the businesses in which they invest as long-term passion projects, but rather as a short-term strategic position, adopted when advantageous and discarded just as easily. This approach can be taken towards services, but the authors also recommend using it with regard to your organisation's internal procedures. As they say,

> corporate-control systems must be built that can manage both to control operations and to increase the rate of creative destruction. Control what you must, not what you can; control when you must, not when you can. If a control procedure is not essential, eliminate it.

All of the factors described earlier tend to make public sector organisations disinclined to do this; nevertheless, if methods aimed at forcing them to do so are incorporated as part of standard procedure, it is possible to go a certain way towards correcting this tendency. In the following sections, we will look at some of these methods in greater detail. However, in practice, the approach has been used more often to try to work out how to convince citizens and businesses to accept policy change rather than necessarily to change government or administrative practices. One example of this would be in the dairy industry in Norway, where the approach was applied to search for ways to convince dairy farmers to accept climate change mitigation measures that run counter to their immediate interests.[7]

2. The Innovator's Dilemma

The innovator's dilemma suggests when an organisation falls behind it is the result of conscious decision-making. What's more, its proponents argue, these are not necessarily bad decisions: often they appear to all reasonable observers to be entirely reasonable and rational. While the formulation stage of the policy process appears to be functioning perfectly, it is producing sub-optimal results.

This idea was developed by Clayton Christensen, who observed that the failure to keep up with disruptive changes is equally likely to afflict well-managed and successful organisations as poorly run and inefficient ones.[8] He cites various examples from the corporate world. Sears was praised for years as not just an exemplary company but an innovative one. It pioneered supply chain management, store brands, catalogue selling and credit card sales, all approaches that were later picked up by almost all other retailers. However, even as Sears was receiving plaudits for its efficiency and ability to stay ahead of the competition, it was actually falling behind; it failed to anticipate the development of discount retailing and home centres, and when online retail companies began to eat away at its market its fate was sealed.[9] IBM experienced a similar reversal: having dominated the mainframe market it was perfectly placed to do the same on the desktop PC market, but failed to do so, convinced that size simply was not an issue for computer buyers. Instead, the new market was captured by Digital Equipment Corporation, which in turn was undermined just when it seemed most successful as it failed to anticipate the rise of low-cost personal computers.[10] The same phenomenon is often present in the public service but is far harder to identify without the presence of market indicators to do so. Thus, for example, it is not uncommon to see government departments use their proficiency with outdated methods to justify their reluctance to adopt newer ones. Thus, many government departments tend to cling resolutely to paper-based systems in the face of the development of e-government modalities, both because they are unfamiliar with the latter and because there were often relatively low numbers of citizens interested in and equipped to use them in the early days. During the COVID-19 pandemic, for example, the French authorities did not adopt mobile-based track and trace approaches on the basis that this was new technology for them and many older citizens did not have smartphones. The result was a paper-based system that was highly inefficient.

Christensen argues, based on these examples, that large organisations do not fail because they are poorly managed, but precisely because they are well managed. The organisations he describes all listened assiduously to those that they were supposed to serve and conducted wide-scale research to identify key trends, allocating R&D budgets to the development of innovations that will bring in the greatest possible returns. However, existing users are unable to indicate a demand for a service that does not yet exist. As Henry Ford put it, "If I had asked the public what they wanted, they would have said a faster horse".

When internet retailing began, it was a minority pursuit that made most people highly nervous concerning the security of their payment information. For Sears to have shifted resources away from its core catalogue sales business to pour into a technology that seemingly engaged very few potential customers would have been illogical. Similarly, IBM's customers were large businesses that were used to putting money into room-sized computers and had made their business plans on the basis that this would continue to be necessary for the foreseeable future. Companies that might appreciate smaller computers were not a lucrative enough part of the market to make it worth IBM's effort to target them. DEC faced a similar situation: selling low-cost PCs would have involved accepting much lower margins on all of their products, something that seemed actively self-sabotaging. This can often be the case in government organisations. In World War I, the Allies had focused principally on improving their existing technologies, into which they had already sunk a large amount of money, while Germany poured its energies into new technologies such as submarines and aircraft. The result was that a war that the Allies believed they could win easily dragged on for over 4 years.

The problem is that a disruptive technology generally does not look like a disruptive technology when it first emerges. Air BnB famously struggled to raise initial funding because venture capitalists were simply not convinced that its core concept was feasible, and who can forget Paul Krugman's famous quote about the internet:

> The growth of the Internet will slow drastically, as the flaw in "Metcalfe's law" – which states that the number of potential connections in a network is

> proportional to the square of the number of participants – becomes apparent: most people have nothing to say to each other! By 2005 or so, it will become clear that the Internet's impact on the economy has been no greater than the fax machine's.[11]

In a corporate context, this can lead to losing money, but in government the consequences can be far more grave. In World War I example given earlier, the misunderstanding of the impact that changing technologies would have on warfare led to millions of needless deaths. Moreover, the naturally risk-averse nature of the public sector means that staff are less inclined to take a punt on new technologies. Individual agents are more likely to suffer censure if they make a change than if they stick to old-established methods.

For an established organisation, neglecting important sectors, in order to focus on small ones would be ridiculous. For a small start-up, however, these are often the only strategies available to them. While most will continue to struggle on the margins of a bigger market, occasionally one will hit upon an innovation for which there exists a huge and previously unsuspected market. While this is less often the case in the public than in the private sector, it is not entirely unknown. When the British National Health Service was introduced, for example, the idea of healthcare that was free for all at the point of use was a revolutionary idea. The same thing can be said for the various experiments on universal basic income that have taken place in recent years. Both were hugely popular initiatives for which there nevertheless existed no real demand until the idea was proposed to people, simply because they had not considered it a possibility until then.

On this basis, Christensen distinguishes between sustaining and disruptive innovations. Sustaining innovations may be novel, but what makes them distinctive is that they serve to improve the performance of existing products and services, rather than creating new products and services in and of themselves, and they do so along the dimensions of performance that customers in major markets have traditionally valued. Thus, for example, IBM's effort to speed up its mainframe computers was an example of sustaining innovation. In the government sector, electronic payment of benefits would be considered a sustaining innovation. The Indian shift towards electronic transfers was designed to reduce the opportunities for corruption in citizens' interactions with government, as well as saving time and money in delivering public services, and enabling more efficient management of the population. However, while the technology was revolutionary, the goal was to provide old services in a new way, rather than to devise entirely new services.

Disruptive innovations are different. While these innovations may offer poor performance in the short term, they also provide a very different value proposition to existing options. Thus, in the early years of the automobile, cars were expensive, slow and unreliable – no competition at all for horses and buggies. On the other hand, cars had a potential that horses simply did not possess. Cars could be improved incrementally, with each part progressively growing more efficient, and the whole growing ever faster and cheaper. This is not the case for horses, which had already been improved as much as was feasible through selective breeding. Often, disruptive products are cheaper, simpler, smaller and more convenient to use – the desktop computers described earlier are one example, but one may also cite the small, cheap, off-road motorcycles introduced to the United States by Honda and Kawasaki, edging out Harley Davidson and BMS's heavy, high-power off-road bikes. In the government sector, universal basic income would be considered a disruptive technology; while it can be provided using existing technologies, the concept itself is entirely new. This distinction between sustaining and disruptive innovations can easily be represented on a graph:

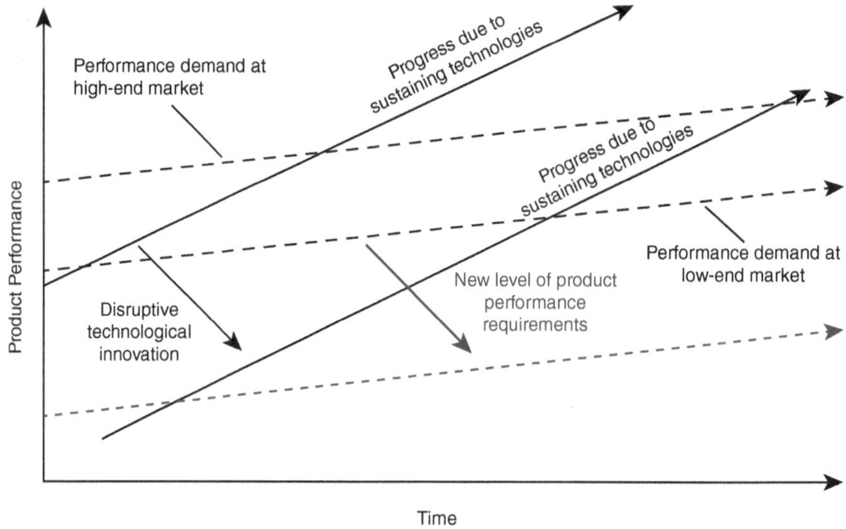

FIGURE 7.1 Disruptive Innovation (Inspired by Christensen, 2013)

While a disruptive innovation may not currently be capable of competing with existing products and services, they have the potential to completely change your organisation's raison d'être. Usually, innovations such as this are carried out by small companies that have technical expertise and a belief in their technology but lack the capacity to compete in the main market with large existing companies. However, they occasionally emerge from government too. In the universal basic income example, the idea was originally espoused by fringe candidates only, or tried in small experimental runs in specific areas. Over time, however, as citizens became more aware of the idea, it soon came under consideration by serious political heavy hitters.

This may seem to paint a bleak picture as far as innovation by large organisations is concerned. They do not innovate because it would be illogical for them to do so: end of the story. However, the fact that some companies and governments have successfully adapted to disruptive innovations that they did not create suggests that it is not entirely impossible. Various strategies can be adopted to enable organisations to serve their existing users and search for new opportunities. It is, for example, possible to establish a specific unit dedicated to "thinking outside the box" and investigating potentially disruptive technologies in your field, while the rest of the organisation continues to focus on your current core activities. Alternatively, some companies – including state-owned and state-linked industries – have created extensive acquisitions programmes, making a habit of buying up promising-looking companies in their sector, knowing that while some will turn out to be poor deals, others are the unicorns with the potential to change the entire industry. Establishing such a unit will at least give you a chance of foreseeing change, though it provides no guarantee that you will correctly identify developments that will revolutionise the way in which you deliver your services.

To improve your chances of "doing an HBO", Christensen advises several other strategies.

1. Seek independent advice. The ways in which your money is spent will be directed by existing stakeholders, and these tend to be the people who benefit most from the status quo. To find a reason to do anything else, you will need to solicit outside input. This can be done in various ways. Companies sometimes spin off subsidiaries or advisor groups. In the public sector, it is possible to solicit recommendations from independent consultants or auditors, to conduct focus groups among non-users, or to constitute independent advisory boards.
2. Bear in mind that small is not necessarily trivial. This is a particular problem for large companies: a $40 million company needs to find an extra $8 million in revenue to grow by 20%, but a $4 billion company needs to make an extra $800 million. It is impossible to achieve this by targeting small markets, meaning that these tend to be ignored. Public sector organisations should not face this problem, since their objective is service rather than growth. However, it is often the case that small user segments are ignored in favour of bringing the greatest good to the greatest number.
3. Remember that you can't analyse what doesn't exist. Many large hotel chains conduct regular strategic market research exercises. These failed to anticipate the rise of Air BnB, however, because there was no market for Air BnB rentals until Air BnB was created. Prior to this, the market size was $0, but this does not mean that it should have been ignored. The National Health System in the United Kingdom would soon come to be one of the major components of the national budget and an issue upon which governments may stand or fall, but at the time it was created it was an entirely new initiative, and there was no way to predict how well it would work or what the public reception would be.
4. Abilities in one context are disabilities in another. Remember that your organisation's habits and processes were developed, in order to carry out the tasks that you currently undertake. You will naturally be less equipped to perform other tasks and will handle them less efficiently. This does not mean that they should be ignored, however.

5. The size of a new market is determined by supply, not demand. Proponents of disruptive innovations are usually only able to target a small segment of their potential market: when Bitcoin was first launched, it was accessible only to people with the technical know-how to mine coins and enough of an interest in cryptography to be aware of the idea, but as knowledge spread the use of cryptocurrencies expanded massively. The market for secure online stores of value always existed, it was simply not easily visible – even to its future participants – until an appropriate product was created and publicised. The initial market for bitcoin was in no way an indicator of what the bitcoin market was destined to become. Once again, one may cite the example of healthcare in the United Kingdom: prior to the advent of the National Health System, the effective demand for healthcare was relatively small. If you were sick and too poor to pay for treatment, you simply had to endure it. When supply began to be rationed via a queueing system and not purely by price, however, demand shot up to meet or even exceed it.

This approach has been taken by multiple governments to try to anticipate technological changes that they will likely have to deal with in the near future.[12] However, in order to make a reasonable job of it, it is necessary to do proper research into the sectors of society that one is serving – as described earlier. New insights can help break through the deadlock and move towards new strategies, as described later.

3. Blue and Red Oceans

Rather than dividing technologies into sustaining and disruptive, the Blue Ocean theory of innovation, as developed by W. Chan Kim and Renee Mauborgne in 2015, divides the world into existing industries and potential industries – the red and blue oceans of their book's title.[13]

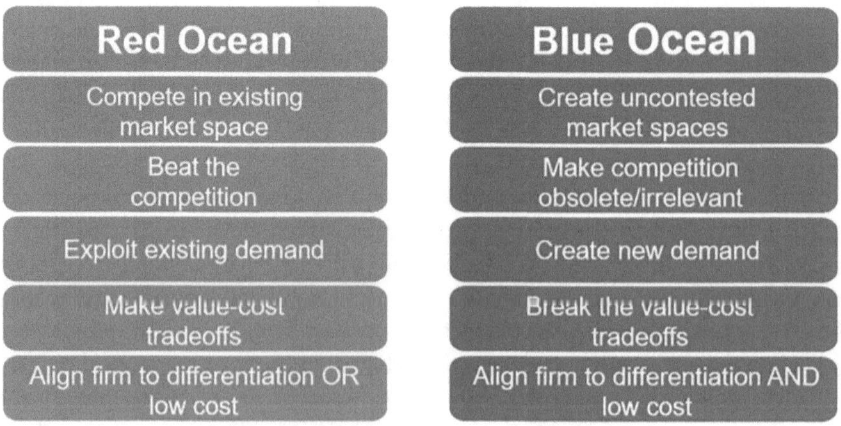

FIGURE 7.2 Red vs. Blue Ocean (Inspired by Kim and Mauborgne, 2015)

They suggest that the way to anticipate or even drive the emergence of disruptive innovations is not simply to research or buy up new technologies indiscriminately, but rather to look for potential demands that are not being addressed or are being inadequately addressed. The central example the authors give is that of Cirque du Soleil. The group was founded by a group of street performers in 1984. While their skills would have enabled them to enter the travelling circus market, this was an industry in long-term decline. Instead, they created an entirely new kind of show, targeting adults rather than children and audiences that would be willing to pay Broadway theatre prices for a novel kind of show. After Cirque du Soleil grew into a multimillion-dollar phenomenon, many other similar troupes attempted to copy its formula with greater or lesser success – Cirque du Soleil had effectively distinguished itself so much from other alternative entertainment options that it created its own market. In the government sector, one may once again cite the examples of the National Health Service in the United Kingdom, or the various universal basic income experiments that have been conducted across the world. While these had not been considered as an option by most citizens until the idea was raised, as soon as it was put forward, the demand emerged. Nowadays, providing healthcare is seen as one of the key functions of many governments, and any attempts to reduce or restrict it are immensely unpopular at the ballot box.

In addition to the factors described in the previous sections, the authors suggest that organisations find themselves becalmed in red oceans because they focus too much on competition. With only a limited amount of strategic bandwidth, executives tend to focus on outperforming other similar organisations in the same sector, rather than looking for new areas of demand to address. In contrast with other theories of innovation, the Blue Ocean concept insists far less on technological innovation. Instead, they argue that many successful blue ocean organisations create their own demand by simplifying current technologies rather than elaborating upon them. This is how DEC managed to conquer the desktop PC market from under the nose of IBM, for example – while IBM focused only on improving its technology, DEC simplified it to bring it within the price range of ordinary buyers. Once again, the parallel may be drawn with the National Health Service: while the treatments, facilities and bedside manner offered were nowhere near that provided in private healthcare settings, the no-frills approach made it possible to offer it to everyone free at the point of use.

The Blue Ocean authors are less pessimistic than the other theorists described earlier. They note that blue oceans are often created by large organisations. This was the case when Honda and Kawasaki effectively created the market for small off-road bikes in the United States, for example. They suggest that the key to opening up blue oceans lies less in research than in strategic awareness. The authors contrast their vision of markets with Porter's vision described earlier. They argue that rather than aiming to distinguish themselves based on either cost or product differentiation, blue ocean companies often do both. Thus, Cirque du Soleil simplified the traditional circus concept by removing the animals, the star performers and much of the infrastructure – all sources of significant costs – while also distinguishing itself by providing a more theatre-like experience with narratives and themes, and by developing entirely new shows for every tour. Rather than succumbing to environmental determinism and seeing industry structures as set in stone, they created a product for which a market existed only *in potentia*.

This is often phrased in terms of an ERRC (eliminate, reduce, raise, grid). Thus, Cirque du Soleil eliminated the animals and star performers, reduced the infrastructure, raised the ticket prices and created completely new themed shows every 6 months. Another example of this process would be Netflix. Netflix became successful by distinguishing itself from current cable TV stations. It eliminated commercials, news and live sports, reduced the price and infrastructure, increased accessibility and user control, and created the binge-watching concept and multi-device accessibility.

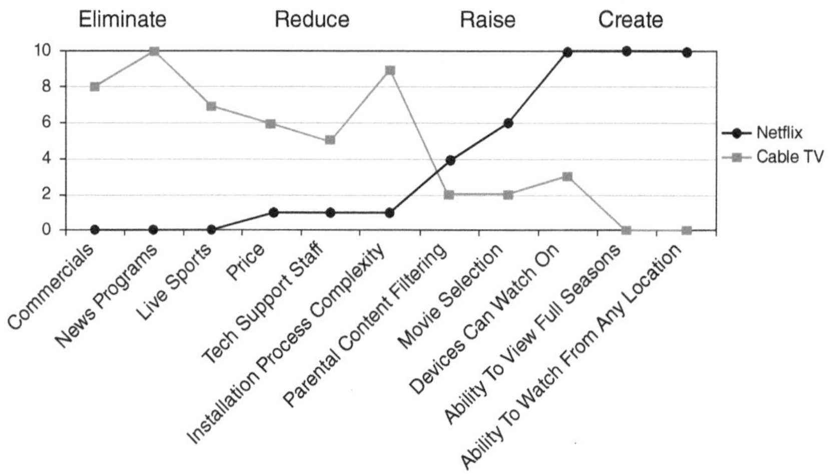

Step 1: Find one to two cases of solutions
Step 2: Identify the key pros and cons of the cases and collate into factors on the X-axis
Step 3: Plot out how the case(s) would look like on the graph
Step 4: Engage stakeholders on factors (ask what they REALLY want) and plot a third line to show the potential "Blue Ocean" solution

FIGURE 7.3 Author's Own Design

To use this approach, it can be helpful to plot your existing services on an Eliminate, Reduce, Raise, Create (EERC) grid to try to work out how they could be improved by eliminating, reducing, raising or creating various attributes. If your service requires in-person visits to an office, possibly you could look into providing online access (where feasible). If your website requires an ID and a PIN and a token, possibly you could try enabling mobile-based logins.

This approach has become extremely fashionable in recent years, and while its applicability is more readily evident in the private sector, it has also been used in various public sector contexts. It has been used to drive the creation of innovation clusters in the Greek region of Attica.[14] It has also been used extensively in Malaysia:

> In 2010 the Malaysian government introduced the National Blue Ocean Strategy (NBOS), to reduce the cost and maximizing the output in the public sector. Reports indicated these projects gave benefits to society and government through its projects. As the National Blue Ocean Strategy has gained its momentum, their activities and impacts have been subject to closer review and evaluation.[15]

There are various theories to explain the ways in which disruptive innovation happens. In this chapter, we have run through a few of the principal ones, all of which share a certain level of overlap. This overlap means that they can often be used in conjunction. Thus, for example, the diamond model can be used to situate your organisation in its operational landscape, and the ideas of cultural lock-in and the innovator's dilemma can be borne in mind to help you remain more aware of the potential pitfalls that your organisation faces, while the blue ocean theory can be used to open up new areas of demand in which to maximise the number of people served by your organisation, and the amount of benefit that you deliver.

While many of these theories seem to paint a relatively pessimistic picture of the prospects for innovating within large organisations, both their authors and various other experts have put forward a variety of suggestions for how to minimise your organisation's chances of being left behind by others' innovations. In the next chapter, we will set out some of these and explain how they can potentially be applied within public sector organisations.

After everything we covered so far in this chapter, it may seem that innovation is entirely impossible for public sector organisations. They're simply too big and subject to too few pressures to make innovation possible. Whether for reasons of cultural inertia or for ones of solid strategy, it is difficult for a large and successful organisation to turn away from the approaches and systems that made it large and successful in the first place, in order to take the kind of risks that lead to the failure of so many small and unsuccessful organisations.

While it may not be possible to give your organisation the speed, hunger and willingness to take risks of a small start-up, it is possible to oblige your staff to adopt some of the behaviours that prevail in these organisations, enabling them to propose innovations that will let you remain ahead of the game.

It is likely that the majority of your staff will spend most of their careers carrying out the same old standard tasks as they have for the past 20 or 30 years (give or take a few technological changes). After all, a public hospital will always have to cure illnesses and injuries, and while the drugs they use may change over time, there will only ever be so many possible ways to deliver healthcare: people come in, they are seen by a doctor and then they leave. Nevertheless, around this central activity, huge changes may be going on. Records can be computerised, services can be moved from in-patient to out-patient and diseases can be wiped out or evolve. Not everyone in the organisation will have to spend their entire working lives thinking about these things (unlike in a start-up), but it can be helpful to have at least a part of the management team try to integrate innovative mindsets to help the organisation strive for constant improvement and anticipate and prepare for environmental changes.

Some large organisations will give this task to a dedicated team. In Singapore, for example, the government began experimenting with "futures" teams, whose entire job consists of speculating about the future and trying to anticipate demand for public services. While this began as a small unit within the civil service, it gradually spread throughout public organisations, and now many ministries and even smaller organisations such as universities have futures thinking teams.[16] As well as trying to predict and anticipate future trends, these teams often – as a natural consequence of this – end up thinking of new ways to improve public services in the here-and-now, since the best way to prepare for future disasters is to optimise one's present capacities.

In this section, we will look at ways in which you can oblige your team members – or even your entire organisation – to behave in more innovative ways. We will begin by following on from the design thinking approach described in Chapter 6 and look at the job-to-be-done methodology. We will then go on to look at Lean and Agile approaches – two well-known ways to try to push large organisations into more innovative behaviour. Finally, we will go on to look at Blue Ocean thinking – a way for organisations to identify entirely new groups of consumers for their goods and services.

4. The Job-to-Be-Done

The job-to-be-done approach was developed by Harvard Business School professor Clayton Christensen.[17] As a technique relevant to the agenda-setting stage of the policy cycle, it has a lot in common with the design thinking methods described in Chapter 6. However, while design thinking is centred on empathising with the user or the customer's wishes, the job-to-be-done approach takes it up a level, asking why they want this thing. It asks two main questions: "Why?" to elucidate the strategic objectives and "How?" to clarify the operational objectives. Thus, for example, someone may go to the barber's because they want to get their hair cut, but they are not doing this simply for the joy of having their hair cut. Assuming that they are not doing it for work requirements because they are in the police or the military, the assumption is that they wish to improve the way that they look. Knowing this, it is possible to think of potential alternative solutions. While it may be in the barber's immediate interests to simply give the customer what he wants and cut his hair, he could also conceivably suggest other solutions: sell him a hat, persuade him to grow his hair out and get a Mohawk, propose electrolysis so that the customer will never need to have his hair cut again. None of these are likely to receive a favourable reply from a customer who is merely there for a short back and sides, but it is by running through other potential solutions to the problem that innovative new products and services can be developed. After all, fashions change – a few years back a barber suggesting beard care products to someone coming in for a shave would have been laughed out of his own shop, but in recent years it's been a rare adult male who hasn't experimented with facial hair at one point or another.

Jobs to be Done can be broken down into two principal types:

1. Main jobs to be done: The tasks that the service user or customer wants to achieve (getting a haircut).
2. Related jobs to be done (having better-looking hair).[18]

Within each of these two types there are two aspects:

1. Functional job aspects: The practical and objective customer requirements. ("I want my hair to look like Tom Cruise's".)
2. Emotional job aspects: The customer's feelings surrounding the process. ("I want that style in order to look good".)

And within the emotional aspects are two dimensions:

1. Personal dimension: How the customer feels about the solution. ("Looking like Tom Cruise would make me feel sexier".)
2. Social dimension: How the customer believes he will be perceived by others as a result. ("My girlfriend is always watching Tom Cruise movies; she'll think I'm hotter if I do this".)

The idea behind this exercise is that a solution that provides the customer with satisfaction on all of these levels is more likely to be successful on the market. Obviously, this is not necessarily a useful exercise in all parts of the public sector. If you are a Captain of a nuclear submarine, then your job is to patrol the oceans and wait for a signal to launch the missiles. The main job to be done is providing citizens with a nuclear deterrent, and there are no real alternative ways to do this. In other sectors, however, the approach can work surprisingly well. For example, imagine that you manage your country's national parks agency. For hundreds of years, your organisation has been conducting patrols to catch poachers and illegal loggers.

However, the goal in itself is not simply to catch criminals. The goal is to preserve the environment for future generations. This could be done by patrolling to catch those set on exploiting the land illegally, but other options are available. For example, local villages could be made responsible for safeguarding particular stretches of forest and allowed to take a certain number of trees in return. Alternatively, legislation could be passed to transfer the assets of anyone caught logging illegally to whoever provided information about the crime leading to a successful prosecution. Alternatively, it is worth considering that citizens simply do not wish to protect the natural environment. The poaching and illegal logging could be a sign that ordinary citizens do not care about preserving the environment.

The goal of many of the theories outlined earlier – such as blue ocean strategy and design thinking – is to create win-win solutions, which offer good results for all stakeholders. This can be possible if all stakeholders are willing to compromise on certain things, in order to maximise their utility in other areas.[19] However, in the real world, this is not always possible. In the event that every possible solution has defects, the idea of the triune brain comes into play. This is the idea that the human brain has three layers: reptilian (to do with survival and biological needs), emotional and intellectual. When these come into conflict, it is usually the lower layer that will win. Thus, when service users have to decide between their biological and intellectual preferences, it is usually their biological needs that will win out. Thus, for example, people may understand on an intellectual level that preserving the environment is a good idea, but if they rely upon illegal slash and burn agriculture for their livelihood, this will fall by the wayside. The approach can be applied following well-defined steps:

1. **Identify how you might serve your existing users better or find new users to serve**. This can be done in four ways: core growth (finding unmet desires among your existing users – "preserve forests *and also* plant new trees following forest fires"), related job growth ("preserve forests *and also* maintain trails so that people can appreciate them"), new job growth (look for ways in which new technologies may change the ways in which you fulfil your functions – "preserve forests *and also* install surveillance cameras to spot illegal loggers") and disruptive growth (focusing on opening up entirely new functions for your organisation: "preserve forests *and also* plant new stands of trees on behalf of wealthy companies who wish to offset their carbon output").
2. **Identify the jobs your customers/users are trying to get done**. This is the design thinking component that we covered in Chapter 6 – use empathy to imagine yourself in service users' shoes and use this to work out what they expect or desire from you.
3. **Categorise jobs to be done**. Are they main or related jobs? Do they satisfy basic, emotional or intellectual needs? How urgent are they? How easy are they to complete?
4. **Create job statements**. These could "protect the environment", "prevent illegal logging" or "manage the countryside".
5. **Prioritise the jobs to be done**. To do this you can rank jobs according to the level of satisfaction your users have with the solutions available to the problem currently, and according to the importance of the problem in their day-to-day lives. They can also be classified according to whether a particular area is underserved, well-served or overserved.

However, this effort to think outside the box can seem like a chore or a waste of time if the organisation is large, successful and under no significant pressure to change. While the sudden appearance of existential risks can be transformative to an organisation, inflicting a disaster upon oneself simply in the hope that it will encourage improvement is a rather drastic step. Nevertheless, it is possible to adopt other ways to foster a more proactive approach to innovation. Two well-known approaches are the Lean and Agile frameworks, which we will go into in the next section. While these are better-known for their application in business contexts, they can also be used in public sector contexts to create start-up-style cultures and practices of innovation.

It is important to apply job-to–be-done concepts in exploring blue and red ocean approaches, finding the right survival/emotional/intellectual components upon which to focus, working to create new audiences for your services. It is important to bear in mind that emotional and intellectual levers are relatively weak as compared to survival ones – hence, there is generally more demand for emergency medicine than preventative medicine, for example.

1. Think Small to Think Big: Lean

The Lean Methodology was first laid out by the Toyota Company in the 1930s, in a manual called *The Toyota Way*.[20] It was not given the name "Lean Methodology" until US businesses started to take an interest in the approach in the 1980s.[21] It has since become a key part of policy implementation in both public and private sector organisations.

The process involves five key ideas:

1. Specify the value desired by the users. (This can be done via design thinking and the job-to-be-done approach.)
2. Analyse the value stream, and identify places where waste is occurring. This can be done using value chain analysis.
3. Make sure that the steps that go into process flow unimpeded from one to the next – blockages or delays are a source of waste.
4. Introduce "pull" between steps where possible. This refers to the "kanban" or "just in time" system, only producing or ordering supplies when they are demanded downstream.[22] This minimises the amount of stock maintained at any given time, which is also a source of waste.
5. Strive for continuous improvement. As with most of the methods in this book, this is intended to be iterative, rather than a one-time exercise. This idea is often referred to as the Kaizen Methodology – a focus on quality control and continuous improvement ("kaizen" is Japanese for improvement).

The key to the approach is step two: to minimise waste at all costs. This is not just a good thing for its own sake but also serves as a driver to eliminate inefficiencies.

Traditionally, seven types of waste have been identified:

1. **Faulty goods or services**. Producing output that does not meet user demand is a waste of everyone's time and resources. When government produces services or facilities that are not used, this is a waste of taxpayer money.
2. **Waste of skills**. Miss-allocation or misuse of human resources. If government recruitment and training policies do not keep up with environmental changes, this often results in the redeployment of staff to roles for which they are not suited. This often happens in emergency circumstances, with armed forces members being redeployed to fight forest fires or firefighters being asked to serve as paramedics.
3. **Under-use of capabilities**. This can happen when environmental changes have not been anticipated. Thus, for example, the British government overestimated the number of COVID-19 patients hospitals would have to treat during the early days of the pandemic, and pushed off all non-emergency treatment, leading to deaths from untreated cancers as hospitals sat empty waiting for a wave of cases that would not come in until much later.
4. **Delegating tasks with inadequate training**. This is often related to point two, as staff are allocated to jobs for which they lack the appropriate skills.
5. **Applying the wrong metrics or using no metrics to measure results**. This is a particular problem in the public sector, as mentioned earlier. Public organisations tend to be reluctant to conduct evaluations or fudge their evaluations in order to show themselves in the best possible light. Often proper evaluation will not be conducted until popular outrage forces politicians to begin evaluation exercises.
6. **Inadequate participation (not inviting ideas and contributions from other stakeholders)**. If you have not worked out exactly what your service users and others with an interest in your organisation genuinely expect from you, then it is likely that you will get it wrong and provide a service that is poorly adapted to their requirements.
7. **Improper or inadequate use of computers**. Public IT procurement and use is often particularly badly done, since there are often few people in a public organisation with the expertise to assess and check up on private suppliers of IT solutions.

There is an abundance of evidence concerning the ways in which waste reduction has assisted companies to innovate – whether applied inside or outside of the lean framework. In the late 1990s, for example, BP began a programme of "looking for carbon" in an attempt to reduce emissions and improve its public profile. While the initiative cost $20m to implement, it saved the company $650m over its first few years in operation, with the company developing new methods, products and processes in the name of reducing the amount of carbon produced.[23] This process relies on having a very clear perspective on your organisation's flows. This can be extremely difficult to do, and every organisation's value stream map will be different, and usually highly complex. Here is an example.

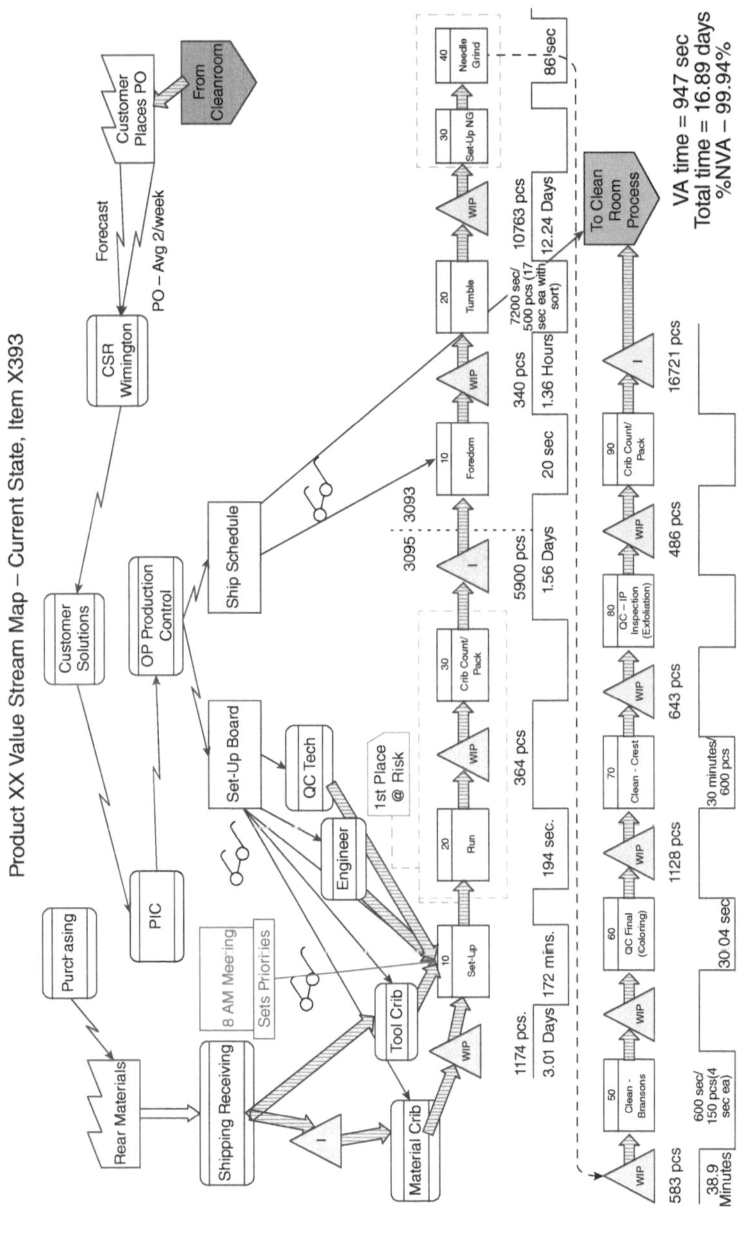

FIGURE 7.4 Lean Sample (Adapted from Aaron Hunt/Lean Enterprise Institute)

6. Think Small to Think Big: Six Sigma

One way to approach this is via the Six Sigma method, which focuses on reducing waste by reducing defects and failures.[24] Six Sigma involves two methodologies: DMAIC (for improving current outputs) and DMADV (for creating new ones). DMAIC has five stages:

1. Define the system and the user requirements. What services do you provide? What do service users expect from you?
2. Measure the current process and collect relevant data. How is your organisation currently performing?
3. Analyse this to identify causal chains. Why do you perform well in certain areas and badly in others?
4. Improve the process on this basis. Change what is not working and improve what is.
5. Control the process to make sure that the improvements are not lost and that it stays up to date with current requirements; continue to evaluate and iterate.

DMADV is similar but adapted to create something entirely new:

1. Define the system and the user requirements. What services do you provide? What do service users expect from you? How is your organisation currently performing?
2. Measure your capabilities and risks and set quantifiable goals for the project. What can you achieve with the organisational capabilities that you have? What might go wrong?
3. Analyse ways to solve the problem presented. How can you achieve the goals set out?
4. Design a solution;
5. Verify the solution at a small scale to test its efficacy. Roll out to a small subset of users and evaluate both its effectiveness and their responses to it.

The Six Sigma concept has spawned a vast number of quality control systems and procedures, however, which can tend to make its implementation somewhat cumbersome. This can make it actively counterproductive if your goal is to innovate quickly. However, the approach is useful when it comes to connecting sustaining innovation and disruptive innovation, providing as they do a way to link means and goals.

While the Lean Methodology has been criticised for increasing stress among employees, this is also – to a degree – the point of the method. It creates an artificial sense of pressure in an attempt to replicate the conditions that compel smaller companies to be nimble, adaptable and – above all else – innovative. The approach has also been widely applied in public sector organisations. A study in 2019 showed it being employed in the United States, Canada, Mexico, the United Kingdom, the Netherlands, Italy, France, Sweden, Portugal, Denmark, Spain, Saudi Arabia, Taiwan, Israel, Iran, India, Turkey, Jordan, Australia and Brazil, with the list being a non-exhaustive one. The vast majority of experiments with the systems took place in the health and education systems, with local government also employing the methods.[25] A study carried out in the United Kingdom found "no firm evidence that Lean implementation improves performance at an organisational level".

However, the researchers noted that adoption of the method had often been cursory and made with a focus on short-term gains. They concluded that,

> Lean should not be adopted as a "magic bullet" solution to organisational performance issues. The Chief Executive asserts that after six years of implementing Lean the organisation is only just starting to see the impact of a systemic approach to Lean implementation on the "bottom line"; thus, organisations implementing Lean in order to make short term financial savings are likely to fail in their endeavour, as illustrated by ELHT. In summary, the impact of Lean upon organisational performance should be measured at a local level in the short to medium term and should include subjective views of impact as well as more objective measures.[26]

7. Think Small to Think Big: Agile

Another approach based on the idea of artificially creating a start-up ethos is the Agile Methodology. Agile began in the software development industry but has since expanded to other areas. The basic idea behind the approach is to replicate within large companies, behaviours that are second nature in small start-ups. Projects are carried out by small, cross-functional teams that collaborate closely at all stages of a project, from planning through analysis, design and testing. The *Manifesto for Agile Software Development* sets out 12 principles:

1. Customer satisfaction by early and continuous delivery of valuable software
2. Welcome changing requirements, even in late development
3. Deliver working software frequently (weeks rather than months)
4. Close, daily cooperation between business people and developers
5. Projects are built around motivated individuals, who should be trusted
6. Face-to-face conversation is the best form of communication (co-location)
7. Working software is the primary measure of progress[27]
8. Sustainable development, able to maintain a constant pace
9. Continuous attention to technical excellence and good design
10. Simplicity – the art of maximising the amount of work not done – is essential
11. Best architectures, requirements and designs emerge from self-organising teams
12. Regularly, the team reflects on how to become more effective and adjusts accordingly

The driving belief behind this is that small teams of competent individuals can be trusted to handle small, incremental jobs without requiring rigid rules and procedures to guide their decisions and behaviour. As one of the authors of the Agile Manifesto put it,

> The Agile movement is not anti-methodology, in fact many of us want to restore credibility to the word methodology. We want to restore a balance. We embrace modeling, but not in order to file some diagram in a dusty corporate repository. We embrace documentation, but not hundreds of pages of never-maintained and rarely used tomes. We plan but recognize the limits of planning in a turbulent environment.[28]

While the Agile system aims to abandon many of the heavy frameworks and procedures that tend to slow down work in large organisations, the idea is not to simply have everyone wander off in their own direction and hope that something good comes of it. As described earlier, the Agile approach does recognise that projects and groups should have particular features: projects should be small and incremental and be conducted in clear stages. Groups should include individuals with all the skills required to fulfil the brief and should neither be too small to complete the work nor so large that their work becomes inefficient. In fact, the Agile approach has spawned a variety of different procedures to help people implement it, among which the best known is Scrum. Under the Scrum framework, teams of ten or fewer members break their work into smaller goals that are intended to be completed in short iterations called "sprints". Usually, a sprint is no longer than 2 to 4 months. The team should ideally share a physical location and work together in a single room most of the time. They hold 15-minute daily meetings to update the team on their progress and consider any problems, and at the end of the sprint a review meeting is held to assess their performance. The group has a Scrum Master – who is responsible for organising and facilitating meetings and processes and dealing with any obstacles to productivity. It also has a Product Owner – who is responsible for bearing in mind the user requirements and recalling them to the other members in case of uncertainty or dispute. Otherwise, the members of the group are free to organise themselves as best they see fit.

As in the design thinking and job-to-be-done approaches described previously, a key part of the Scrum approach involves a clear focus on the user's needs, which are presumed to change regularly over time. In a Scrum context, this is known as a User Story. These User Stories are usually elaborated on and maintained by the Product Owner and written in the form of a narrative. This narrative can be constructed based on data collected via market research in the context of a design thinking or a job-to-be-done exercise. Typically it would take the form "As a <role> I want to <goal> so that I can <purpose>. I know that I am done when <acceptance criteria>". In a public sector context, a typical User Story may be something along the lines of,

> As a commuter I want to travel quickly and easily so that I can waste a minimum amount of time on transport. I know that I am done when my daily journey is at least 20% faster than it is now.

Unlike many of the previous approaches described in this book, the Agile methodology tends not to be applied as an occasional exercise. An organisation that relies on rigid structures and procedures will find it difficult to allow employees to break away from their present roles to join a Scrum group, for example. This means that Agile tends to be an all-or-nothing choice – either an entire organisational unit adopts the approach or no-one can. Agile being an approach originally developed in the IT world, it is most frequently used in the public sector by IT departments and contracting companies employed to develop software for public organisations, even in contexts where one would not necessarily expect it to be implemented. For example, in the early 2000s, FBI employees and contractors came together to create a case management system known as Sentinel,[29] while the Israeli Air Force adopted agile metrics in an attempt to speed up its development cycles.[30]

However, lean methodology tends to generate sustaining change rather than disruptive change. The idea behind it is to make innovation-generating approaches such as design thinking into an organisation's fundamental structures. To create disruptive innovation, it is necessary to adopt a different approach.

8. Charting Your Own Opportunities: Blue Ocean Strategy

We already covered the theory behind the blue ocean strategy, but to summarise the idea is that the key to innovation is to make a new product or service that creates its own market. Under the theory, every industry and product that already exists is referred to "red ocean" space, while industries that exist *in potentia* are referred to as "blue oceans". In this way, an organisation can create a product that people do not yet know that they want. Bubble tea, for example, has grown to be a massive market across the world in recent years, but until quite recently many people in the West had no idea that it existed or that they would want to buy it. Elsewhere, new processes have created markets: in the early 2000s, meeting people on the internet and getting into strangers' cars were both seen as being incredibly dangerous. Now many of us regularly use apps such as Uber and Grab to summon strangers from the internet with the goal of riding in their cars.[31]

The blue ocean strategy is not just a philosophy of innovation. It is also associated with a particular set of implementation approaches and methodologies. While the authors of the concept acknowledge that large organisations often find it difficult – bordering on impossible – to spot and create blue ocean opportunities, there are steps that they can take to make such an outcome more likely. The blue ocean strategy is often explicitly contrasted with the Diamond/Five Forces model described in previous chapters. This approach tries to assess the levels of competition within an industry, while the blue ocean strategy tries to identify new industries that do not yet exist. Nevertheless, while being separate from the ideas described earlier, it can also complement them. An organisation that is working to develop a blue ocean strategy can also employ Lean and Agile approaches in its day-to-day existence and design thinking to understand the perspectives of its stakeholders.

The first and most important step in developing a blue ocean strategy is to change deciders' mindsets. Often, public service managers merely ask themselves "How can we provide better service?" rather than "What new services can we provide?" Thus, for example, education department managers may be so focused on improving exam results among school children that they do not bother to look at alternative ways of fulfilling their core goal: that of improving knowledge and skills among all parts of the population. While this can be done by improving school results, the same goal can also be achieved by employing a job-to-be-done approach to search for educational Blue Oceans. Maybe the overall national skills level could be improved by offering free subscriptions to online courses. It's possible that mid-career employees are keen to improve their education but cannot find time to do that and their jobs at the same time. Perhaps people are already training themselves in how to use new technologies, but this is not being recognised by the qualifications system.

The conventional distinction between blue and red ocean spaces is based heavily on business experiences.

Red Ocean Strategy (focus on existing users)	*Blue Ocean Strategy (focus on non-users)*
Compete in existing markets	Create uncontested markets to serve
Beat the competition	Make the competition irrelevant
Exploit existing demand	Create and capture new demand
Make the value-cost trade-off	Break the value-cost trade-off
Commit to either differentiation or cost competition	Pursue differentiation and low cost

While most public sector organisations do not face the pressure of competition in the same way as corporations, it is nevertheless possible to adopt a blue ocean strategy to facilitate continuous improvement.

It can be difficult to get management into the Blue Ocean mindset, but not necessarily more difficult than convincing them to accept any of the other approaches described in this book. Only once this preliminary step has been undertaken, however, can the next stages be contemplated. Blue ocean strategy guides list five of these, which can also incorporate approaches described earlier in the book:

1. Choose where to start and build your team. Value stream analysis can be helpful here.

2. Clarify the current situation and gather data. The issue redefinition and job-to-be-done approaches described earlier can be helpful in this stage.
3. Search for hidden pain points among existing users and search for blue oceans of non-users. At this point, design thinking is very useful to help in empathising with key stakeholders.
4. Redraw the boundaries between users and non-users, based on the groups of current non-users that you intend to target in the future. Ask yourself which component part of the problem needs rethinking and where in the world has best practices for that component. Study those best practices with the intent of breaking down conceptual boundaries and re-drawing the boundaries of what can be done.
5. Implement your changes, test them and seek feedback. This iterative approach links back to design thinking, as described earlier. If interventions are successful, then they can be integrated into day-to-day functioning through an approach such as the Agile framework.

Thus, in the example given previously, managers of a public education department may decide that given the prevalence of ageism and the increasing reliance upon technology in modern companies, mid-career professionals constitute a key target group of non-users of their services, and – as a result – decide to design courses that are intended to improve IT skills and are delivered in small modules that can be completed during the evening or at weekends.

The blue ocean strategy has been adopted in public sector organisations in various countries. In Malaysia, 80 different public sector agencies have experimented with the idea, leading to 118 Blue Ocean projects intended to improve public service delivery. Agencies and departments were invited to submit projects for consideration, and these were accepted for trial if they met six criteria:

1. Bring substantial benefits to the target group of citizens who are currently underserved or unserved;
2. Deliver a novel solution at a lower cost; Encourage interagency collaboration including the sharing of resources;
3. Be rapidly executable in between 3 and 6 months;
4. Be replicable across the public service; and
5. Observe the principles of fair process, that is, engage employees by asking for their inputs on how services could be improved and clarifying what is expected of them in executing the BOS.

The Ministry of Health, for example, introduced a pharmacy-by-post scheme aimed at saving time for both pharmacists and customers.[32]

Looking at successful examples we can see how the various theories described in this book are not necessarily mutually exclusive. A blue ocean strategy can serve as a framework upon which to hang all of the others, turning to a different methodology for every stage of the strategic process in order to gain maximum benefit from each.

Conclusion

Improved public service is a benefit to everyone, and it should be every public manager's goal not merely to improve the services that they provide but also to investigate ways in which they can provide new services and target new audiences.

In this chapter, we have looked at a variety of ways to encourage your organisation to achieve the most difficult of goals for public service organisations: innovation. This can be done either by artificially creating the sort of pressures that create innovation in small and nimble companies or by encouraging your staff to adopt a mindset that strives continuously to find new ways to target new audiences for your services.

While all of these approaches can be applied individually, better results can be obtained if they are used in a coordinated way, so as to complement one another. Thus, for example, it is possible to use a scenario-planning approach to plan for the distant future and a blue ocean strategy to take advantage of unknown unknowns. At the same time as doing this, it is possible to use a design thinking approach to empathise with service users and deal with their current pain points, and an Agile approach to improve efficiency. Simultaneously, an effective organisation will carry out repeated environment scanning and stakeholder analysis exercises in order to remain up to date on the stakeholders surrounding your organisation.

While these exercises may seem like an additional burden to already-busy teams, over time they will become second nature, being ingrained within your organisational DNA. The first iteration of a blue ocean strategy or design thinking exercise is usually immensely difficult, but the second is always easier, and by the time the third iteration rolls round, people can barely remember having done things in any other way.

The goal in this should always be to create a win-win situation, in which every stakeholder emerges from the changes in a better position than that in which they began. In such a way, it is possible to create a public sector organisation that is not afraid of risk and innovates like a high-tech company, even without the financial pressure that drive innovation in commercial contexts. Thus, your organisation will remain relevant to its users and continue to justify its own existence by providing excellent services that meet high demand from all those who benefit from them.

Notes

1 Nicholas, Tom. "Why Schumpeter was right: Innovation, market power, and creative destruction in 1920s America." *Journal of Economic History* (2003): 1023–1058.

2 Davis, Todd, and John Higgins. "A blockbuster failure: How an outdated business model destroyed a giant." (2013). Accessed from: https://www.semanticscholar.org/paper/A-Blockbuster-Failure:-How-an-Outdated-Business-a-Davis-Higgins/f578acdf0863b65491d9587af7ea346f4b9df1c7. Accessed on 20 November 2020.
3 Howlett, Michael, Michael Ramesh, and Anthony Perl. *Studying public policy: Policy cycles and policy subsystems* (Vol. 3). Oxford: Oxford University Press, 2009.
4 Foster, Richard, and Sarah Kaplan. *Creative Destruction: Why companies that are built to last underperform the market–And how to success fully transform them*. New York: Currency, 2011.
5 Gavetti, Giovanni, Rebecca Henderson, and Simona Giorgi. *Kodak and the digital revolution (A)*. Cambridge, MA: Harvard Business School Publishing, 2005.
6 Foster, Richard, and Sarah Kaplan, *op cit*, 2011.
7 Burton, Rob J.F., and Maja Farstad. "Cultural lock-in and mitigating greenhouse gas emissions: The case of dairy/beef farmers in Norway." *Sociologia Ruralis* 60, no. 1 (2020): 20–39.
8 Christensen, Clayton M. *The innovator's dilemma: When new technologies cause great firms to fail*. Cambridge, MA: Harvard Business Review Press, 2013.
9 Weitzel, William, and Ellen Jonsson. "Reversing the downward spiral: Lessons from WT grant and sears roebuck." *Academy of Management Perspectives* 5, no. 3 (1991): 7–22.
10 Schein, Edgar H., J. Paul, H. Edgar, Peter S. DeLisi, Paul J. Kampas, Michael M. Sonduck, S. Peter, and M. Michael. *DEC is dead, long live DEC*. Oakland, CA: Berrett-Koehler Publishers, 2003.
11 Krugman, Paul, "Why most economists' predictions are wrong." *Red Herring Online*, 10 June 1998.
12 Misuraca, Gianluca, and Gianluigi Viscusi. "Digital governance in the public sector: Challenging the policy-maker's innovation dilemma." Proceedings of the 8th International Conference on Theory and Practice of Electronic Governance, pp. 146–154, 2014.
13 Kim, W. Chan, and Renée Mauborgne. *Blue ocean strategy, expanded edition: How to create uncontested market space and make the competition irrelevant*. Cambridge, MA: Harvard Business Review Press, 2015.
14 Bourletidis, Dimitrios. "The strategic model of innovation clusters: Implementation of blue ocean strategy in a typical Greek region." *Procedia-Social and Behavioral Sciences* 148 (2014): 645–652.
15 Ramli, Anis Safwan, Jasmine Binti Ahmad, and Norhafizah Mohamed Harith. "Blue ocean strategy in Malaysian public sector: An analysis of the four-action framework." *Advanced Science Letters* 22, no. 5–6 (2016): 1702–1706.
16 Inayatullah, Sohail. "Six pillars: Futures thinking for transforming." *Foresight* 10, no. 1 (2008): 4–21.
17 Christensen, Clayton M., Taddy Hall, Karen Dillon, and David S. Duncan. "Know your customers' jobs to be done." *Harvard Business Review* 94, no. 9 (2016): 54–62.
18 Silverstein, David, Philip Samuel, and Neil DeCarlo. *The innovator's toolkit: 50+ techniques for predictable and sustainable organic growth*. New York: John Wiley & Sons, 2013.
19 Phua, Charles Chao Rong. *Towards strategic pragmatism in foreign policy: Cases of US, China and Singapore*. Oxon: Routledge, 2021.
20 Liker, Jeffrey, and Gary L. Convis. *The Toyota way to lean leadership: Achieving and sustaining excellence through leadership development*. New York: McGraw-Hill Education, 2011.
21 Krafcik, John F. "Triumph of the lean production system." *MIT Sloan Management Review* 30, no. 1 (1988): 41.
22 Monden, Yasuhiro. "Adaptable Kanban system maintains just-in-time production." In *Toyota production system*, pp. 15–35. Boston, MA: Springer, 1994.
23 Esty, Daniel C., and Andrew Winston. *Green to gold: How smart companies use environmental strategy to innovate, create value, and build competitive advantage*. New York: John Wiley & Sons, 2009.

24 Harry, M.J. "Six sigma: A breakthrough strategy for profitability." *Quality Progress* 31, no. 5 (1998): 60.
25 Rodgers, Bryan, and Jiju Antony. "Lean and six sigma practices in the public sector: A review." *International Journal of Quality & Reliability Management* 34, no. 9 (2019): 1402–1411.
26 Burgess, Nicola, and Zoe Radnor. "Evaluating lean in healthcare." *International Journal of Health Care Quality Assurance* 26 (2013): 220–235.
27 Beck, Kent, Mike Beedle, Arie Van Bennekum, Alistair Cockburn, Ward Cunningham, Martin Fowler, James Grenning et al. "Manifesto for agile software development." (2001): 2006. Accessed from: https://www.semanticscholar.org/paper/Manifesto-for-Agile-Software-Development-Beck-Beedle/3edabb96a07765704f9c6a1a5542e39ac2df640c. Accessed on 20 December 2020.
28 Highsmith, Jim. "History: The agile manifesto." Accessed from: http://agilemanifesto.org/history.html (2001). Accessed on 19 November 2020.
29 Fulgham, Chad, Jeffrey Johnson, Mark Crandall, Leo Jackson, and Nathan Burrows. "The FBI gets agile." *IT Professional* 13, no. 5 (2011): 57–59.
30 Dubinsky, Yael, David Talby, Orit Hazzan, and Arie Keren. "Agile metrics at the Israeli air force." Agile Development Conference (ADC'05), pp. 12–19. IEEE, 2005. Accessed from: https://www.semanticscholar.org/paper/Agile-metrics-at-the-Israeli-Air-Force-Dubinsky-Talby/dc712288e5a3514ed4175ab8f8a106851519275f. Accessed on 20 December 2020.
31 De Wit, Bob, and Ron Meyer. *Strategy: Process, content, context: An international perspective.* New York: Cengage Learning EMEA, 2010.
32 Ramli, Anis Safwan, Jasmine Binti Ahmad, and Norhafizah Mohamed Harith. "Blue ocean strategy in Malaysian public sector: An analysis of the four action framework." *Advanced Science Letters* 22, no. 5–6 (2016): 1702–1706.

Bibliography

Beck, Kent, Mike Beedle, Arie Van Bennekum, Alistair Cockburn, Ward Cunningham, Martin Fowler, James Grenning et al. (2001). "Manifesto for agile software development." Accessed from: https://www.semanticscholar.org/paper/Manifesto-for-Agile-Software-Development-Beck-Beedle/3edabb96a07765704f9c6a1a5542e39ac2df640c. Accessed on 20 December 2020.

Bourletidis, Dimitrios. (2014). "The strategic model of innovation clusters: Implementation of blue ocean strategy in a typical Greek region." *Procedia-Social and Behavioral Sciences* 148: 645–652.

Burgess, Nicola, and Zoe Radnor. (2013). "Evaluating lean in healthcare." *International Journal of Health Care Quality Assurance* 26: 220–235.

Chobanyan, Armen, and Laurence Leigh. (2006). "The competitive advantages of nations: Applying the 'Diamond' model to Armenia." *International Journal of Emerging Markets* 1(2): 147–164.

Christensen, Clayton M. (2013). *The innovator's dilemma: When new technologies cause great firms to fail.* Cambridge: MA: Harvard Business Review Press.

Christensen, Clayton M., Taddy Hall, Karen Dillon, and David S. Duncan. (2016). "Know your customers' jobs to be done." *Harvard Business Review* 94(9): 54–62.

Curran, Paul J. (2000). "Competition in UK higher education: Competitive advantage in the research assessment exercise and porter's diamond model." *Higher Education Quarterly* 54(4): 386–410.

Davis, Todd, and John Higgins. (2013). "A blockbuster failure: How an outdated business model destroyed a giant." Accessed from: https://www.semanticscholar.org/paper/A-Blockbuster-Failure:-How-an-Outdated-Business-a-Davis-Higgins/f578acdf0863b65491d9587af7ea346f4b9df1c7. Accessed on 20 November 2020.

De Wit, Bob, and Ron Meyer. (2010). *Strategy: Process, content, context: An international perspective*. New York: Cengage Learning EMEA.

Dubinsky, Yael, David Talby, Orit Hazzan, and Arie Keren. (2005). "Agile metrics at the Israeli air force." Agile Development Conference (ADC'05), pp. 12–19. IEEE. Accessed from: https://www.semanticscholar.org/paper/Agile-metrics-at-the-Israeli-Air-Force-Dubinsky-Talby/dc712288e5a3514ed4175ab8f8a106851519275f. Accessed on 20 December 2020.

Esty, Daniel C., and Andrew Winston. (2009). *Green to gold: How smart companies use environmental strategy to innovate, create value, and build competitive advantage*. New York: John Wiley & Sons.

Foster, Richard, and Sarah Kaplan. (2011). *Creative Destruction: Why companies that are built to last underperform the market – And how to success fully transform them*. New York: Currency.

Fulgham, Chad, Jeffrey Johnson, Mark Crandall, Leo Jackson, and Nathan Burrows. (2011). "The FBI gets agile." *IT Professional* 13(5): 57–59.

Gavetti, Giovanni, Rebecca Henderson, and Simona Giorgi. (2005). *Kodak and the digital revolution (A)*. Cambridge, MA: Harvard Business School Publishing.

Harry, M.J. (1998). "Six sigma: A breakthrough strategy for profitability." *Quality Progress* 31(5): 60.

Hodgetts, Richard M. (1993). "Porter's diamond framework in a Mexican context." *MIR: Management International Review*: 41–54.

Hosein Rezazadeh Mehrizi, Mohammad, and Mohammad Pakneiat. (2008). "Comparative analysis of sectoral innovation system and diamond model (the case of telecom sector of Iran)." *Journal of Technology Management & Innovation* 3(3): 78–90.

Howlett, Michael, Michael Ramesh, and Anthony Perl. (2009). *Studying public policy: Policy cycles and policy subsystems* (Vol. 3). Oxford: Oxford University Press.

Inayatullah, Sohail. (2008). "Six pillars: Futures thinking for transforming." *Foresight* 10(1): 4–21.

Kim, W. Chan, and Renée Mauborgne. (2015). *Blue ocean strategy, expanded edition: How to create uncontested market space and make the competition irrelevant*. Cambridge, MA: Harvard Business Review Press.

Kim, W. Chan, and Renée Mauborgne. (2017). *Blue ocean shift: Beyond competing, proven steps to inspire confidence and seize new growth*. New York: Hachette Books.

Krafcik, John F. (1988). "Triumph of the lean production system." *MIT Sloan Management Review* 30(1): 41.

Krugman, Paul. (1998). "Why most economists' predictions are wrong." *Red Herring Online*, 10 June 1998.

Liker, Jeffrey, and Gary L. Convis. (2011). *The Toyota way to lean leadership: Achieving and sustaining excellence through leadership development*. New York: McGraw-Hill Education.

Misuraca, Gianluca, and Gianluigi Viscusi. (2014). "Digital governance in the public sector: Challenging the policy-maker's innovation dilemma." Proceedings of the 8th International Conference on Theory and Practice of Electronic Governance, pp. 146–154.

Monden, Yasuhiro. (1994). "Adaptable Kanban system maintains just-in-time production." In *Toyota Production System*, pp. 15–35. Boston, MA: Springer.

Nicholas, Tom. (2003). "Why Schumpeter was right: Innovation, market power, and creative destruction in 1920s America." *Journal of Economic History*: 1023–1058.

Phua, Charles Chao Rong. (2021). *Towards strategic pragmatism in foreign policy: Cases of United States of America, China and Singapore*. Oxon: Routledge.

Porter, Michael E. (1996). "Competitive advantage, agglomeration economies, and regional policy." *International Regional Science Review* 19(1–2): 85–90.

Ramli, Anis Safwan, Jasmine Binti Ahmad, and Norhafizah Mohamed Harith. (2016). "Blue ocean strategy in Malaysian public sector: An analysis of the four-action framework." *Advanced Science Letters* 22(5–6): 1702–1706.

Rodgers, Bryan, and Jiju Antony. (2019). "Lean and six sigma practices in the public sector: A review." *International Journal of Quality & Reliability Management* 34(9): 1402–1411.

Schein, Edgar H., J. Paul, H. Edgar, Peter S. DeLisi, Paul J. Kampas, Michael M. Sonduck, S. Peter, and M. Michael. (2003). *DEC is dead, long live DEC*. Oakland, CA: Berrett-Koehler Publishers.

Silverstein, David, Philip Samuel, and Neil DeCarlo. (2013). *The innovator's toolkit: 50+ techniques for predictable and sustainable organic growth*. New York: John Wiley & Sons.

Tsiligiris, Vangelis. (2018). "An adapted porter diamond model for the evaluation of transnational education host countries." *International Journal of Educational Management* 32(2): 210–226.

Weitzel, William, and Ellen Jonsson. (1991). "Reversing the downward spiral: Lessons from WT Grant and Sears Roebuck." *Academy of Management Perspectives* 5(3): 7–22.

8

CONCLUSION

Towards Strategic Pragmatism in Policy Strategy–Innovation, a Research Agenda for Complexity

The goal of this book was to provide anyone interested to learn – policymakers, but also students and citizens – with a toolkit of ideas from the private sector that can potentially be used to improve the functioning of public policy processes. We began by providing a brief introduction to the history of public policy and the conventional depictions of the policy process, before going on to look at a variety of tools from the private sector that may be plugged into various stages of this process in order to improve its efficiency.

However, it is important to reiterate that these approaches should not simply be ported over from the private to the public sector with no regard for specific circumstances. It is important to judge in every case whether the method is appropriate to the circumstances, and what – if any – modifications it will need to go in order to be apposite for use. Moreover, it is crucial to bear in mind that the kind of wicked problems that are currently the focus of policymakers cannot be resolved via any one approach alone. If they could, then they would not be wicked problems. Instead, a variety of approaches much be combined in a flexible manner in order to get the best possible outcome out of each of them. This requires pragmatism on the part of all those involved.

This being so, we draw the link between this and our previous work, which lies in the importance of "strategic pragmatism". This refers to the practice of remaining firm and consistent with regard to one's goals once they have been set, while remaining flexible as far as the means used to achieve them are concerned. This is often not the case in the public sector, as bureaucracy naturally tends to focus on procedures rather than outcomes. However, this must soon change if the organisations involved are to survive. The low-hanging fruit of industrial and post-industrial growth has long gone, and only the most difficult problems are left for governments to target. If they are to continue to provide their citizens with the

DOI: 10.4324/9781003307228-8

kind of improving quality of life that they have come to expect, they must become as or more innovative than the private sector.

1. Strategic Pragmatism Framework in Policy Strategy–Innovation Process

In a previous book (*Towards Strategic Pragmatism in Foreign Policy*),[1] I set out a definition of strategic pragmatism:

Grand strategy and pragmatism are not antithetical and can co-exist. Strategic pragmatism exists when one has a rigorously devised grand strategy (potentially guided by principles/ideology) that is realistic in its analysis and policy options, and flexibly implemented to adapt to the situation, including tactical adjustments and strategic reversals, to achieve the desired vision and goals. Without an overarching grand strategy, it is likely that feedback loops will lead to knee-jerk responses. This is the gold standard for Pragmatism. For parsimony's sake, it can be summarised in terms of five key features:

(1) Realistic analysis: Fact-based analysis of reality; reality as it is, not as one wishes.
(2) Duality: Striving for policy innovation or hybrids; breaks the either/or construct, moving towards a both/and construct (duality) where co-existence, mutual wins are possible and desired. This combines principles and pragmatism. Fitzgerald aptly surmised the essence of duality: "The test of first-rate intelligence is the ability to hold two opposed in mind at the same time and still retain the ability to function".[2]
(3) Grand strategy: Having a grand strategy to achieve desired strategic vision. Grand strategy has to demonstrate foresight (scenario planning) and insight (systems thinking) in analysis, and long-term planning to achieve long-lasting goals. This is differentiating factor between Strategic Pragmatism and Pragmatism.
(4) Flexibility in implementation: Adopting an experimental, trial-and-error approach during implementation which acknowledges that the initial plan may not be perfect. This entails tactical adjustments, operational changes, strategic policy reversals and tight feedback loops. This is a response to the dynamism inherent in complex reality.
(5) Contextualism: Having a propensity to reject universal application of particular principles/ideology regardless of context. Having a sensitivity to context allows one to better solve problems in a systemic and long-lasting manner.

At the opposite end of the scale, non-pragmatism is directed by ideology: driven by wish-based analysis and with principle predominating over being realistic when the two enter into conflict.

The corporate strategy approaches described in this book have proved themselves in the real world of praxis, having served their purpose for generations of business leaders. However, this does not necessarily mean that they will be appropriate for use in all public sector contexts. While clinging blindly to old traditions is not pragmatism, neither is throwing oneself upon every novelty. Judgement is required.

The goal of this book is not to instruct you to use these toolkits come what may, but rather to offer them up for your consideration. Some may be appropriate for your circumstances, others may not. However, you will only discover this by considering your circumstances and your stakeholders, evaluating your environment and probable future changes, prototyping solutions and adopting a process of continuous evaluation, iteration and improvement. In the end, you may even decide not to use any of the approaches we describe, and conclude that your traditional approaches are actually perfectly well adapted to your situation. While we are presenting corporate methods, we are doing so for the public good, and thus the best solution is not the one we like most, but rather the one that turns out to work best in any particular situation. We are not here to proselytise in favour of a particular idea but to help build better policy for all of us.

2. Policy Strategy–Innovation With Strategic Pragmatism + Complexity

Following on from Chapter 1, at the macro-level, strategic pragmatism framework (Phua, 2021) offers itself as a possible partner of complexity framework in public policy (Bourgon, 2011; Cairney, 2012; Morcol, 2012). As Mitleton-Kelly (2015) put it,

> Complexity's great strength is that it crosses the boundaries of disciplines in both the natural and social sciences. It may one day provide us with a unified approach capable of linking those disciplines, because understanding the behaviour of complex systems in other subjects helps one gain deeper insights into phenomena in one's own field. Much work now being done on complexity in a variety of fields, from anthropology and psychology to economics and organisational science, will in due course change the way we see organisations, will help us understand their nature as complex systems, and ultimately will change the way that we manage organisations.

The "New Synthesis" (Bourgon, 2011) applied complexity to public policy and hence offers a suitable comprehensive macro-framework to be adapted for complexity in smart city governance (one level down from national governance). This

> intellectual framework integrates past practices and lessons learnt from 30 years of public sector reform and reality of practice in a post-industrial era, . . . to prepare government to serve the public good and collective interest in face of increasing complexity, uncertainty and volatility.
>
> *(Bourgon, 2011a)*

It "presents public administration as a dynamic system with the capacity to adapt to changing circumstances and to co-evolve with society: government transforms society and is transformed by it" (Bourgon, 2010); it is an "enabling framework that helps to frame questions and explore a space of possibilities" (Bourgon, 2011b). It argues that "public results are a combination of public policy results and civic results" and public servants, as stewards, are to "mediate and leverage on collective capacity (of public, private and civic spheres) for better results" (Bourgon, 2011a). Innovation is hence strongest when "synergistic sharing of roles and responsibilities between people, government and society' in this open concept of governance" (Bourgon, 2011a).

This **adaptive** system of government would require four sub-systems (Bourgon, 2011):

(1) Efficient **Compliance** sub-system include constitutions, conventions, rules and norms that govern how we live in society and help to "set priorities, forge societal and political **consensus** and conserve energy within a context of constrained actions and behaviours".
(2) Effective **Performance** sub-system transforms public purpose into **concrete action**. It "thinks across systems and work across boundaries, sectors and disciplines" to "reconcile hierarchical accountability with **shared responsibility** to achieve system-wide, government-wide and societal public results".
(3) Strong **Emergence** sub-system helps build government's capacity to "**anticipate and detect** emerging issues and phenomena and introduces proactive interventions to mitigate the risks associated with undesirable events". It also "taps **collective intelligence** to shape emergent solutions and **co-create** responses to complex policy issues".
(4) Powerful **Resilience** sub-system provides the "reality check to adaptive capacity of government and society". It seeks to "**co-produce** public results, encourage **active participation** of citizens, families, communities as value creators and build the **adaptive** capacity of society to prosper and adapt in all circumstances".

Separately, there are scattered micro-theories on complexity. Several theorists wrote on complexity at the micro-level initiatives covering sustainability (Trindade et al., 2017), data security (Giest, 2017) and governance (Pereira et al., 2018). The neighbourhood case is instructive. Lara et al. (2016), for example, suggest deploying smart city initiative primarily at the neighbourhood level, while Ekman (2018) suggests modelling changes before implementing them. At the neighbourhood level, complexity encourages local governance, exploration and self-organisation. Instead of having the central government producing tailor-made policies for every neighbourhood, different local governments can experiment with different ideas and learn from one another. Alternatively, several neighbourhoods can explore the possibility space, adopting different ways of doing things and learning from their experiments as they experiment with different ways of doing things. In a complex context, it is not possible to copy best practice without regard for its context. The learning necessitates crystallising the underlying principles of success within the particular context. In doing this, one can adapt the principles to different contexts. Modelling becomes useful as a way to explore counterfactuals, particularly when the modeller and the problem owner work together and try out various subsequent experiments.

However, it is important to note that there has been – as yet – no comprehensive and successful attempt to reconcile the top-down control required for smart city initiatives, with the decentralisation required for the smooth functioning of complex systems. While critiques of smart city initiatives from a complexity viewpoint are relatively common, far fewer efforts have been made to reconcile the two concepts. As more and more cities move towards a smart city model, this is an important gap to fill (Colding et al., 2020). Specifically, the bottom-up and top-down interactions that are necessary for central government organisations to produce technological systems that are capable of accommodating the decentralised nature of complex systems. In this, it can be compared to the design thinking approach used in corporate settings, which relies upon the practice of seeking continuous feedback to improve centrally designed products (Dorst, 2011).

3. Strategic Pragmatism as Meso-Enabler for Complexity in Smart City Governance

Complexity lacks an operational-level partner in bringing the meso-enabler (policy process) that connects the micro- and macro-levels (Almaguer-Kalixto et al., 2014). That is where this volume on Policy Strategy–Innovation using the Strategic Pragmatism framework is a useful foundation. Regardless of the policy problem, there is a reasonably standard policy process covering agenda setting/problem-finding, policy formulation (user data collection, data analysis and idea generation), decision-making, implementation and evaluation in the policy literature, and it is within this policy process that policy strategy–innovation, strategic pragmatism and complexity concepts may be applied to enrich smart city governance. The ensuing paragraphs offer a glimpse of that vision.

Problem-Finding

In this stage, the process of finding the right problem to solve requires more targeted user data and collaborative exploration. On user data, when smart city with internet-of-things data architecture and tech-enabled analysis allows for adaptive and anticipatory governance in near-real time according to dynamic changes of data (Geyer and Cairney, 2015). With such networks of data at the multilevel systems of international–national–city–municipal–neighbourhood, a problem-finding exercise can be precisely directed at a specific problem involving multiple stakeholders in neighbourhood X for experimentation (Johnson et al., 2018). Part-whole systems are important in this context, where intermediate-level systems may constitute parts of a higher-level system or have sub-systems of their own. This supports the understanding of the past and current patterns of behaviour, and big data allows for sub-aggregation analysis.

On collaborative exploration, Mitleton-Kelly et al. (2018) proposes a method to identify a multi-dimensional problem space, stakeholders and its co-evolutionary dynamics across time before considering the enabling environment needed to address challenges as the problem evolves and changes. This in turn can lead to changes in organisational culture, behaviour and relationships necessary for a multi-dimensional enabling environment addressing all inter-related dimensions simultaneously (Mitleton-Kelly, 2011, p. 1).

Data Collection and Analysis

At this stage, data are collected to validate assumptions and address information gaps for analysis. Smart cities have an advantage in continual and dynamic data collection through IoT devices, which could track and monitor their users' actions and behaviour (aggregated) to identify patterns of behaviour (pending privacy concerns). Besides IoT, deliberate and consented public engagement data collection through focus groups, surveys, interviews and observation research can be conducted and interpreted via effective visualisations (Richardson and Tait, 2018). Visualisation accentuates significant relationships and dynamics to support analysis. If data are collected and analysed longitudinally, it allows for deep study of the smart city for benchmarking and iterative improvements (Wolf-Branigin et al., 2018).

Idea Generation

At this stage, the insights gained from the data analysis can then be used for "modular exaptation" (Andriani and Carignani, 2014), defined as "co-opting of a technology or biological trait for a function for which it was not designed or selected through novel associations". It is contrasted with adaptation, which is the improvement of an existing trait through natural selection. To achieve this, it is necessary to have regular contradiction between the intentional function/purpose of a feature and the proper function, leading to the conclusion that the SAME function is also tenable for another purpose/task, for example, CD-ROM originally intended as music singles became hard-disk. The same task can be approached from a radical novelty perspective, for example, cassette player that walks is a Sony walkman (Goldstein, 2001).

Implementation and Evaluation

During policy implementation, it may be possible to disaggregate data in a top-down manner and create synthetic micro-populations for large-scale computer models to experiment with conditions and effects (behaviours) before actual live experiments in neighbourhoods. Therein, continuous consultation at the neighbourhood level offers feedback required for implementing effective smart city initiatives (Berntzen and Johannessen, 2016), as would be utilised in design thinking exercises as prescribed by Bourgon (2011). Harnessing big data on public opinion and behaviour is the only way to bridge the gap between the top-down development of technological governance systems and the decentralised ontological nature of complex urban environments. Moreover, feedback can also happen iteratively at different stages of the policy process.

4. Conclusion: The Best Is Yet to Be

The best is yet to be. The fusion of policy strategy–innovation in strategic pragmatism and complexity merits a full monograph in itself. The strong vision of smart cities worldwide necessitates a pragmatic approach towards complexity in smart city governance. As Mitleton-Kelly (2003) puts it:

> If organisations are seen as complex evolving systems, co-evolving within a social "ecosystem", then our thinking about strategy and management changes. With the changed perspective comes a different way of acting and relating which could lead to a different way of working. In turn, the new types of relationship and approaches to work could provide the conditions for the emergence of new organisational forms.

"Complexity in smart city governance" is itself an emergence, and this emergence has potential growth for academics and practitioners. Smart city cannot simply be a smart city of smart devices as existing micro-literature suggests. Smart city must involve the integration of technology with traditional infrastructure, and smart city governance must be embedded by a suitably comprehensive macro-framework as new synthesis and yet tightly integrated with micro-studies through application of complexity concepts in meso-policy processes.

Further research would contribute to operationalisation of this macro–meso–micro-framework with neighbourhood/municipal micro-cases working with big data networks to better understand citizen's aspirations in smart city living, privacy needs and government's aspirations for big data for governance. We hope this volume, having fused corporate strategy into policy process, serves as an integrated government-business strategy–innovation foundation towards that research vision.

Notes

1 Phua, Charles Chao Rong. *Towards strategic pragmatism in foreign policy: Cases of US, China and Singapore.* Oxon: Routledge, 2021.
2 Fitzgerald, F. Scott. *Great Gatsby.* New York: Charles Scribner's Sons, 1925.

Bibliography

Almaguer-Kalixto, Patricia, José A. Amozurrutia, and Chaime Marcuello Servós. (2014). "Analyzing policy processes as complex systems: The case of Mesoamerican Sustainable Development Initiative." *Journal of Sociocybernetics* 12(1/2).

Andriani, Pierpaolo, and Giuseppe Carignani. (2014). "Modular exaptation: A missing link in the synthesis of artificial form." *Research Policy* 43(9): 1608–1620.

Batty, Michael, Kay W. Axhausen, Fosca Giannotti, Alexei Pozdnoukhov, Armando Bazzani, Monica Wachowicz, Georgios Ouzounis, and Yuval Portugali. (2012). "Smart cities of the future." *The European Physical Journal Special Topics* 214(1): 481–518.

Berntzen, Lasse, and Marius Rohde Johannessen. (2016). "The role of citizens in 'smart cities'." Management International Conference.

Bourgon, Jocelyne. (2010). "Reclaiming public administration." *Ethos*, No. 4, April 2008. See also Jocelyne Bourgon, "Serving beyond the predictable." *Ethos*, No. 7, January 2010.

Bourgon, Jocelyne. (2011a). "The new synthesis: Preparing government for challenges of the 21st century." *Ethos*, No. 10, October 2011.

Bourgon, Jocelyne. (2011b). "Exploring new frontiers of public administration: The new synthesis project." *Canadian Government Executive* 17(3) (March): 16–18.

Bourgon, Jocelyne. (2011c). *A new synthesis of public administration: Serving the 21st century*. Montreal: McGill-Queen's University Press.

Cairney, Paul. (2012). "Complexity theory in political science and public policy." *Political Studies Review* 10(3): 346–358.

Cavada, Marianna, D.V. Hunt, and C.D. Rogers. (2014). "Smart cities: Contradicting definitions and unclear measures." World Sustainability Forum, pp. 1–12. MDPIAG. Accessed from: https://www.semanticscholar.org/paper/Smart-Cities%3A-Contradicting-Definitions-and-Unclear-Cavada-Hunt/25758d220bf0ca5a6e2d2ed22b76b664302119c2. Accessed on 20 December 2020.

Colding, Johan, Magnus Colding, and Stephan Barthel. (2020). "The smart city model: A new panacea for urban sustainability or unmanageable complexity?" *Environment and Planning B: Urban Analytics and City Science* 47(1): 179–187.

Cortés-Cediel, María E., Iván Cantador, and Olga Gil. (2017). "Recommender systems for e-governance in smart cities: State of the art and research opportunities." Proceedings of the International Workshop on Recommender Systems for Citizens, pp. 1–6. Accessed from: https://www.semanticscholar.org/paper/Recommender-systems-for-e-governance-in-smart-state-Cort%C3%A9s-Cediel-Cantador/12d2cc2c7cbe249997e86fa593f70df0b4c3b179. Accessed on 20 November 2021.

Dickinson, Helen. (2016). "From new public management to new public governance: The implications for a 'new public service'." In *The three sector solution: Delivering public policy in collaboration with not-for-profits and business*, p. 41. Accessed from: https://www.researchgate.net/publication/318230714_From_New_Public_Management_to_New_Public_Governance_The_implications_for_a_%27new_public_service%27. Accessed on 20 November 2021.

Dohler, Mischa, Ignasi Vilajosana, Xavi Vilajosana, and Jordi Llosa. (2011). "Smart cities: An action plan." *Proc. Barcelona Smart Cities Congress*, Barcelona, Spain, pp. 1–6.

Dorst, Kees. (2011). "The core of 'design thinking' and its application." *Design Studies* 32(6): 521–532.

Edelenbos, Jurian, Fadi Hirzalla, Liesbet van Zoonen, Jan van Dalen, Geiske Bouma, Adriaan Slob, and Alexander Woestenburg. (2018). "Governing the complexity of smart data cities: Setting a research agenda." In *Smart technologies for smart governments*, pp. 35–54. Cham: Springer.

Ekman, Ulrik. (2018). "Smart city planning: Complexity." *International Journal of E-Planning Research (IJEPR)* 7(3): 1–21.

Fernández-Güell, José-Miguel, Silvia Guzmán-Araña, Marta Collado-Lara, and Victoria Fernández-Añez. (2016). "How to incorporate urban complexity, diversity and intelligence into smart cities initiatives." International Conference on Smart Cities, pp. 85–94. Springer.

Geyer, Robert, and Paul Cairney (Eds.). (2015). *Handbook on complexity and public policy*. Cheltenham: Edward Elgar Publishing.

Giest, Sarah. (2017). "Big data analytics for mitigating carbon emissions in smart cities: Opportunities and challenges." *European Planning Studies* 25(6): 941–957.

Goldstein, Jeffrey. (2001). "Emergence, radical novelty, and the philosophy of mathematics." *Nonlinear Dynamics in the Life and Social Sciences* 320: 133–152.

Johnson, Jeffrey, Joyce Fortune, and Jane Bromley. (2018). "Multilevel systems and policy." In *Handbook of research methods in complexity science*. Cheltenham: Edward Elgar Publishing.

Lara, Alexander Prado, Eduardo Moreira Da Costa, Thiago Zilinscki Furlani, and Tan Yigitcanla. (2016). "Smartness that matters: Towards a comprehensive and human-centred characterisation of smart cities." *Journal of Open Innovation: Technology, Market, and Complexity* 2(2): 8.

Mitleton-Kelly, Eve. (2003). "Ten principles of complexity and enabling infrastructures." *Complex Systems and Evolutionary Perspectives on Organisations: The Application of Complexity Theory to Organisations* 1: 23–50.

Mitleton-Kelly, Eve. (2011). "Identifying the multi-dimensional problem-space and co-creating an enabling environment." *Emergence: Complexity and Organization* 13(1/2): 1.

Mitleton-Kelly, Eve. (2015). *Urban governance: A complexity theory approach*. LSE Cities/MacArthur Foundation Seminar 2014 (Unpublished paper).

Mitleton-Kelly, Eve, Alexandros Paraskevas, and Christopher Day (Eds.). (2018). *Handbook of research methods in complexity science: Theory and applications*. Cheltenham: Edward Elgar Publishing.

Morcol, Goktug. (2012). *A complexity theory for public policy*. New York: Routledge.

Peltan, Tomáš. (2015). "Smart cities as complexity management." 2015 Smart Cities Symposium Prague (SCSP), pp. 1–5. IEEE. Accessed from: https://ieeexplore.ieee.org/document/7181551. Accessed on 20 December 2020.

Pereira, Gabriela Viale, Peter Parycek, Enzo Falco, and Reinout Kleinhans. (2018). "Smart governance in the context of smart cities: A literature review." *Information Polity* 23(2): 143–162.

Phua, Charles Chao Rong. (2021). *Towards strategic pragmatism in foreign policy: Cases of United States of America, China and Singapore*. Oxon: Routledge.

Rhodes, Mary Lee, Joanne Murphy, Jenny Muir and John A. Murray. (2011). *Public management and complexity theory: Richer decision-making in public service*. New York: Routledge.

Richardson, Kurt A., and Andrew Tait. (2018). "On the visualization of dynamic structure: Understanding the distinction between static and dynamic network topology." In *Handbook of research methods in complexity science*. Cheltenham: Edward Elgar Publishing.

Scott, John. (2000). "Rational choice theory." *Understanding Contemporary Society: Theories of the Present* 129: 671–685.

Thompson, Emine Mine. (2016). "Smart city: Adding to the complexity of cities." 651–660. Accessed from: https://www.semanticscholar.org/paper/Smart-City%3A-Adding-to-the-Complexity-of-Cities-A-Thompson/8dd2433dd864eaef2d91380db1343e10e50ec2ea. Accessed on 20 December 2020.

Trindade, Evelin Priscila, Marcus Phoebe Farias Hinnig, Eduardo Moreira da Costa, Jamile Sabatini Marques, Rogério Cid Bastos, and Tan Yigitcanlar. (2017). "Sustainable development of smart cities: A systematic review of the literature." *Journal of Open Innovation: Technology, Market, and Complexity* 3(3): 11.

Vedung, E. (1998). Policy Instruments: Typologies and Theories. In M.L. Bemelmans-Videc, R.C. Rist, and E. Vedung (Eds.), *Carrots, sticks & sermons: Policy instruments & their evaluation*. New Brunswick/London: Transaction Publishers.

Wiesel, Fredrika, and Sven Modell. (2014). "From new public management to new public governance? Hybridization and implications for public sector consumerism." *Financial Accountability & Management* 30(2): 175–205.

Wolf-Branigin, Michael E., William G. Kennedy, Emily S. Ihara, and Catherine J. Tompkins. (2018). "Applying complex adaptive systems to agent-based models for social programme evaluation." In *Handbook of research methods in complexity science*. Cheltenham: Edward Elgar Publishing.

INDEX